FIGHTING FOR HOPE

FIGHTING FOR HOPE

Organizing to Realize Our Dreams

JOAN NEWMAN KUYEK

**BLACK
ROSE
BOOKS**

Montreal/New York

Reprinted in 1992

BLACK ROSE BOOKS No. T154
Paperback ISBN: 0-921689-86-1
Hardcover ISBN: 0-921689-87-X

Canadian Cataloguing in Publication Data

Kuyek, Joan Newman, 1942 -
  Fighting for hope

Includes bibliographical references.
ISBN: 0-921689-87-X (bound). --
  ISBN: 0-921689-86-1 (pbk.).

1. Community organization--Canada. 2. Community power--Canada.
3. Social Action--Canada
 I. Title.

HN49.C6K99 1990   361.8′0971   C91-090032-9

Library of Congress Catalog No. 90-83629
Cover design: Pierre-Paul Pariseau
Design and Photocomposition: Nat Klym

Editorial Offices
BLACK ROSE BOOKS
3981 St-Laurent Boulevard,
Suite 444
Montréal, Québec H2W 1Y5
Canada

Mailing Address
BLACK ROSE BOOKS
P.O. Box 1258
Succ. Place du Parc
Montréal, Québec H2W 2R3
Canada

U.S. Orders
BLACK ROSE BOOKS
340 Nagel Drive
Cheektowaga, New York
14225

Printed and bound in Québec, Canada
on acid-free paper

TABLE OF CONTENTS

ACKNOWLEDGEMENTS

This work is woven from the lives and work of many people and groups. It is impossible to name them all. However, I want especially to thank my aunt and dear friend, Jean Newman, for her support and careful editing; Laurie McGauley, Heather Smith, Carol Rowland, and Jean Trickey for their constructive criticism of the original manuscript; Dimitri Roussopoulos for urging me to write this book; my partner, Jos, for his belief in me; and my children, Devlin and Andree, for their patience.

The Canada Council provided a grant which made it possible for me to take the time to write it.

I don't believe that any ideas are truly original. Certainly my own are nourished by the many people across the country who have shared their stories, their work and their homes with me over the years. To respect these contributions, I name Bronwen Wallace, who began the community organizing project that was to change the direction of my life, cooked meals for me in her kitchen when I was too freaked out to feed myself, who wrote poetry that I carry around like holy text, and Steven Lisson, who lived every day with strength, kindness, honesty, sharing and humour.

This book is dedicated to the healing of Anishinabai-Aske.

PREFACE

This is a book for people who are actively engaged in working for a better world, and for those of you who want to be. It will describe the context in which work for justice, freedom and the protection of the earth takes place in Canada, and discuss action, ideas and examples.

I have spent most of my life trying to find ways to build the capacity of poor and marginalized people to act for their own long term interests. This book is a product of that work and of the work of other organizers from all over the world.

Perceptions and strategies of social change vary from writing letters to government asking them for help, to blowing up an environmentally destructive factory; from putting on a church supper, to squatting in vacant housing; from starting a worker co-operative, to organizing a union. The work we take on to heal the planet and the human family depends on our analysis of the problem, the context in which the problem exists, and who we are socially, historically and geographically.

Since the perspective of this book is a product of my history let me tell you a little bit about my life and why I wanted to take on this project.

I began my work in the "movement" (as we called it then) in 1965, as a researcher with the Company of Young Canadians — an attempt by the Canadian government to contain young radicals and put them into community service. They had hired me to research what national organizations thought young Canadians should be doing. For some people I interviewed, polishing statues was what they had in mind.

This work also put me into contact with a number of people who were to change my life. First were a few experienced adult educators who introduced me to something called "community development," and, because of the abysmal lack of knowledge in the CYC, I became in two short months the CYC's expert on it.

Second, were the student radicals in the Student Union for Peace Action (SUPA). I fell in love with the Movement. After five months, converted to participatory democracy and community action, I quit my job and went to work for $75 a month on the Kingston Community Project in Kingston, Ontario. We organized tenants associations, a teenage drop-in centre, two residents' associations, a food co-op and a range of other activities with the people of Kingston. It was an exciting and vibrant time in all our lives. I was even elected to City Council. I have always felt that my real education came from those people in Kingston who had the patience to spend some time with me.

During that time, too, the womens' liberation movement started up, and it felt like the logical extension of the work we already did. I became an active member, and have remained one ever since.

Applying the learnings from community organizing work and from the women's liberation movement to other activities just made sense. The principles were the same after all: helping people achieve their own goals, building co-operatives, taking care of the earth, taking care of one another.

I moved to Sudbury in 1970 — a vibrant town at that time. INCO and Falconbridge, the two enormous mining companies that dominate this community, were expanding rapidly. INCO had 20,000 miners on its payroll, most of them young, from all over the country. Within three years, the payroll had been reduced by half, and many of the young people had left.

Some of us started the first daycare centre in Sudbury in 1972. When I was a teller at the Royal Bank we tried to organize a union; we supported union organizing at lumber companies, department stores, white collar workers at INCO. Our Sudbury women's group put out a guide to Sudbury women in crisis called *Alternatives to Hysteria.* We demonstrated and submitted briefs about health care and abortion issues. My friend Sue Byron and I ran an unsuccessful but interesting bookstore. During a nine month strike at INCO in 1978-9, we organized strike support in the community and across the country. With my friends, I have organized recreation programs, co-operative housing, strike support activities, worker co-operatives, peace rallies, and environmental groups, in my own community.

Because you don't usually get paid to organize, I have worked in a variety of jobs over the years. Every one of them has been a great learning experience. I worked in legal clinics, hospitals, retail stores, the telephone company.

From 1986-9, as the national staff person for a three year project of the United Church of Canada called *The Church and the Economic Crisis,* I had the privilege of travelling all over the country assisting folk to develop programs for economic justice in their church and community.

If I've learned anything from this eclectic experience, it is that we all have within us the ability to be kind, co-operative and honest, just as we all have the ability to be greedy, vicious and treacherous. Who we become in the world depends on the context of our lives. We are inter-dependent with one another and with the earth.

If we set up a workshop that valued the experience of all the participants and made it safe to say "I don't know," then people would be gentle and co-operative and would leave saying "Everyone here is so diverse, interesting and wonderful." On the other hand, if we set up the meeting with a few star speakers, the speakers and organizers would have a good time and make lots of contacts whereas most participants would leave saying "So-and-so gave a really interesting talk but we haven't met anyone and don't know how to use the information." A number of participants would be frustrated and angry.

When we worked collectively to put on a demonstration or to organize a community event, people were excited, put in lots of extra time and energy and were full of creative ideas. If one person started bossing them around, or took credit for the work, then the others voted with their feet.

Some organizational forms bring out the good in us, and some bring out the bad. Organizations are systems of power relations: they can be equalitarian or hierarchical. When the system provides a few with power over others it corrupts the judgement of those who have that power and marginalizes those who don't.

Over centuries of human existence, peoples have organized themselves in different ways to accomplish the social project. With very few exceptions, co-operative and earth-based peoples have been conquered or dominated by peoples who were organized hierarchically and who treated the earth as a resource to be exploited. Where history is not about this conquest and resistance to it, it is about the battles between rival hierarchies for power over resources, peoples and territories. The unwritten story of the last three thousand years is the efforts of ordinary people to build some kind of life for themselves and their children despite the battles for power that have raged in their midst. Resistance is not new. It has gone on for centuries, and it still goes on today.

Those who do not understand history are doomed to repeat it. History is full of stories of the oppressed rebelling against the oppressor, only to reinstitute an equally oppressive system. What we learn from oppression is how to oppress. If we want a truly transformative politics, then we take up methods that embody the kind of world we want to create.

At this time we are confronted with the need to reconstruct a society that can live in harmony with the earth, that sees human beings as one part of the creation: we have to recognize, understand, and transform the systems that have fostered destruction and exploitation.

I start from the assumption that it is in our long-term self-interest to live in harmony with the earth and one another and that most people try to do this. But we have forgotten how, and have taken many roads that look very seductive, but lead to injustice, ecological destruction and misery.

All too often as an organizer I hear people say that others are "apathetic" or "too comfortable" or "lazy" when they do not get involved in social change. I don't believe that this is true, and in fact think that it is just another way of blaming the victim.

The economic, social and political systems we live in have been created and are maintained by human labour, and they depend on our consent. Our consent to do work that is against our long-term self-interest is manipulated in a variety of ways: by hiding or ignoring the actual products of our work; by providing seductive short-term rewards; by making it very difficult for us to reflect on what we are doing; by creating an atmosphere of hopelessness, and where all else fails, by fear of starvation and force.

There is a vital and growing movement for social change in Canada. To be part of healing the earth and the human family, we are learning how to free ourselves and others from the social, economic, political and cultural prison that is the context for our work.

This book is a very personal reflection on my own experience, and on the histories of other organizers. Activists in Canada have experienced dismal setbacks, unexpected victories and carefully planned successes. I have tried to take the common threads and weave them into a multipurpose cloth.

The book is in four parts and seven chapters.

The Bars of the Prison, Part I, looks at the context of community organizing work in Canada. What are the structures and systems here that bring out the greedy, competitive and oppressive side of us all? How do they work? How are they located in our day to day reality?

Fighting for Hope, Part II, looks at strategies for change in a holistic perspective: cultural, social, economic and political. Organizers use all four when they work effectively: the strategies complement one another.

Doing Analysis: Thinking Like an Organizer, Part III, provides five exercises for looking at ordinary life situations from a community organizer's perspective, and developing a social analysis that makes possibilities for change visible.

Get Real or Get Lost, Part IV, pulls together some of the ideas in the book and puts forward suggestions for the future of community organizing in Canada. Print resources are listed at the very end for those who want to read more.

NOTES

1. Swift, Jamie, *The Big Nickel: INCO at Home and Abroad,* Between the Lines, Toronto, 1977 provides a detailed history of INCO.
2. Women Helping Women, *Alternatives to Hysteria: A Guide to Sudbury Women in Crisis,* Sudbury, 1977. We also made two films by the same name, Parts 1 and 2, that are available from DEC Films in Toronto.
3. Bissonnette, Rock and Duckworth, *A Wives Tale.* Available from DEC films in Toronto. A film about the organizing of Wives Supporting the Strike made during the 1978-9 strike.
4. Kuyek, Joan. *The Phone Book, Working at Bell Canada,* Between the Lines, Toronto, 1979.
5. Kuyek, Joan, *Managing the Household: A Handbook for Economic Justice Work,* United Church of Canada, Toronto, 1990, records the learnings from the Economic Crisis project.

I

THE BARS OF THE PRISON

This section looks at the structures that "keep us in our place." The way our communities, our work and our schools are organized quite frequently seem "neutral" to us. In fact, they are a product of the ongoing struggle between the demands of those who live by extracting wealth and labour from others and the needs of people wanting to live their lives, raise their families and care for the earth.

The kind of structures that we end up with reflect the intensity of that struggle: they are always in a state of flux. As Margaret Randall writes, "If you are not part of the solution, you are part of the problem."

To those who presently hold power-over, the rest of us are an unruly bunch who are always refusing to do as we are told: skipping work, building squatter settlements, refusing to pay our rent or our taxes, sassing the teachers, demanding higher wages and just generally trying to do our own thing. Some of us don't even have any ambition, we don't care how we dress or how much money we save. When we get together to resist their demands, we are rebellious, tree-huggers, or anarchists.

We become so accustomed to the way the power structure likes to organize things, that we take on their language and are unable even to name our own needs, let alone organize around them. This chapter attempts to disclose some of the ways that social control operates in Canada, to set the context for the organizing work that continues despite the difficulties.

Chapter One

THE BOGEY-MAN

A few years ago, I had a dream that I was at a women's conference where we were given topographical maps and asked to use them to find our way to the "centre." The centre was the core of evil in a particular man's brain. The map was of his brain. The man to whom this brain belonged was, however, living, and the same size as the rest of us. We were sent out alone on this quest. We were not told what the centre was, or what the man looked like. Before we set out we asked a lot of questions of the game organizers: could we have compasses, were there trails, how would we know the centre or the man when we found him etc.? No answers were supplied, except that "we would know when we found it."

So I set out with the map in my hand, and tried to follow it. At first I thought the topography was of a forested area, but soon discovered that it was in fact a city. Many of the hills were staircases in buildings and tunnels. At first, walking down a corridor, I was accosted by a really horrible looking person, whom I took to be the villain. He chased me up and down staircases (my having no idea where I was going) until he collapsed with exhaustion. At that point, I realized that he was not the enemy I was to seek.

I kept going in a direction that felt right, and found myself in a sordid bar, full of alien looking creatures and drunks. When I entered I was introduced to Sid, the owner. He looked like an amiable businessman, fit and handsome. To my shock and horror, I knew at that moment that he was the enemy we sought. The need to hide my identity from him overwhelmed me, and I said I was there to audition as a dancer. As I auditioned all I could think about was: how did I find out where the centre really was...was this bar, in fact, it? and how would I continue to conceal my identity from Sid as one of the searchers? Or was he so arrogant that he thought we presented no threat at all? I felt very alone and very scared. I woke up covered with sweat...

* * *

After I wrote the first draft of this book, I gave it to my friend Carol to read. During the feedback of her comments, she said that the book read as though I thought there was a "bogey-man" and that if I thought there was, I had better explain who it is. I have been struggling with that concept most of my life. Is there a bogey-man that makes all the bad things in the world happen, or are we all equally responsible, or is there another way to analyze reality?

I had just come back from Taiwan, where I visited political prisoners jailed for twenty-five years for doing nothing more than advocating free elections, where I met workers who had been stabbed by company-employed thugs for protesting layoffs, and where I saw twelve and thirteen year-old Philippino girls who had to turn forty tricks a day just to keep from being murdered by their pimps.

Returning from that same trip, I rode on the airplane beside a pleasant man in blue jeans — lean, fit, interesting — who told me he had just been in Seoul on business. He was an engineer in the Pentagon and he had been there as part of a sales team, along with some generals. He said that he had replaced his passport three times this year, because he had visited so many different countries to sell military equipment. His next visit would be to Canada in April: he had a "deal" for the Canadian government on some radar equipment to go on the F-18 jet. He said he liked his work: it was interesting, challenging and he really liked to visit all these foreign countries. He acted like he had had a moral lobotomy.

There are real people who do real evil things in this world: they murder children, they torture and rape and steal from the poorest. They are willing to do anything to hold on to their money or their position.

Then there are other people who make it possible for this evil to continue, sometimes with active support, sometimes unknowingly or passively. The evil that these people do is made possible by human labour, consent, and ignorance.

What is the relative responsibility, for example, in the use of a nuclear bomb for the following: the shareholders of the company that want a good return on their investment; the workers who assemble it; the miners who produce the uranium; the pilot who flies the plane; the president of the country that issues the order to drop it; the wife of the pilot who let him go to work that day?

Don't tell me we are all equally responsible. We are not.

Any talk of change is talk about the organization of the way power is distributed. "Politics" means the organization of power. There is a politics of the family, of the church, of the classroom and of the community just as there is a politics of the state or the global economy.[1]

When we try to talk about "getting power" or "power structures" in community groups, we often find that people are very uncomfortable with the discussion. "Power" is synonymous to them with domination and oppression, and they will deny that anyone in the group holds it, or that they themselves seek it.

Or they will protest that there are "no enemies" only people who need to be changed. The discussion gets confused and unhelpful. "When power becomes a dirty word, so that no one can name it or talk about it, then those who seek it can operate without controls on their behaviour. If we want to make the flow of power truly equal, then we have to understand it."[2]

In her important book, *Truth or Dare,* Starhawk names three distinct kinds of power: power-over, power-with, and power-from-within. They are very different from one another.

"Power-from-within" is the personal power I have, my energy, self-knowledge, self-discipline, character.

"Power-with" sees the world as made up of changing relationships and is our collective energy and ability to act together. It includes influence and leadership as legitimate forms of power.

"Power-over," on the other hand, *requires* the domination or oppression of others. Unlike the other two forms, "It has to have a clear material base, as it is grounded in the ability to punish by imposing physical or economic sanctions."[3]

> Domination is not the creation of some evil force, but the result of millions of human choices, made again and again over time. Just so can domination be undone, by shaping new choices, by small and repeated acts of liberation... Domination is a system, and we are part of it, and in that lies hope. For any system is always in delicate balance, dependent for stability on the feedback of its parts. When the feedback changes, so does the system. At first it reacts to

regain its stability, but if the new feedback is sustained, the system will be transformed.[4]

By allowing ourselves to be dominated we collude with power-over. Every act of freedom diminishes the strength of the power structure. That's why those who hold power-over are so threatened by talk about organizing the dominated and oppressed for justice and self-empowerment.

Power-over is not confined to large structures, it can exist anywhere that some people have access to the material means of dominating someone else: in the family, the school, the church, in a social change organization. As long as some people have the ability to control the lives of others, they have the ability to use power-over.

If our goal is *transforming* politics, then these particular characteristics of power-over are significant:

- Power-over is based in control of capital, resources, military force and government.
- Power-over is structured in a hierarchy of domination. It is international in scope.
- The structure of power is not monolithic. It's very nature means that those at the top of the structure compete with one another for more power, resources, land and labour and those further down the ladder compete for the favours of those above them.
- It cannot function without the labour of the people who work to maintain and extend it, and without the consent of the majority of the dominated.
- Power-over creates fear not only in the oppressed but in the oppressor, and she/he reacts quickly to any indication of rebellion.
- Power-over corrupts all who use it to control others.

The most pervasive form of power-over is found in the world economic system, precisely because power-over depends on control of capital, resources and force. In capitalist countries like Canada the very purpose of the economy is to provide the accumulation of capital for the owners of private corporations. In simple language: to provide a steady flow of income to shareholders.[5]

The greatest limitation of this system is that it can only measure and record services and things that have monetary value (in dollars, yen, rubles). The success of any enterprise or activity is judged by its ability to show an excess of measurable benefits over costs. This is called "showing a profit." If the benefits are not measurable in money, then they are deemed not to exist.[6]

The world economy is shaped by the decisions of human beings in corporations and states and is made possible by the day-to-day work we all do. It is dependent upon consenting human labour, unending resources and smoothly functioning technologies. It functions because people are "just doing their job."

Each enterprise, project, corporation and individual is assumed and encouraged to have a cost-benefit ledger, and to be seeking to show a profit in the same measurable way. Corporations and persons are expected also to compete with one another for labour, time and energy, raw materials and markets.

The basic organizational unit of our society is the corporation. In law, corporations are treated as individuals, although they might be made up of thousands of workers. Any corporation is designed in a hierarchical fashion to facilitate control from the pinnacle and rapid response from the bottom of the pyramid. Each corporation, like each household, maintains its own ledger, and a healthy corporation is considered to be one where income exceeds expenditure.

In a corporation, the only way to measure job satisfaction is in terms of higher productivity, and the only way to measure impact on the environment is through potential loss of income to the corporation. Although concern is often expressed for other factors there is no way to have them enter into the accounting system.

As an example, INCO is a multinational mining company active in northern Ontario. They are a profitable enterprise and considered successful in the corporate world. Their success, however, has been built on the destruction of over 900 square miles of whitepine forest; the production of war materials that were sold to both sides during the first and second world wars; at best, ignoring state terror in Guatemala and Indonesia during the time the company was expanding there; and working conditions that have resulted in cancer, crippling back injuries, whitehand or deafness for the majority of its workforce. It's "Superstack" is the single largest source of acid rain in North America.[7]

As a response to public pressure, the company has now developed a method of reclaiming the sulphur dioxide that it produces from the air: it wants to use it for fertilizer, which is almost as destructive to the environment. They have known how to do this for a long time, but it only became attractive to them economically when they found they could market the reclamation technology to other companies. The company does keep an "environmental audit." This audit will show up on the bottom line as a benefit when the company begins to market pollution control technologies; and it will continue to show up as a "community relations" cost.

Most of the real environmental and justice costs of the enterprise do not appear on the INCO ledger: they are either completely unrecorded or they appear in the ledgers of individual households or in the "social programs" of governments.

Our economy in Canada is "advanced capitalism." With a few exceptions, control is in the hands of transnational corporations owned outside the country. The base of Canadian wealth is the mining of the earth's resources: fossil fuels, fish, lumber, metals, soil. What secondary industries we have are related to these primary products.

In the 1990's, this continues to be true as a new growth industry is added to the roster: the consulting and manufacture of environmental protection technologies. Canada continues to have some of the highest energy consumption and garbage production in the world, most of it because of the enormous energy requirements and waste byproducts of resource extraction industries. It is ludicrous in the extreme that economists can only imagine dealing with the problem by creating new enterprises to profit from the waste. Many of these new "green" businesses will be owned by the same people who create the problem in the first place.

A very few people in Canada, the owners of the large multinational companies, become rich by extracting wealth from the rest of us.

Linda McQuaig develops a wonderful image in a book called *Behind Closed Doors*. She describes the distribution of wealth in this country by asking you to imagine a parade that is one block long and one hour long. The first ten minutes of the parade are underground, because the marchers are in debt. At fifteen minutes, people are 3 feet high. At 30 they reach 5 feet high. At 54 minutes they are 14 feet high. At 59 minutes they are as tall as the CN Tower. But in the last one tenth of a second, there are marchers that range from 3 miles to 198 miles high. The average wealth per Canadian, if it were distributed equally would be $78,000![8]

In Canada, the Business Council on National Issues is the organization that represents the interests of the corporate leaders in this country. Its membership, by invitation only, is made up of the Chief Executive Officers of companies like INCO, and all the major financial institutions. It has an agenda for Canada, and it works vigorously to have it implemented by governments. The agenda includes the Free Trade agreement with the United States, user fees in health care, cutbacks in the social security network, reduction of the minimum wage, the hobbling of trade unions, and the restriction of dissent. The structure of the "Canadian Corporate Elite" has been carefully studied by academics like John Porter, Jorge Niosi, and Wallace Clement. There are nine families who control most Canadian wealth, and their loyalty is to their corporate interests not their country. Their interests are allied with those of transnational corporations in other parts of the world.

Because these companies make profits by keeping costs down, keeping wages low is one of their concerns. If there is lots of competition for scarce jobs, they benefit. For our economic system to function, ten per cent or more of those capable of working must be looking for jobs in this country.

For each of us, with our own needs, desires and visions, our lives become battlegrounds for the competition between different balance sheets. It is our time they want, our dollars and our energy. When we have trouble getting to meetings, being loving to our friends and families, spending three hours a day getting to and from work or finding that we are always having to move to find affordable housing or work, these are economic and political problems, not "social" ones. The problems of our economic system are located in the very real stuff of our lives.[9]

So, to come back to Carol's question: is there a bogey-man? There is not an individual bogey-man or group of bogey-men, but there are systems of human organization that bring out the very worst in human beings and turn evil into virtue. Some people are so corrupted by those systems that it is difficult to see any good in them at all. Often the most corrupt are the very people our culture celebrates — the chief executive officers of corporations that plunder and pollute, or who make their profits off the misery of the poor.

NOTES

1. This discussion of power is informed by the work of a number of different writers. In particular :

    Starhawk (Simos, Miriam). *Truth or Dare,* Harper and Row Publishers, New York, 1987.

    Speeter, Greg, *Power: A Repossession Manual,* Citizen Involvement Training Project, Massachusetts, 1978.

    Gaventa, John, *Power and Powerlessness,* University of Illinois Press, 1980.

    Kahn, Si. *How People Get Power,* McGraw-Hill, New York, 1980.

2. Starhawk, *op.cit.,* p.314

3. *ibid.,* p.16

4. *ibid.,* p.314

5. The following analysis of the Canadian economy is particularly informed by the work of:

    Clement, Wallace, *The Canadian Corporate Elite, an Analysis of Economic Power,* McClelland and Stewart, 1975.

    Porter, John, *The Vertical Mosaic,* University of Toronto Press, 1965.

    Niosi, Jorge, *Canadian Multinationals,* Between the Lines, 1985.

    Marchak, Patricia, *In Whose Interests,* McClelland and Stewart, Toronto, 1979.

    Burstyn, V. and D. Smith, *Women, Class, Family and the State,* Garamond Press, Toronto, 1985.

6. Rees, William E, *Sustainable Development and How to Achieve It,* An Address to a conference on "Our Common Future in British Columbia," Vancouver, 1988.

7. Swift, Jamie. *The Big Nickel: INCO at Home and Abroad,* Between the Lines, Toronto 1977.

    Clement, Wallace, *Hardrock Mining,* McClelland and Stewart, Toronto, 1981.

    Luoma, Jon R., *Troubled Skies, Troubled Waters: The Story of Acid Rain,* Penguin, 1984.

8. McQuaig, Linda, *Behind Closed Doors,* Penguin, 1987, pp.34-40.

9. Jesuit Centre for Social Faith and Justice. "Understanding Economics, Starting With Our Lives," *The Moment,* Spring, 1989.

Chapter 2

THE DESTRUCTION OF COMMUNITY IN CANADA

"Community" is a word that can mean many things. People use it to refer to the people and buildings in their immediate vicinity, or their peer group, or those people with whom they have interests, work, or a neighbourhood in common. But we also attach a yearning, visionary meaning to the word. "Community" becomes the name we give a geographically-based human relationship between a number of people who know each other quite well, share a sense of purpose and values, and interact in their work, play, and family, and share power to shape their lives.

The cheapening of the meaning of "community" in North America reflects the destruction of human community in this place. As economic development, capitalist-style, has progressed in North America, its corollary has been the pillage not only of natural resources but of natural human relationships.[1]

When the colonizers came to North America, they left rural areas and cities where they had lived for centuries, and came to a continent where the original inhabitants still lived in community. A person's community was recognizable in many cases just by their dialect or the slope of their brow. Just as industrialization, conquest and private property destroyed communities in Europe and drove people to North America, the settlers applied these hard earned lessons in oppression to the indigenous people's communities here.[2]

"Canada" is the name given by the early colonizers from Europe to the northern half of America. Originally it was the homeland of a number of aboriginal nations with different lifestyles and languages. Some of these, like the Beothuk, were wiped out by the Europeans. Others were decimated by disease, starvation and war. But some survived. There were two initial waves of settlers: the French and then the English. The French had almost two hundred years to become part of the northern landscape before the English conquered them. Many of them had been assimilated by indigenous culture and became known as Métis.

The country of Canada was founded as a business agreement between the white colonizers in various parts of the northern continent in order to extend their control over the exploitation of raw materials and to assure the creation of an infrastructure to facilitate this exploitation. This infrastructure was to be supported by taxing the white and Metis landholders and labourers. The taxation system tied the white population to wage labour and to cash cropping in order to have dollars with which to pay their taxes.[3]

The indigenous population was restricted to certain parts of the country and were exempt from taxation. This, however, left them with no vote and no right to own property or business until 1959 (they got the vote in 1968 in Québec).

In most cases, the move left them without an adequate base to pursue the traditional occupations of hunting, fishing and trapping. Even where land agreements were made, the federal and provincial governments frequently failed to pay up. Their lands taken from them, these previously nomadic people were forced into villages. Their language, culture and often their work were made illegal. Their children were taken from them and sent to residential schools and white foster homes. Alcoholism was encouraged by white traders and businessmen.[4]

Any economic development for indigenous people then became dependent on loans and grants from the federal government. The reserves became tied into a wage economy and an acceptance of the narrow definition of "economy" understood by the state. The poverty of the reserves drove many aboriginal people into the white cities, where they faced cultural alienation, racism and greater poverty. They became "enfranchised" and lost any aboriginal rights they had. Until recently any indigenous women who married a white man, gave up her ability to return to the reserve. Many indigenous nations were partitioned by the founding of the Canadian nation, and still refuse to recognize the U.S.-Canada border.[5]

In less than one hundred years, the original inhabitants saw disease and starvation reduce their numbers by 90%.

At the present time, about 50% of indigenous people live in separate sections of the downtown core of cities marked by terrible housing conditions, illegal economies, horizontal violence and despair.[6]

In the early 17th century, New France became a reality. French settlers traded furs and farmed in the fertile Maritime and St. Lawrence valleys. The government of France and the Catholic church were very conscious of the dangers of colonial rebellion, and put down any independence very quickly. No printing presses were allowed in the colony. The fur trade brought the men of the community into intense contact with indigenous people, transforming both cultures.

In the late 18th and early 19th centuries, English-speaking people began to arrive in great numbers. Most of the early settlers were Scottish and Irish immigrants who had been driven out of their homeland by sheep-grazing, industrialization and famine, or they had left the colonies in New England to avoid the independence movement.[7] In the West, the Hudson Bay Company had achieved hegemony over the fur trade and wanted to settle the region to hold it for themselves against the Indians and Metis.[8]

It was not until the early 20th century that immigration from other countries massively increased the white population. Starving peasants came from Poland, Italy, the Ukraine, Finland. From the beginning, Canada's immigration policy discouraged non-white settlement. The building of a railroad, "from sea to sea" by the Canadian Pacific Railroad, and the development of a monopoly controlled telecommunications system uneasily held the country together: a country where the population is strung out over 5,000 miles in a band about 100 miles wide. The forests, tundra, prairies and waters that make up the great expanse of the rest of the country were seen as one big opportunity for resource exploitation by our founding fathers.

* * *

The European settlers quickly formed communities to protect themselves from the environment and the indigenous people. They organized themselves around defense, need for food, shelter and mutual aid of many sorts. As these original settlements became larger, a number of factors were at work that militated against a deepening of the bond between the citizens.

First, the settlers were not encouraged to be self-reliant amongst themselves, but to be a market for goods produced outside their town, village or neighbourhood. Increasingly they produced for an export economy, and imported the essentials of life. This produced profits for the owners of the businesses, but did not encourage co-operation among the settlers.[9]

Second, the pattern of settlement was not in the interests of the newcomers or the original inhabitants, but was determined by the needs of trade, the railway, or resource extraction companies or the most power-ful members of the community — the largest property owners and in-dustries. The most cost effective route for the Canadian Pacific Railway determined the pattern of settlement of most towns in Manitoba and Saskatchewan.[10]

Cities and villages were usually a grid design with no town centre and few natural gathering places. The business elite and local land-owners were worried that gathering places might enable the poor and working people to loaf about or organize. The grid survey system was the quickest way to survey large tracts of land for sale: it had nothing to do with how the people who were there at the time lived, or how the future occupants might want to live.[11]

Unlike more organically evolved towns and cities in the "old world," Canadian urban spaces clearly reflect the interests of retailers, the grain trade, the auto industry, resource extraction companies and booze manufacturers.

Third, religious, ethnic and racial antagonism was encouraged in order to keep the workforce from organizing against the employer. Laws forbidding Chinese workers from bringing their families to Canada, the hiring of Polish, French-Canadian and Finnish miners who had no com-mon language, school yard fights between Catholics and Protestants leave their mark on our cities and towns.[12]

Fourth, where there is no sense of common purpose, there can be no community. In the earlier days, the common purpose was quite simply to survive, and people saw that they would have to co-operate with one another to do it. In more recent years, our "common purpose" has been reduced to having a winning team in sports or some kind of boosterism for tourists. Increasingly, our personal goals have to do with the acquisi-tion of material goods and property or status; we compete with one another. It is the need for a sense of purpose, I think, which makes Canadians remember times of disaster or crisis with such nostalgia. A flood, a tornado, a major strike, are opportunities for people to work together and share their material possessions and their time.

* * *

In February 1987, I was in Cross Lake, Manitoba, an indigenous community about 400 miles north of Winnipeg. Cross Lake is one of a number of Indian reserves and Métis communities that was transformed by a Manitoba government project in 1975. Before that time, Cross Lake was a fairly self-reliant community, that supported itself with hunting, fishing and trapping. It had one of the most profitable commercial fisheries in Manitoba. There was little alcoholism, and little real poverty. There were definitely problems, of course, since the children were all sent out to residential schools. They came back unfamiliar with their own language, and culture. Often they wanted to live in the city. They had no models for parenting, except the institutional relationships and abuse they had experienced in the schools.

Before the introduction of wage labour and capitalism, people were much more aware of the different kinds of work that make human existence possible: the work of transforming raw materials into food, shelter and clothing and of returning them to the earth; the work of raising children and caring for the infirm; the work of building community and spiritual life. Aboriginal people were forced to live within the limits and loops of nature. They knew that if you over-fished an area, you could not fish there next year. They knew that they held the earth in trust for seven generations.

In 1975, the NDP government in Manitoba began construction of a series of dams on the Nelson River system that were to produce hydro electric power for the midwestern United States. These dams changed water levels in all the northern reserves. There was opposition to the dam in the cities and up north, but it did not succeed. So in 1975, Cross Lake saw its fishing and trapping seriously disrupted; the ice became unsafe in winter; a road for the first time connected Cross Lake with a liquor outlet; and television came to the community. The compensation package that was to reimburse the community for the loss of its principle sources of income is so poor that the community has still not signed it.

In this village with unemployment at over 60%, people work harder than I have seen people work in a long time. But now their work is directed toward trying to keep the community from falling apart. The diseases of poverty debilitate the adults. Women spend hours nursing the sick, helping their children learn the lessons they do not understand, worrying and struggling over the drug and alcohol problems of their teens and the rest of the community, trying to support neighbours and family members whose lives are in chaos. Keeping skidoos and fishing boats in repair is a nightmare of searching for parts and retooling others. The Band Council wrestles with trying to scrape up enough capital to develop any kind of income for the community: grant applications, consultants, negotiations.

Throughout Canada, we see the Cross Lake story repeated, but often without the same dramatic clarity. Daily we work to maintain some community among ourselves in spite of the increasing disorganization of our lives by the plans of interests beyond our neighbourhood.

NOTES

1. For my understanding of the nature of community in Canada, I am particularly grateful to:
    Jacobs, Jane, *Cities and the Wealth of Nations,* Random House, New York, 1984.
    Bookchin, Murray, *Toward an Ecological Society,* Black Rose Books, Montréal, 1980.
    Newman, Peter C., *Company of Adventurers,* Penguin, 1986.
    Lorimer, J. and E. Ross, *The Second City Book,* James Lorimer and Company, Toronto, 1977
    Park, Libby and Frank, *Anatomy of Big Business,* James Lewis and Samuel, Toronto, 1973.
    Davidson, Basil, *Africa, A Modern History,* Penguin, 1978.
    Stelter, Gilbert A., *Community Development in the Sudbury Area,* Laurentian University Review, June 1974.
2. Prebble, John, *The Highland Clearances,* Penguin, Great Britain, 1963.
    Etienne, Mona and Eleanor Leacock, eds., *Women and Colonization,* Praeger, 1980.
    Ryerson, Stanley, *Unequal Union,* Progress Books, Toronto, 1973.
    Lipset, S.M., *Agrarian Socialism,* Anchor, 1968
    Richardson, Boyce, *Drumbeat,* Summerhill Press, 1989.
3. Myers, Gustavus, *A History of Canadian Wealth,* James Lewis and Samuel, Toronto, 1972.
    Glazebrook, G.P.deT., *A History of Transportation in Canada,* McClelland and Stewart, Toronto, 1967.
4. Interviews with Art Soloman, Alban, Ontario; Noel Knockwood, Halifax, Nova Scotia; Don Ryan, Hazelton, British Columbia; Heather Ross, Toronto, Ontario. Richardson, Boyce. *op.cit.*
5. Interview with Lynda Edzerdza, June 1988.
6. Brascoupe, Pat and George Erasmus, "Index on Native Canadians," *Canadian Forum,* April, 1990, page 32. According to this reliable source, the registered "Indian" population of Canada is 466,337 of which 260, 337 live on reserves. 284,000 of these live on social assistance. Indigenous income in Canada averages 54% of Canadian income. Native joblessness is about 70%. Federal expenditures on aboriginal programs have declined by 11% in real dollars over the last five years. Indigenous infant mortality rates are more than double the Canadian rate (17.2 per 100). Functional illiteracy is 45%.
7. Prebbles, *op.cit.*
8. Newman, *op.cit.*
9. Myers, *op.cit.*
10. Skelton, Jacie, *Settlement of Southwestern Manitoba,* unpublished paper, 1989.
11. Writes Kent Gerecke: "One main function of colonial government in Canada was to administer policies regarding alienation of land from the crown and the

extraction of revenue from the land. Under the British, land policy was seen as a means to develop a society with the right kind of social, political and religious institutions to serve British interests. For example, the practice of granting townships to individuals or companies was done explicitly in hope of creating a feudal society of 'country gentlemen' and serfs...The chequered plan...was consciously done to 'tie a government, a church and a people to the land as a conservative bulwark against the liberal ideas of the American revolution.'...the gridiron plan's dominance is due to its preference by land speculators because it is simple to layout and survey." Gerecke, Kent, "The History of Canadian City Planning" in Lorimer and Ross, *op.cit.*, p.156-7.

12.   Solski, Mike, John Smaller, *Mine Mill: The History of the International Union of Mine, Mill and Smelter Workers in Canada Since 1985,* Mutual Press, 1984.

Bird, Pat. *Of Dust and Time and Dreams and Agonies,* John Deyell Company, 1975.

Chapter 3

VIOLENCE AND FEAR

INTERVALS: Entry

Enough people come to tell you how comfortable it is
and you come to believe it
this city opening up
like the map it hands out to tourists,
the parks and the reasonably priced restaurants
enclosed in circles, innocent and reassuring
as the arrows lead you back to 401,
the songs on the radio tracing
the same old terrain, love's body
where the prince and the princess live
happily ever after.
Your own childhood. A small girl
eating her spinach out of duty
to the starving, those ragged figures
who still lurk at the edges of polite conversation
like the cities they inhabit, the televised names,
the pictures where women walk through markets
full of soldiers, and kids play
near a parked car, where anything
can happen any minute; though when it does
there's always somebody there
between you and the damage, a voice
over the shots of the bodies, letting you look
up from the screen
to the square of street outside,
and back to the weather
which will be fine, tomorrow rising
as it always has, with those

who are never asked.

All that talk, what was it
but a need for safety, your life
running on automatic
for as long as you let it,
right up to that night (exactly like any other,
you think now, exactly) when a neighbour
knocked on your door, some figure
from a backyard painting of blue arms,
white squares on a clothesline
suddenly there, a woman, coming to you
her face full of blood, the night
spilling out from her hair
to the street, the man, light glinting
off the metal in his hand
as you pull her inside.

Where that night's taken you ever since.
This city, an edge like any other;
its dark, the border territory between houses
where violence holes up in men's hands, the shadows
that fall between a woman's breasts, the kids born
already knowing. Like time bombs, all those childhoods
huddled in corners, these houses
wired to the world, the hum you hear
when you pass, the TV's blue light
spreading into the street and inside
the people, frozen by it,
just sitting there
waiting.[1]

I was raised in a quiet suburban part of Winnipeg, but during the early
1950's, I can remember being afraid to walk home from school because
the Koreans might drop bombs on us. I was luckier than my friend, who
was afraid to walk home because her dad was going to beat her if she
"did anything bad." And I remember a teacher going berserk in the
class room and throwing one of my girl class mates up against a wall,
until another teacher came in and stopped it. Like most young women, I
learned very quickly when and where you could be out at night with
some degree of safety. I was lucky. It wasn't until I left this cocoon behind that I was able to see how fragile this security was.

Violence is a very real part of Canadian society. For many of us, fear of physical injury, pain and humiliation are a way of life. The institutionalized violence of the state is often hidden from white middle-class people, but it is very obvious to native people and blacks. Canada is also a participant in NATO and has supported American aggression in Central America and elsewhere. Over $1.3 billion of our gross national product is for war materials, most of which are sold to the U.S. military machine and Third World dictatorships.

Violence Against Women

Violence against women received a great deal of attention in the media after the shootings of 14 young women at the University of Montréal in December 1989. But it is not a new problem. Even conservatives estimate that one in ten Canadian women have been physically assaulted. The Ontario Native Women's Association estimates that eight out of ten aboriginal women experience physical abuse at some time in their lives.[2]

Certainly poverty and race affect the kind of protection women will get from police and other authorities. I remember receiving a call from an indigenous woman friend, who said that her white boyfriend had beaten her up (in fact he had fractured her skull), and that she was afraid to call the police because they would not keep him in jail, and they might dismiss what she had to say as coming from "another drunken Indian." The hearing into the Betty Osborne case in Manitoba made it clear that life for indigenous women in Canada is very dangerous indeed.[3]

When women want to become active outside their own home in the community or the workplace, they often face the damaged pride of their husbands and boyfriends. Often they are risking their lives. Or at least they are risking being beaten or shunned by their families for breaking with the traditional role of women. Sometimes they are said to be unfit mothers and their children are taken from them.[4]

When women do lay charges, or fear for their lives or their children, they have to leave home; they become dependent on welfare and the police for protection. In most cases they have to live in transition houses, while the batterer walks the streets. If they cannot afford to rent or buy another home, they will have their living circumstances and that of their children substantially reduced.

Violence Against Indigenous People and Blacks

As I write this book, the Canadian army has occupied Kahnasetake and Kahnawake — Mohawk land — with tanks, armoured personnel carriers, and almost four thousand troops. Freedom of the press has been curtailed. Aboriginal people are being tortured and imprisoned in unprecedented numbers.

Even before the events at Oka in the summer of 1990, it had become very clear to white society that blacks and indigenous people are treated differently by the police and the state. Aboriginal justice inquiries in Alberta, Manitoba and Nova Scotia produced scathing indictments of the justice system in those provinces in 1989. Hearings into the police shootings of black youths in Montréal and Toronto in 1988-9, made it very clear that the problems were systemic.[5]

A disproportionate number of people in the prisons are non-white, especially aboriginal. There is hard evidence to show that prison sentences for non-whites are longer, harsher and much more frequent. Indigenous people are more likely to be physically abused by the authorities.[6]

In sovereignty struggles, aboriginal people have been actually engaged in a war over the retention of their land. They have waged this with non-violent direct action. The response of the Canadian state has been to show enormous military strength. The Innu people of Labrador have been arrested in large numbers and held in jail for sitting on runways to prevent low-level NATO flights over their traditional hunting grounds. The Gitska'an and Wet'suwet'en people have had full military patrols chasing them in their fishing grounds. During a five month blockade of the Red Squirrel logging road on the ancestral lands of the Teme Augama Anishnabai over 370 people were arrested. The OPP spent over $1 million on "protection" during this action. The government sent 40 officers and a helicopter to arrest 5 of us one snowy Saturday.

When police decided to act on the Kahnawake Reserve in 1988 over the smuggling of cigarettes they ringed the reserve with 225 officers armed with submachine guns. In Akwesasne, on October 13, 1988, 250 police officers and 75 vehicles, a helicopter, 2 tow trucks and patrol boats were sent to arrest 7 people.

Although the United States has dealt out much more direct violence to indigenous activists like Leonard Peltier and Anna Mae Aquash — falsely imprisoning Peltier and arranging the murder of Aquash — we should not forget that they are Canadian citizens and the

Canadian government has done nothing to seek a redress of these heinous crimes.[7]

Violence Against Labour and Community Activities

The Canadian state has never hesitated to move swiftly and viciously whenever social control breaks down, and Canadians do not react with shock when it happens.

Uprisings such as the Winnipeg General Strike, the Estevan strike, the On-to-Ottawa trek, the treatment of Doukhobours, the October crisis in Québec in 1970, and the heavy sentencing of the Squamish Five are only a few of the more shocking incidents in Canada.[8]

The Canadian secret service maintains files on many activists that are not obtainable through the Privacy act. Several environmental and peace groups suffered breakins in 1989, including the Ontario Environmental Network in Toronto, the Toronto chapter of Science for Peace, the Green Party of British Columbia in Vancouver. They were robbed of information and computer equipment. Filing cabinets were opened and rifled.[9]

Over the years, many labour and community activities have been the target of police spying and disruption.[10] Police agents and informers have played a significant role in disorganizing trade unions in Canada. In the early 1970's, it was discovered that the violence attributed to the Front d'Action Politique in Québec, was in fact the work of RCMP agents provocateurs.[11]

When the G-7 summit was held in Toronto, the waterfront area was turned into an armed camp. Army officers cordoned off the area from Front Street south, and harassed passersby and people going to Toronto Island for picnics. A peaceful demonstration during that time was met with riot police, helicopters and armed force.

Unions in Canada were only organized after difficult and violent struggles in most Canadian communities in the 20th century. In my own community of Sudbury, miners still talk about the mass layoffs of workers who tried to organize in the forties, and of the interference of the American State Department, and the Catholic church in union affairs in the late fifties. Activists in the Mine-Mill Union were blacklisted, and beaten up in the streets just thirty years ago.[12] Today, workers trying to organize still face intimidation, firings, and blacklisting.

In Québec in 1990, the CSN faced a multi-million dollar suit for damages, loss of their rights to a compulsory dues check-off, and members in the union lost their seniority, after they defied a provincial government order to terminate a legal strike.

Non-union workplaces are not at all democratic, and the power of an employer on the shop floor is absolute. Any worker can be expelled from a workplace for "disruptive" behaviour. Even in such benign workplaces as the church, fired employees are routinely told of the firing in a supervisor's office and escorted out of the building without being allowed to say good-bye to fellow workers, or pick up their belongings.

The "Social Safety Net"

At a workshop on the "Feminine Face of Poverty" in Sudbury, we were looking at the life of a single parent on family benefits and trying to diagram all the forces that serve to disorganize her life. We talk about transportation scheduling and the location of housing. We talk about lack of credit and costly medications. Her children's inability to participate in school activities and recreation because it costs too much. All the nightmare problems that come out of having too little money in a city that assumes you have enough. And then her voice breaks. "The worst part," she says,"is when it's the last week of the month and you find out they are holding your cheque."

Canada has an elaborate system of security for those who are unable to earn a living through wage labour. It has been there since relief and the dole in the Thirties. Working people and organizations of the unemployed fought hard to get it: riding the rails and getting shot up on the On-to-Ottawa trek, demonstrating and lobbying and struggling in elections. It is kept in place by the continuous vigilance of the ordinary folk in this country. When an effort was made to change the old age pension, seniors across the country mobilized and demonstrated on Parliament Hill. In the last few years, every province except Ontario has tried to gut their welfare system, and thousands of people have dropped what they are doing to petition, lobby, demonstrate and organize. That the cutbacks have not been worse is a tribute to this effort.[13]

There are a whole lot of people who visibly make their living as helpers in the welfare system: social workers, income maintenance officers, psychologists, family therapists, administrators, book-keepers, clerks and so on. But there are also a lot of other interests that benefit: computer manufacturers, paper companies, communications companies, sell to the administrative apparatus. And then there are all the merchants, gas companies, landlords, and services where welfare cheques are spent. Even on skid row, there are pawn shops, barber colleges, Christian missions, used clothing and furniture stores, cheque cashing outfits, and rooming house/hotels. And poor people also pay taxes, in fact more, percentage-wise, than the rich. Welfare is an important part of our economy.[14]

However, the government has transformed demands for redistribution of wealth into a punitive and complex system that serves other interests better than it serves the poor. Although it provides a very minimal income to most poor people in Canada, it does little to shift wealth from those who have to those who don't, and nothing at all to redistribute power.[15]

Despite some rhetoric to the contrary, most social policy in Canada "blames the victim" and maintains the powerlessness and poverty of the bottom 20-30% of the population. Even our much-vaunted job creation programs are short-term, minimum wage, under-capitalized efforts that serve only to shift the costs of unemployment from municipal ledgers to federal ledgers for short periods of time. Most training programs for the unemployed fill the needs of industry for semi-skilled or unskilled workers. Although they might move some individuals from unemployed to employed categories, they do nothing to change the percentage of the population that is without paid work.

Basically, the welfare system takes what might once have been the concepts of "caring for your neighbour as yourself," or "sharing what we have," and turns them into a set of relationships where some people in our society get to be professional helpers and others get to be professional helpees. Which you get to be is determined by your income and birth as much as it is by your abilities. That's because you have to go to secondary school to get to be a helper and that costs money. On the other hand, low-income people get to be the helpees, and they are trained in the school of hard knocks.

The professionalization of helping relationships in our society is really quite extraordinary. You would think that people never did know how to get along with one another or to solve human problems before the advent of the social worker. People no longer get together to stop someone from beating his kids; they call in the Children's Aid Society. People who are in despair or emotional pain are treated by psychologists and psychiatrists and drugs. Some welfare families see five or more social workers or services at one time. Every one of these services has different rules, structures and powers that make them confusing and frightening even to the most sophisticated helpee.

Often the central message communicated by these services to clientele is "we will teach you how to fit in with our world and then you and/or your children will be happy." In fact, what they do teach is that the client does not have sufficient skills to get along, that she/he has to depend on the good will of these professionals to survive, and that she/he better be "good" (however that is defined by the agency) or she/he will be punished: be institutionalized, have her/his kids taken away, be kicked out of the program and so on. The client's own survival skills and street smarts are devalued and undermined.

On the other hand, the system is also hard on the professional helpers. Day after day, they see people in crisis, who they have only limited ability and power to help. The burn- out rate amongst workers in the helping professions is very high.[16]

The welfare system itself doesn't even pretend to "help" the poor anymore. Now they call their frontline workers "income maintenance officers," and they administer files, interview clients, and act like fraud police. For many welfare recipients, the fear of getting cut off and potentially ending up starving and homeless, or losing your children because you cannot support them any longer is a very real threat. In Woodstock, Ontario, in 1987, emergency shelter was handled by the Salvation Army but Social Services wouldn't pay their share on a per diem basis unless the applicant first went to the police and got booked as a vagrant. Said a worker at a church sponsored drop-in centre there, "People at Social Services call them transients, but they aren't. They are local people with no place to live." [17] The amount of social assistance received in real dollars has been shrinking for a number of years now, and the only way that most recipients survive is to earn income babysitting or at part-time work or to have a boyfriend on the side, or a secret roommate. Undeclared income is a criminal offense for someone on welfare as are other means of income supplement: theft, pushing drugs, bootlegging and prostitution.

For low-income people, the social safety net looks like an irrational system of spying and terror. For them to stick their necks out and organize with one another under these conditions takes great courage indeed.

NOTES

1. Wallace, Bronwen, *The Stubborn Particulars of Grace*, McClelland and Stewart, 1987.
2. Ontario Native Women's Association President Susan Hare, speaking in Sudbury, January 1990.
3. Reports in the *Winnipeg Free Press* throughout 1988-90.
4. Rodriguez, C. and L. Wise. *Organizing with Women of Colour*, a paper presented to URM-North America, October 1989.
5. Ample documentation of these injustices can be found in the report of the Donald Marshall Inquiry, the Aboriginal Justice Inquiries in Alberta and Manitoba, and the report on the death of Millie Sutherland in Ottawa in 1988.
6. Walkom, Thomas, a series of articles in the *Toronto Star*, April 15-20, 1990.
7. Richardson, Boyce, *Drumbeat*, Summerhill Press, 1989.
8. Bird, Pat, *Of Dust and Time and Dreams and Agonies*, John Deyell Company, 1975.
9. "Break-ins Against Activist Groups," *Connexions Digest*, Issue 50, December 1989,p.19.
10. Brown, Lorne and Caroline, *An Unauthorized History of the RCMP*, James Lewis and Samuel, 1973.
11. Chodos, Robert and Nick Auf Der Maur, *Québec, A Chronicle, 1968-72*, James, Lewis and Samuel, 1972.
12. Solski, M. and J. Smaller, *Mine Mill: The History of the International Union of Mine, Mill and Smelter Workers in Canada Since 1985*, Mutual Press, 1984.
13. Riches, Graham. *Food Banks and the Welfare Crisis*, Canadian Council on Social Development, 1986.
14. Ward, James, *Organizing for the Homeless*, Canadian Council on Social Development, 1989.
15. Ross, David P. and Richard Shillington, *The Canadian Fact Book on Poverty*, Canadian Council on Social Development 1989.
16. Carniol, Ben, *Case Critical: The Dilemma of Canadian Social Work*, Between the Lines, Toronto, 1988.
17. Interview with Marg Murray at the Meeting Place, Woodstock, Ontario, Feb. 5, 1987.

Chapter 4

MANAGEMENT OF INFORMATION AND
COMMUNICATION

It's Saturday morning in my house. The kids are lying on their stomachs in front of the television, watching Roger Ramjet kill off one more bad guy. In between five minute segments of the cartoons there are ads for toys, sugary cereal, and the occasional message about being nice to your family from the Mormons. The telephone rings constantly as the kids make their plans for the rest of the day. They watch TV while they talk to their friends. If the TV wasn't on, it would be radio pop-songs at full blast. Tonight, Dev wants to watch the hockey game on TV, Andrée would like to see the new movie in town, some stupid Hollywood comedy.

We all know that THE MEDIA has a lot of power. It is folk knowledge now that kids are more influenced by TV than by the classroom; that media makes or breaks political campaigns; that polls matter more than votes in deciding public policy; that our perception of the world is shaped by what the media presents as information.

Community groups worry constantly about how to get their points across in the media; how to protect themselves from media stereotyping. Politicians use media images to sell themselves and their ideas to the public. Any corporation or person with something to sell tries to buy time in the media. How does "Media" work anyway?

In Canada, we get information from many sources. We talk things over with our friends, neighbours and co-workers, in person, on the telephone, through letters, and sometimes with interactive computers and facsimile machines, or by attending meetings and workshops. This is "interactive communication." Or we attend lectures, watch television, read books, newspapers, magazines, listen to the radio and tapes, watch films, videos and theatre. These are "one-way communication."

Since there are so many sources of information, one might think that it is easy to find out what is going on around us, or to inform people. In fact, we all know how difficult this is, and we know that it is getting harder. Why?

There is a famous saying that "Freedom of the press is reserved for those who own one." Getting your message out depends on access to a channel of communication.

Most television and radio stations are owned by a few multinational corporations. The programming they carry is determined by what potential advertisers pay to support. What they will support are programs that viewers who might be interested and able to consume their product will watch. Poor people are not big consumers, so they are not a potential market and their needs and tastes in television viewing hold no weight. Middle-income people are big consumers, so their interests in viewing are important to the owners of the medium. Teenagers like rock music, so radio stations carry hours of this music and are supported by advertisers that appeal to adolescents.

Experiments in alternative programming are described later in Chapter 8 of this book. At this point, let me say how very difficult it is to compete with the expensive and glossy productions that the mass media crank out. Their format and presentation are scientifically designed to fit the short attention span of most viewers, and to hold us mesmerized. The programs and ads over-stimulate us with violence, sexuality and suspense. Advertisements for new cars, beer and soft drinks are given more attention and time than reports on children dying in Africa.

Books, magazines and newspapers are much less expensive to produce, but it is increasingly difficult for small publishing houses to survive at all in Canada. Newspapers (with a few exceptions) are controlled by Thomson, Irving or Southam Industries.[1] Most books and magazines are also published by a few large companies headquartered in the United States. Until recently, Canadian magazines were protected by "Tariff Item 9958," which restricted the access of U.S. magazines. The Free Trade deal is changing all of that.[2] Now print media that are vertically-integrated and have access to national advertising contracts and economies of scale dominate the market. Recent cutbacks in Secretary of State and Canada Council funding to publishers have decimated women's, indigenous and multicultural publications. Rising costs of the postal service have made it worse.

Distribution of books, magazines and newspapers is by retail sale or subscription. Outlets in stores and malls are controlled by distributors who prefer to stock high volume products like the *National Enquirer*, Harlequin Romances, the local Thomson paper. Even if an alternative publication gets access to the distribution network, it will probably be displayed in a "low visibility area." Subscriptions are expensive to maintain. Most commercial magazines and newspapers are paid for by their advertisers and depend on the size of their readership for economies of scale. Even bookstores are dominated by chains, who are interested in books that will turn a large volume quickly. Smaller bookstores which are more likely to carry alternative publications struggle to meet the rent with a tiny margin of 15-20% per book, often not enough to meet the shipping charges.

Although simple interactive forms of communication like conversation, telephone, mail are still available to most of us, there are significant shifts in their power and accessibility.

To speak of the postal service first, we all know that it is much more expensive and takes much longer to receive a letter than it used to. The reduction of operating hours, rural postal service and the line-ups in post offices have made it harder to send letters. More and more Canadians are illiterate, or at least uncomfortable with the written word, and this reduces the effectiveness of postal communication. What most of us don't know, is that the new technologies in the post office are manufactured by the same companies that produce electronic communications equipment: facsimile machines and telephones. A friend of mine who worked as a mechanic in the post office told me a few years ago that it was his opinion that the post office equipment was made to break down, so that people would become impatient with it and use private couriers and privately-owned electronic services instead.

These electronic forms of communication — telephones, computer networks, facsimile machines — are not available to everyone. They all represent a capital investment. Although the telephone is the cheapest of these tools, the deposit required by telephone companies for installation (sometimes as high as $500) makes them inaccessible for poor people. The other technologies are simply unavailable to people who have trouble paying the rent or feeding their children.

What we increasingly see is the class division of communication. The service gets worse and more expensive for the poor and faster and more efficient for the wealthy. This leaves conversation, meetings and other face-to-face kinds of information exchange, which are dependent on people being in one place at one time. Even our ability to do this has been disrupted by the design of cities, the pervasive presence of television sets, and the increasing amount of time we spend in "shadow work" — the time getting too and from the workplace, shopping, caring for children, waiting in line, filling out forms — that is essential to keeping our lives together but not rewarded with a paycheque.

All-in-all, it is no wonder that ignorance (not stupidity) is one of the greatest problems facing Canadian activists. We don't know very much, and what we do know is often inaccurate, a-historical, or disconnected from the real world. The development of a critical consciousness in this country is more difficult than it is with Latin American peasants.

Social and Cultural Effects

Language and forms

Control of information goes beyond the ownership of newspaper and television chains, to the question of the language and forms in which information is kept and exchanged.[3] In Canada, most research is done by corporations and academics.

Knowledge is divided into disciplines and specialties each of which has its own vocabulary and jargon. The windows on the world of these specializations appear to be framing very different animals. The description of the same forest by an economist, a biologist, a lumber company, and an indigenous person would sound like completely different things, but in fact they are all important to understanding the past, present and future of that forest and to understanding what needs to be done to protect it.

These different languages are related to socio-economic class, and bring with them certain privileges. Ethnic accents, grammatical differences and size of vocabulary are instant indicators of one's position in society. It is difficult to imagine a person who has been trained to think and talk like a bank president having to argue with a welfare administrator over his/her cheque. Conversely, it is almost impossible to imagine someone who talks like a Toronto street kid running a bank.

The ways in which information about the world is compartmentalized is obvious in a newspaper. In one issue of the *Globe and Mail* for example, there might be six different stories, all reflecting parts of the same reality:

- Interest rates going up after a lull;
- Housing starts for suburban homes increased last year;
- More families seeking emergency shelter in Toronto;
- Crack trafficking causing crisis in the inner city;
- Increased car accidents on highways linking city core with suburbs;
- Crisis in emergency wards in hospitals.

Chances are that there are little groups meeting all over the city to discuss these separate "issues," but no one is looking at the larger picture. Even if we put the key actors in these events together to discuss what they had in common, they would be unable to understand what one another was saying.

Selective information

Those who can afford to buy radio, television and print time can by and large determine what people think the important things in the society are. They manipulate us with images and slogans. Very little time or space is given to news of the world or our local communities. When it is, it is often confusing and piece-meal. A great deal more time is given to sports, situation comedies, soap operas, advertisements. Almost all the soap operas and sit-coms are set in upper-middle class American homes. You rarely see people doing real work. The problems are all personal and not related to socio-economic conditions. The city streets are portrayed as filled with random and inexplicable violence.[4]

From time to time, a good show or news report appears on television, but they are the exception.

Recently I have been struck by the lack of distinction between fact and fiction in newspapers and magazines. The continuing sagas of soap opera plots, the ridiculous headlines in the *National Enquirer*, the sex lives of movie and sports stars are given greater billing than First Nations sovereignty struggles.

Interestingly enough, it is the most colourful and simply written papers that carry this bunk. Newspapers written for the literate carry the news of the mergers and acquisitions of the ruling class.

Although Canadians seem to get a fair amount of information about problems with our economic, social and political life, we get very little information about how people are working for change in this country. It is really common to hear people say "nobody is doing anything about…"

Unless an activist subscribes to a variety of alternative publications: *Canadian Dimension, Pro-Canada Dossier, This Magazine, Our Generation, Earthwords, The Moment,* and others like them, you really have no idea that anyone but government is involved in working for change. The history books and sociology texts used in schools also represent the point of view of the establishment. Popular history has been written so that change appears to be the beneficence of the state, or the work of a few extraordinary individuals.

Most Canadians feel an overwhelming sense of their own powerlessness and despair. In the present, the steadfast refusal of the media to report the successful struggles of ordinary folk in Canada against oppression, makes popular groups feel that they are the only ones doing anything, and makes those who are not active feel very lonely indeed.

Contradictions

In many community groups, as we struggle to get our voices heard, we forget that within the corporations that control the media, there are also workers just like us. These people struggle on a daily basis to present real information to the public. In recent years, the *Globe and Mail* fired most of its editorial staff. Many small town papers, like the *Sudbury Star* are locked in union fights with management over editorial control and the time to do a decent job. There are many martyrs and heros.

Attempts at alternate newspapers, television broadcasting, magazines and books compete for market space and support with these giants. Because corporate media take these efforts very seriously, they continuously lobby the government for changes that will undercut the alternative media, such as increasing the hurdles to obtaining charitable status for tax deductions and increasing mail costs.

The Education System

At an Ontario Federation of Labour conference in 1989, entitled aptly *It's Our Knowledge,* long-time education activist George Martel said:

Everyone knows how hard it is to stand up for your dignity
in school. You know how hard it is to keep faith with your

intelligence, with your knowledge that you are as smart and able as anyone else. This knowledge should be obvious when we look at this room full of union leaders who have proved their competence and their smarts in the real world. But to those who wield power in this society and who control its education and media, working class intelligence in not one bit obvious. The recognition of this intelligence is something you have had to fight for ever since you were kids...

...There are, it seems to me, three main ways in which those who run our schools try to keep workers' kids at the bottom and which we in turn have to resist. (These administrative and political initiatives are resisted I want to add here, by lots of good teachers; the worst thing we can do is scapegoat teachers for a system largely outside their control).

The first thrust is the labelling — at different levels and degrees — of more and more working class kids as dumber and crazier than middleclass kids...Usually there's a lot of fancy pseudo-scientific language in these definitions. Someone once figured out there were 52 euphemisms for "stupid."

Then there is the placement — or streaming — of these kids (defined as dumb or crazy in varying degrees) according to how dumb and crazy they are judged to be.

Finally there is the programming that is laid onto the labels...[5]

Martel goes on to explain that the testing that determines the abilities of children, particularly the IQ test, is class-biased. It asks children to sort in general categories instead of asking for answers to do with relationships and change. This same critique of testing methods is made by Carole Gilligan in *In a Different Voice*, which debunks the notion that boys develop morally at an earlier age than girls.

Our education system has produced little in the way of critical consciousness. Working class children are systematically humiliated and made to feel inadequate in a system that devalues their own experience, and teaches them they are failures. This has become increasingly scandalous as class size increases, and teachers' organizations are undermined. Illiteracy even among high school students is growing rapidly. In Newfoundland it is over 40%.

The fact is that for a lot of kids — working class, poor, disabled, native, immigrant — the school system is a place where you learn to hide what you don't know from the teacher, and where you only preserve your dignity and self-respect by rebellion. Unfortunately, many kids throw the baby out with the bath water, and rebel not only against the school system but against knowledge and book learning.[6] When my own daughter was moved to a French school at the age of ten and found she could not understand the teacher, her interpretation of the problem was to say she "hated school," was "too stupid to try." She began to cut classes and act up.

I remember stopping a young indigenous kid who was staying with us, and for whom school had been a frustrating and humiliating experience, from burning some books on the porch. I remember how many young people at drop-in centres that we set up like the Do-Drop-Inn and Murut were unable to read and write.

Children, like the rest of us, have fragile egos and lots of pride. Scars left from the education system prevent us from learning as adults; interfere with our ability to say "I don't know"; and destroy confidence that would enable people to organize together for change.

A few years ago, I, along with Lillie MahSen and Alyson Huntley from CUSO, was asked to facilitate a gathering of development educators from the Prairies. We were asked to help participants integrate their learnings about oppression in the Third World with an understanding of oppression in Canada. So we developed a role play called Kasup, B.C. The central character was a person recently returned from Nicaragua anxious to "educate" local people. He chose to do it through the schools. But at the time, in this hypothetical town, the community was convulsed by a conflict between the teachers' union, the province and the local school board. And the students, many of whom were low income, indigenous or immigrant, were bored and frustrated. The participants' job was to develop a strategy for social change in Kasup.

Although many of the participants were able to develop a strategy that worked with the teachers' union and some low-income town people, none of them were able to see the classroom situation itself as oppressive to the students. They still developed strategies for "teaching" more progressive information through means that marginalized kids who had a hard time in school.

In the debriefing from the exercise, we discovered that all the development educators there had been straight A students, and that most of them were from privileged backgrounds — an interesting finding.

NOTES

1. Goldenberg, Susan, *The Thomson Empire,* Methuen, 1984.
    MacLean, Eleanor, *Between the Lines: How to Detect Bias and Propaganda in the News and Everyday Life,* Black Rose Books, Montréal, 1988.
2. Canadian Publishers Association Newsletter, #128, quoted in *Connexions,* Issue 50, December 1989.
3. I am particularly indebted to Dr. Dorothy Smith of the Ontario Institute for Studies in Education for her insights in this area, which she has shared with me through numerous conversations.
4. Gordon, Robbie, *We Interrupt this Program...A Citizen's Guide to Using the Media for Social Change,* University of Massachusetts, 1978.
5. Martel, George, "Labelling, Streaming and Programming of Working Class Kids in School," in *Its Our Knowledge,* papers presented at the Ontario Federation of Labour Conference on Education and Training, Toronto, May 1989, p.20-21.
6. Martel, George, *The Politics of the Canadian Public School,* James, Lewis and Samuel, Toronto, 1972.

Chapter 5

PACKAGING DISSENT

Government Support of Social Change

"You have to understand," the Ottawa mandarin said to me, "there are so many people to my right, that I like to have a few people on my left. It keeps me honest."

The man who said this to me in 1965 was one of the architects of the Company of Young Canadians. The CYC — as it was then known — was established by the Pearson government in response to the demands of student activists and others for a radical redistribution of power in Canada. They set up an organizing committee of concerned and pre-eminent citizens and hired a research team (mostly young and full of wishful thinking) in the summer of 1965. The CYC then went ahead and entertained projects from all over the country that were to hire young adults at very low rates of pay (volunteers) to work for social change.[1]

From the beginning there was a struggle between what the activist leaders of the youth movement wanted to do and what the government thought they should do. The leaders of the youth movement wanted opportunities for young people to live and work with the marginalized people in society so that they could learn from each other and then use their shared perceptions and skills to build new bases of power in Canada. This meant leaving the projects open and fluid so that they could take the directions that the community people wanted them to take and having volunteer control of the administration of the Company so it could respond to the needs of the field without establishment interference.

Government spokespeople always claimed that they were in favour of "community development," "empowerment" and so on. At first a number of the projects really did take on the "establishment." Youth took over the streets of Yorkville. They organized with tenants and youth in Kingston. Rocky Jones worked with black people in Nova Scotia. In Montréal, Calgary and many other cities, CYC volunteers really listened to the people in the neighbourhoods and began to build effective community groups. For most of the young people in the CYC it was an intensely radicalizing experience. For the local people it was an exciting time. For the entrenched local elites, it was a nightmare, and they began to demand controls over the CYC and any similar government programs.

In 1969, the conflicts came to a head over the CYC in Québec, where a number of volunteers were said to be members of the Front du Liberation du Québec.

The government's response was to appoint a controller on the pretext that funds were being misused, and to change the criteria and administration of the CYC. The controller, Max Mendlesohn, was "a top-notch administrator and a highly competent manager. His forte was figures, plans, structures, job descriptions, and policies."[2] Within a few weeks, he delivered the CYC program firmly into the hands of the government. Shortly afterwards it was disbanded, and followed by a range of other programs which were administered through the Job Creation Branch and the Secretary of State. These, too, became ways for people to fund work for community empowerment, but as they were successful, new administrative controls were introduced that limited their effectiveness.

What were some of these controls?

- The creation of a board of directors for local projects that represents a variety of community interests and does not include the staff of the project.
- Money only available for special short-term projects and not for long-term funding, and for which the criteria shift regularly.
- A requirement that all staff positions be advertised and only available to very narrow parts of the population.
- Approval for projects from a member of parliament or a committee established by him/her.
- Determining of a goal/issue at the outset of a project including a "needs analysis" and "anticipated outcomes": a method which precludes an issue evolving out of the process of community consultation and action.

- The creation of a number of administrative forms for accountability that require substantial hours of staff time to complete.
- The allocation of funds so that groups that should ally with one another compete for the same funds.
- A requirement for measurable results or output such as clientele, case files, job placements, etc.

In a study by Roxana Ng of an immigrant women's centre,[3] it can be clearly seen how the imposition of these administrative procedures can be used to control community work. The organization she studied had begun as a collective of immigrant women helping one another achieve justice. Once it sought state funding, it was required to have a Board of Directors, to produce regular accounts and funding applications, to show measurable production (i.e., number of clients placed in jobs). It quickly was transformed into a service agency with a tiny staff and a large clientele, delivering a government program.

Corporations and governments are quite happy to "deal with" dissent when it can be packaged and controlled. As another example, in 1990, the Secretary of State department cut core funding to women's centres while continuing to provide program funding. Theresa Mackenzie of the St. John's Women's Centre stated that this was an attempt to determine in which programs and activities women's centres could be involved. "If we think that Meech Lake or reproductive choice are the most important issues for women, we will no longer have the ability to organize around them," she said.[4]

Collective Bargaining

The legalization of collective bargaining in Canada has had a similar story. Collective bargaining was sought by workers for years as a way of gaining control over the conditions and rates of their work. When collective bargaining was legalized during the Second World War because employers needed a secure and stable labour force, workers discovered that the victory was very partial indeed.[5] They could only strike when the contract expired, and in between had to discipline their members if they took matters into their own hands. The negotiations and grievance procedure transformed trade union leaders from militant shop floor stewards to lawyers who haggle with management over the dollars their members will receive for the sale of their labour. What is produced, how it is produced, and how it is distributed are considered to be "management rights" beyond the scope of the contract. A lack of understanding about how this process works leads to disillusionment and charges of "selling out" by rank and file unionists and activists.

The closed shop and the Rand formula granted to recognized trade unions the right to a compulsory dues check off from their membership. This has been an important tool for freeing the union from recruiting members and raising funds on a regular basis. These gains are now under attack, and unions are discovering that they may no longer have the ability to keep their membership and dues in place: they are out of touch with their membership.

The unfortunate fact is that collective bargaining keeps trade unionists so occupied with technical detail and busy work that they are unable to confront the power of management in any basic way. Although it gives workers some power to negotiate wages and conditions of work, it leaves the powers of management intact — powers which enable management to introduce new technologies, change product and move capital from one region to another. For this reason, strikes are often followed by plants closing, or moving to Mexican maquilladores, or by the introduction of labour-saving or deskilling technologies. For this reason, health care workers, teachers, and social service workers continuously see the quality and social utility of their jobs diminished but feel powerless to stop it. Trade unions in Canada are also limited in their abilities to organize with the unorganized or to assist laid-off union members; they become protective of their own position of relative privilege vis-a-vis other workers.

Further, the very special legalistic and research skills required of union leadership in Canada create divisions between the rank and file and the leadership and the staff. No one is immune from corruption, and these divisions make it possible. If your alternative is working shifts on an assembly line, or going back underground, maintaining your position in the union office sure seems attractive. Many working people in Canada have few models of truly democratic organization to draw from, and so are not skilled at creating or running them. The upshot of all this is that, although unions are essential for the defence of workers rights on the shop floor, they have been badly disorganized by the collective bargaining process.

I don't want these comments to be misunderstood. Trade unions are essential to the defence of workers' rights in Canada and elsewhere. This became abundantly clear to me on a recent visit to Taiwan and South

Korea, where workers are struggling for democratic trade unions and workers' rights in the same way North Americans did in the early part of the Twentieth century. In Taiwan, 5 of 13 members of the executive of the new trade union central were in jail charged with sedition for their work. I met fishermen working on trawlers who reported being assaulted by the captain to such an extent that their fellows leapt overboard rather than take any more abuse. I met laid-off workers who had squatted outside a factory for 120 days, because they had nowhere else to turn.

In Canada, I have worked in union and non-union shops. At least in the union shops we had freedom of speech and some protection against the arbitrariness of management. In non-union shops there was nothing. Most non-union workers here owe whatever benefits they have to management's fear of a union coming in. If the trade union movement in Canada is allowed to fall apart, we will all suffer. Their struggle for democracy, relevance and survival is our struggle.

Advocacy Funding

In the late sixties, a number of store front legal clinics were established in Canada. Usually, they were staffed by a mixture of street-wise community people and progressive law students or lawyers who wanted to provide representation and advocacy for the poor. Sometimes they had a board or an advisory committee that was made up of leaders from the poor community, or the injured workers union or some such militant organization. The advocacy took place in the context of this grassroots organizing.

When we first set up the Community Information Service in Kingston, for example, it did workshops for welfare recipients about their rights. It helped organize tenants for collective bargaining. It saw welfare recipients advocating for each other with the welfare department. It participated in running progressive candidates for municipal council. As people came in asking for help in a crisis, they were recruited to help others when they had similar problems. We built a network of committed activists who helped one another; put out a community newspaper and pressured for change.

To some of the law students working in the clinic, it seemed like a good idea to have Queen's Law School take it over and use it to train law students. Although this provided a stable base of funding, the effect of the move was to completely disempower the community people who had worked there. All of a sudden, the skills they brought to the organization were perceived as "unsophisticated, too radical," and so on. Many of them did not even understand the language that the lawyers used in the meetings and felt stupid when they had to ask for an explanation. They voted with their feet.

Quite rapidly, the clinic ceased to get poor people in crisis together for mutual aid, and became a service that called welfare to get cheques released, that launched appeals in administrative tribunals, and/or translated the poor person's situation into legalese or social worker jargon.

Losing control of the clinic was a serious loss to the organization of poor people in Kingston.

Ten years later, I went to work as a community legal worker at a legal clinic that was the progeny of that effort, funded by the Ontario Legal Aid Plan. I was to advocate on behalf of the poor who were having problems with social assistance, the UIC, their landlord and so on. 50% of my job was to be community organizing: helping the clients of the clinic empower themselves for justice. The board that hired me was made up of quite progressive people including representatives from the Union of Injured Workers and some poverty action groups. We were very effective at creating turmoil and pressuring for change.

In the six years I was there, I saw the legal establishment and the Ontario government move to strip clinics of this organizing function and to increase the distance between clinic clients and clinic workers. This was accomplished in a number of ways:

- The administrative requirements of the sole funding body were increased, so that hours of each board meeting and staff time were spent justifying our existence. Many of the less educated members of the board dropped off because they didn't understand the language.
- A means and assets form was introduced so that your first interaction with someone coming into the clinic was to ask them a lot of personal questions that were not directly relevant to their visit. It made an equal relationship impossible.
- The clinic moved its office three times. From a storefront in a working class neighbourhood, to an old house near the courts, to the fourth floor of an office building.
- Requests for increased staff were continuously refused, so that the case load for staff members became unbearable. Since organizing was not quantifiable in the same way, the time allocated to it was squeezed, and I ended up doing it on my own time. When I left the clinic, a

lawyer was hired in my place, and the 50% organizing requirement that was in the collective agreement was therefore dropped.

- Instead of clients dealing with one worker from the moment they came into the clinic they might now deal with three. They would see an intake worker or a duty counsel, and then a legal worker and then a lawyer. It was very disorienting.
- Work around rent review and repairs to slum apartments was dropped, even though the clinic had a very high success rate, and they were one of the key places to teach self-help methods.
- Lawyers were paid a great deal more than community legal workers or support staff. In our clinic we originally had wage parity by mutual agreement. When this began to break down because the lawyers wanted more money, the funding agent stepped in and imposed a director on the clinic as well as higher salaries for lawyers (which had to come out of everyone else's pay).

The clinic ceased to empower its clients or to help people with similar concerns get together to challenge the decision-makers, and became an advocate for individual cases that left the power structure intact. Like the Ombudsman's office, clinics are funded by government to channel the rightful anger of people who are cut off welfare, denied UI, have been unjustly evicted, or treated unfairly by the system in other ways. Were the clinic not there, these victims might be organizing, demonstrating, and generally raising hell in the offices of bureaucrats across the nation.

Packaging Community Development

The term "community development" signals the packaging of a process that ordinary people have engaged in with greater or lesser success for years. This package consists of cataloguing the skills that enable people to develop collective self-reliance by working together in groups, planning activities and carrying them out. Once the process is packaged, it can be purchased, taught, and managed. Community development becomes a component of courses in social work, agricultural extension programs and international development. It becomes a service for which consultants receive salaries.

One of the side-effects is that once someone in a community or group becomes the "community development expert," everyone else starts to feel like they don't know anything about it. They devalue their own knowledge. And often the "expert" thinks it is in their own self-interest to maintain this fiction.

On the other hand, I suppose there is really nothing wrong with demystifying and packaging some of these skills: they are just useful tools. But we need to ask a number of questions before we buy into any community development package:

- Who put the package together?
- What are their interests?
- What will it cost and who will benefit from it?
- Does it lead to an equitable redistribution of power for the community?
- Does it truly enable the community to become more self-reliant?
- Does it help participants become more confident in their abilities to challenge power and conventional wisdom?
- Does it truly encourage the community to develop a long-term vision of where it needs to be in five generations?

Unfortunately, most community development packages don't meet these criteria. Often, the package is an attempt to divert the community from economic development plans that are destroying the community. For example, the U.S. government sent community development workers into Appalachia during the 1950's and 60's while the strip mining of coal was ruining the villages and farms to try to persuade people to accept other kinds of industry, such as textiles and uranium refineries. When the community development workers got involved in protesting the strip mining, the government removed them (not before one was shot).[6]

Community development has enjoyed great popularity with the Department of Indian Affairs in communities where resource extraction was ruining traditional economies. Indigenous people were encouraged to dream about what kinds of small businesses and social programs they would need instead of thinking about ways to stop the plunder of their forests, lakes and fields, or to engage in sovereignty struggles. Most of the community development money went to white consultants in big cities who would fly in, work on proposals, and then fly out to collect their cheques. I remember reading once that "more than one half the $8 billion aid to Africa each year is spent on 80,000 expatriate consultants."[7] Probably the same percentage applies in First Nations communities.

Some community development packages are much too issue-oriented, and are really designed to get community input and volunteer time in a government program. Recently I have been approached by a number of private businesses that are bidding on contracts for public housing redesign or health promotion strategies. When most of them talk about "community development," they just mean setting up a few community meetings and forestalling public protest over the plan.

Sometimes the language of development is used to manipulate acceptance of new technologies and systems that tie communities into dependency on complex and expensive machinery and expertise. Under the guise of community economic development, the green revolution (agri-business farming methods) was brought to Africa and traditional farming methods were lost.[8] Under the guise of community development, indigenous communities became increasingly dependent on a wage economy and were forced to accept economic plans that were based on a profit model. Under the guise of community development, militarism became a much more significant factor in large parts of the Third World.[9]

At present in Canada there is renewed interest in "community economic development" by the state. This is a result, I think, of the problems of single industry towns and the farm crisis. Governments are under pressure from local elites in rural areas to maintain the population base in small towns in the hinterland, by finding alternatives to employment other than the large company (engaged in mining or lumber), fishing or farming.[10]

Government defines the problem as a lack of local initiative and an underdevelopment of the local economy. As a result, they respond with entrepreneurship training and encouraging small enterprises that will preferably generate more dollars in the community by selling to people or businesses outside the community. In technical language this is called an export economy. These are exactly the same "development" ideas that have kept Africa and South America colonized for the last century. We need to define the problem differently: a lot of wealth is generated in all of our communities, but it does not stay there.

Even in poor communities a lot of wealth comes in — welfare cheques, wages from minimal jobs, mortgage money, construction jobs and so on. The problem is that most of it goes out immediately. It goes as profits for the major industries. It goes as rents to landlords who do not live in the neighbourhood, or from local landlords to banks, energy companies and construction firms. Food dollars end up in supermarkets which are owned by big chains and they won't even buy local produce. We buy new cars instead of recycling old ones. We ship out our timber and purchase materials to build a house from outside the community.

Even our recreation and leisure dollars leave the community: bars and bingos and sports teams direct our money elsewhere.

We need to ask not only how do we get more money into our community, but how do we keep it there?

In farming communities, as an example, the problem is the corporate organization of agriculture, not lack of local initiative. Over 40% of farmers have been driven off the land in the last twenty years. This is deliberate government policy, set out in the Task Force on Agriculture Report of 1969. The task force had such noted farmers on it as the chairman of Ralston Purina. For years now, Canadian farmers have been encouraged to grow one or two cash crops largely for an export market. In order to acquire the acreage and equipment they need for this kind of farming, most farmers have gone heavily into debt and now pay out most of their income to the bank for interest and to the seed and chemical companies.[11]

In the long-term that kind of farming is destructive. It kills all the micro-organisms in the soil until it is lifeless and blows away. Large companies begin to patent seeds and other life forms. Rural families are driven off the land, and rural communities die. Their problem is not a lack of local initiative, but an inability to fight effectively the destruction of their land and way of life. This is not for lack of trying. Some of the most brilliant organizing in the country has been undertaken by farm organizations.

For government, community development becomes a way to look like you are doing something when you aren't. It keeps people in the hinterland quiet. In large parts of Canada today, leadership, resources and population are being sucked into the large cities, particularly the golden horseshoe (Toronto, Windsor, London, etc.). Farming communities are being depopulated. Single industry towns are finding that new technology is depleting their workforce. The fishery and the farms are increasingly being run as mechanized companies that require fewer people. Oil, lumber and fish stocks are being mined out.

Community development, as the government plays it, is a way to keep local elites in Sudbury and other cities and towns from screaming. Money is put into investment funds that allow people to start small businesses and to test out expansion ideas. They support the set up of franchises or branch plants of large companies, or they start-up small businesses that are dependent on the computer hardware and software of large companies, or that pay out most of their income to the bank for loans and mortgages. For example, the largest single Innovations grant was made to Tiem Canada, a branch of Control Data corporation.[12] They set up business "incubators" that provide a climate for small business to grow. Control Data is a company that is very active in South Africa. Their interest is in creating markets for wholesalers, banks and computer manufacturers. Most of their profit is from government grants.

In many communities the people who are able to profit from these business schemes are the sons, daughters and friends of the people who make up the local advisory committee to the project. And guess who that is?

Community development in this context can be like giving an aspirin to a woman who is being raped.

NOTES

1. Although most of this information is from my own files, I have also drawn on:
   Hamilton, Ian, *The Children's Crusade,* 1970.
   Daly, Margaret, *The Revolution Game,* New Press, 1970.
2. Hamilton, Ian, *The Children's Crusade,* Peter Martin Associates, Toronto, 1970, page 298.
3. Ng, Roxana, *The Politics of Community Services,* Garamond Press, Toronto, 1988.
4. *The Journal,* CBC, April 6, 1990, an interview.
5. For information on the history of trade unions in Canada, I have drawn on:
   Laxer, Robert, *Canada's Unions,* James Lorimer and Company, 1970.
   Bird, Pat, *Of Dust and Time and Dreams and Agonies,* John Deyell Comapny, 1975.
   Johnson, Walter, *The Trade Unions and the State.* Black Rose Books, 1978.
   Morton, Desmond, *Working People,* Deneau and Greenberg, 1980.
6. Gaventa, John, *Power and Powerlessness,* University of Illinois Press, 1980.
7. *Hard Cash: Man-Made Development and Its Consequences,* Jan 1985.
8. Davidson, Basil, *Africa, A Modern History,* Penguin, 1978.
9. Etienne, Mona and Leacock, eds., *Women and Colonization,* Praeger, 1980.
10. I am grateful to Melanie Conn, Bibiana Seaborn, Dal Brodhead and Ted Jackson for their insights on community economic development.
11. Kneen, Brewster, *From Land to Mouth,* NC Press, 1989.
12. They received $460,000 in 1986 from the Innovations Program.

Chapter 6

THE WORKPLACE

The Line

the line never stops
oh it pauses on occasion
to tease you
or remind you who's boss

life controlled
by a whistle
every movement
a study in time and motion

spot-welded to your press
spot-welded to your job
spot-welded for life
spot-welded for life.[1]

For most of my life, I have not been paid to be a community organizer. Instead, like lots of other people, I've had to do "real work." I've worked as a nurse's aide, a secretary, a bank teller, a research assistant, a service representative for the telephone company, a sales clerk, a teacher, a sod-layer, a gardener and a community legal worker. Because it consumes so much of our time and creativity, the way in which we earn our living changes how we look at and act in the world outside the job.

Working as a bank teller made me very aware of the differences in income between people who came in as customers. I worried about my appearance a lot. I became very careful with money and receipts and bills.

Laying sod made me physically strong and tough and, because the wages were so low, I was constantly worried about money. Loafing behind the boss's back became a game we played to get some needed breaks and self-respect.

Working at the legal clinic, where every client I saw was poor, desperate and facing a terrible life crisis of one sort or another — cut off welfare, eviction, work injuries — turned me into a chronic worrier. I began to see our lives as very fragile indeed. And I became a passionate and effective advocate for the underdog everywhere I went.

In all these jobs, though, there were common threads. Generally, I like work most when I am learning something new, where I have room for individual initiative, where I enjoy my co-workers and where my labour is socially useful. I don't think I'm very different from other workers. But these certainly aren't the characteristics of most jobs.

When I worked at Bell Canada from 1971-73, I simply couldn't understand why anyone would organize work in that way. So I decided to find out and in 1979 put what I learned into *The Phone Book: Working at Bell Canada.*[2] What I learned was this:

Work is organized by the people who own the means of production. Their only interest in the work we all do is to get as much production out of us as possible at the least cost. Over the years the owners have tried out many different ways to organize and plan production, but the way that gives the most control to them and costs them the least has three characteristics.

- Jobs are divided into two basic categories. The owners and upper management do the intellectual planning functions and the workers do the manual, clerical and repetitive functions.
- Decision-making is hierarchical. Structures can be rearranged and policies implemented easily from the top of the pyramid, but at the bottom of the pyramid there is only very limited movement possible.
- Every job is divided into its component parts; each part is given to a different detail worker and a different rate of pay and status is assigned to each part.

The organization of work at Bell Canada in 1979 provided a fine example of this.

All non-management employees fit into the bottom part of a rigidly-structured hierarchy that extends for seven levels, from "line boss" right up to company president. All decisions concerning policy direction and production are made at the top. The lower levels — assistant manager, local manager and district manager — are charged with getting the maximum possible production from the non-management employees beneath them. Managers at the lower levels deal with the customers and the day-to-day problems created by the conflict between customer demands, employee resistance, and company pressure for increased productivity.

The company lists seventeen different clerical occupations and twenty-one associated occupations ranging from detail draughtsman to photographic technician. The employees are trained on the job for these occupations: they are poorly paid and easily replaced...Clerks plugged into computer networks have replaced the skilled book-keepers, draughtsmen and engineers of a few decades ago. The skills required by these clerks are considerably more narrow than those once required by the occupations that are no longer needed. What's more, the skills are cheaper to purchase, easier to impart, and much more easily replaced than those of the highly skilled people who used to perform such tasks.[3]

This idea, of labour being strictly divided into its component parts, was first postulated by a man named Charles Babbage in 1832. Basic to Babbage's then-novel conception of work was the division of a skill or craft into each of its separate parts and the assignment of each part to a different 'detail worker'. Before Babbage's time, each worker would perform all aspects of a task, just as a skilled cabinet maker creates a whole piece of furniture. While workers might divide a process amongst themselves for the sake of efficiency they would never willingly convert themselves into lifelong detail workers.

Charles Babbage predicted the "most important and influential cause" of savings from this division of labour — dividing the job into its component parts makes the jobs a lot cheaper. An appropriate rate of pay can be assigned to each part depending on the amount of training it requires and the number of people available on the market to take the job.

Even during this time, many workers retained the skills necessary to control their work. But new management practices in the first decades of the twentieth century were to change this. The chief theoretician of the new management style was Frederick Winslow Taylor. Its goal was the maximum possible production from employees in the shortest possible time.

It was carried out by relieving employees of all "unnecessary" information about their work and concentrating information in the hands of management. Management could then use it's resulting monopoly over knowledge to parcel out the work and control each step of the labour process.

Taylor believed that the greatest obstacle to production was the loafing, or "soldiering" that workers did on the job, and that the most destructive impulse was "systematic soldiering" — the deliberate effort on the part of workers to conceal just how fast the work could be done.

He insisted therefore that the real task of management was to expropriate from the worker the knowledge of how the task was performed, to study its component actions and details and then, with a view to doing the task in the cheapest way possible, to dictate back to the worker the precise manner in which the task was to be performed.

The basic principles of "scientific management" are:

i. The strict division between mental and manual labour. Manual workers were only to be given the minute specifications of the work done on a daily basis.

ii. All tasks are to be reduced to their simplest components and each component is to be assigned to a different worker. Each worker's task was to be made as simple and repetitive as possible.

iii. Each task was to be consistently timed and analyzed for speed and accuracy so that management might control the pace of work through quotas, piece work and so on.

Taylor's ideas were eagerly embraced and implemented by the two men who had perhaps the greatest impact on modern workplace design in the world: Henry Ford and V. I. Lenin.

For workers involved in this process, it was a direct assault on their autonomy and dignity, an assault that was intensified later by the ability of companies to monitor employee productivity electronically. Detail work and scientific management have now become the basis of the organization of work in advanced industrial countries. The Bell model has become a 'standard' for employee management in modern corporations. Despite talk of job enrichment and team planning, the decisions about the organization of work, product, ownership and control are retained by the owners and managers of the corporation. The impact of this form of organization over a few generations on working people cannot be minimized.

The decision-making process — centralized in management — is mystified and imbues the managers with an aura of competence. Workers at the bottom of the pyramid feel unable to understand or challenge the direction or operations of the corporation. Life-long detail work and rigorous on-the-job discipline makes the employees see themselves as incompetent and ignorant. It undermines the confidence of workers who do the repetitive and low-paid jobs. It divides workers from one another, through differences in wages and status. The hierarchy of skills and status carries over into employees' social acceptance of one another.

We do our community organizing with people many of whom spend at least forty hours of their week in this kind of environment. In the 1990's, most government and non-profit groups work on this model. Sometimes we even inadvertently set it up in our own organizations. If we wonder why tellers and service representatives and frontline civil servants seem so uncaring, we have to look no further than the structure in which they work. Daily, workers are only "following orders" when they continue to carry out work that destroys the environment or builds military equipment or makes others suffer. Any responsibility they feel for the eventual products of their labour has been taken from them long ago.[4]

NOTES

1. Michael Wilson in *Going for Coffee,* ed. Tom Wayman, Harbour Publishing, Madiera Park, 1981, page 15. Michael Wilson is a production worker at Ford Motor Company, Buffalo Stamping Plant.
2. Kuyek, Joan, *The Phone Book: Working at Bell Canada,* Between the Lines, Toronto, 1979.
3. *ibid.,* p.16
4. Some other useful resources for workplace analysis are:
    Rinehart, James W., *The Tyranny of Work,* Longman Canada, 1975.
    Garson, Barbara, *All the Livelong Day,* Penguin, 1975.
    Braverman, Harry, *Labour and Monopoly Capital,* Monthly Review Press, 1974.

Chapter 7

RELIGION AND CULTURE

On February 20, 1988, I am watching the opening of the Calgary Winter Olympics on television. What a spectacle. Over 6000 people performing, over a million watching it. The audience arrives in the stadium to find coloured ponchos on their seats. When they don them, the entire grandstand is turned into a mural bearing the Olympic symbol. There is music and dancing. As the climactic moment for the lighting of the Olympic torch approaches, women in white robes approach a raised dias to the sound of native drums, raising their arms to the centre. A twelve year old virgin runs into the stadium holding the flame and climbs the steps of the enormous concrete altar to light the torch. On cue, a towering representation of a teepee of multicoloured cloth rises into view behind the altar, and airplanes fly over trailing streams of vapour like a rainbow. As the advertisement for Coca Cola, "the Real Thing" comes on the television, I notice that the woman beside me has tears of wonder in her eyes. That evening some young people are arrested and accused of sacrilege for toasting marshmallows on the Olympic flame.

Watching the sports rituals of my culture fills me with despair: so much hoopla about the individual achievements of youthful athletes, so little attention to the meaningful work that dedicated and intelligent kids do to heal this broken planet. How can we ever compete with this?

Canadians are starved for meaning in their lives, and the use of ancient sacred symbols evoke powerful emotions. But in Canada in the 1990's these emotions are manipulated to serve the interests of corporate sponsors and those who would keep us even more imprisoned and afraid.

Healing the earth is dependent upon a re-membering of the natural relationships between people, air, water, energy and matter, and plants and other animals. Most of us have no idea any more how to live in harmony with the natural world. We romanticize it, or we trash it. We hide from the cycle of death, decay and rebirth. We live in a cultural context where salvation is said to be found in the acquisition of wealth and status and where to be poor is to be damned.[1]

Money does not bring happiness in and of itself. Sharing, harmony, co-operation, physical well-being, challenge, beauty do. The problem is not how to get more money, but how to create conditions where material security is equally available to all people.

In Canada in the 1990's, the vision that we are encouraged to seek on television and elsewhere is one of individual happiness through fun, money and the "happy" family. It is represented in the powerful images of beer commercial lifestyle ads and the romantic love peddled in pop-songs. We are led to believe that this vision is not only attainable, but in fact is already the property of "successful" people.

Studying television and magazines tells us that successful people are usually attractive (in a very particular way), white (although they might look like the Cosby family), slim, heterosexual, very clean and economically well-to-do. And they have lots of "fun" and they are "in love" almost all the time.

An "average" point of view of life is as it is seen by a married, upper-middle-income, male Anglo-Saxon with two children. In fact, most of us are not like that. We come from a variety of cultures, races and contexts, which are all depicted as either exotic or marginal.

I remember sitting in a home in northern Manitoba where everyone spoke Cree as a first language, watching Dallas on a television screen while the community radio station asked in Cree for Alice Monias to call her mother. That family thought we were all like the family on Dallas. How many of us have had to pretend to the teacher that Daddy is just like the Daddy in *Dick and Jane*, or that the bruises were from a fall? How many kids can't go on school trips, or miss lunches, or have no one at home who can help them learn to read?

The large majority of the human race are deprived of power and material well-being. It is a tiny minority that manages to live in material comfort, free of fear for survival. Although low-income people in Canada are less than half the population, their interests are aligned with over two-thirds of the world. You would be hard-pressed to find representations in the churches, or the media that treat the poor or the non-white as the predominant cultural influence. Those who do not have access to material well-being are portrayed as pitiful, unhappy objects of charity or as criminals.

I know it certainly doesn't make me want to insist on my difference from the idealized "average" family. I can remember the moment when I realized that the "poor single mom" they were describing was in fact me. I felt shame and then rage...but I sure didn't want to be identified that way.

Our culture makes everyone afraid of being shunned. At one time in my children's lives, they did not want their friends to find out that their parents were not living together, because "it would be too hard to explain." And yet, when they did tell the truth, they discovered that many of their friends had similar stories.

If this weren't enough, a number of much "heavier" tactics can be brought into play when other ways of viewing the world start to take hold. One of these is a kind of ideological name-calling that is taken up by the dominant forces. In the fifties, the cry was "communism," and many people lost their jobs and saw their lives in ruins for being denounced in this way. In some circles, words like "feminist," "queer," "anarchist," "witch" serve the same purpose. Once the label is pulled out, people become afraid to talk anymore, in case they too are labelled with that brush. As Rita MacNeil sings, "You'll find yourself amongst the people you were warned about."

I watched this used with great effect during the INCO strike of 1978-9. The Wives Supporting the Strike group had been extremely effective in gaining country-wide support for the strikers and in helping women in the community support the strike. In March they were asked to participate in the International Women's Day March in Toronto. There they marched with activist women from trade unions, community groups, lesbian organizations and feminist groups. On the way home, one of the husbands who had gone to Toronto with them, started to say that they were being "used" by feminists and communists, and they panicked. By the time the next wives' meeting was held, about one half the women were afraid to stay in the group, because it might "affect the future of their children."

Worshipping the Economy

The Random House dictionary gives as its first definition of religion: "a set of beliefs concerning the cause, nature and purpose of the universe, especially when considered as the creation of a superhuman agency or agencies, usually involving devotional and ritual observances and often having a moral code for the conduct of human affairs…"

The state religion of North America is the worship of the accumulation of wealth. It has all the attributes of a religion:

- A set of beliefs about the nature and purpose of the universe: growth, development and the survival of the fittest.
- It treats the laws of economics as if they were not the creation of human activity, but part of the natural order.
- It has its own devotional and ritual observances: the consumer frenzies of Christmas, Easter and Mothers' Day, and its special festivals, usually centering around sports events and the entertainments that gross lots of money. Its church is the stock market, and its priests are the gurus of the economy.
- It has a code for the conduct of human affairs, based in consumerism, "realism" and the bottom line.

As with the liturgical language and the priesthood of old, most of us are completely bamboozled by the language of the economy. We think of ourselves as economic illiterates: we are so intimidated by the language and concepts that are used by businessmen and economists that we feel powerless to challenge or debate them. When we try to raise issues of the environment, neighbourhood, peace or health, we are told that we are not "realistic" and we "don't understand good business practice."

Often, what they describe as "sound economics" seems like dangerous gobbledy-gook to us.

Economics should be limited to the organization of the material needs in a society. It should be a ground for critical debate about the kind of world we want to live in and how well the society achieves it. Instead, we are served up a value-laden and self-serving justification of the profit motive by economists and businessmen. At the root of this distortion is the premise that only those things that can be measured in dollars have any value or meaning.

In any society, different kinds of work are undertaken by its members: the basic work of survival (food, shelter, clothing); the work of raising children and providing care for the elderly and the infirm; the work of building right relations between people and maintaining community.

You know that all this work is important, but to an economist, most of it does not exist. He can deal only with those activities which are exchanged for dollars. So, for example, my caring for my children and my neighbour's children has no value, unless I sell my services and make sure they are recorded in the government statistics. Clean water has no value, unless it is sold, and then the only value recorded will be its selling price, either as a tourist attraction, a beverage, or an industrial component.

As an example, let's look at the household.

An economist could not measure the contentment of family members or the beauty of the surroundings except as they contributed to the family's productivity. It would mean that everything you produced for yourselves would have value only if it were exchanged for dollars, and even then the economist could not measure things like job satisfaction or quality of production. The economist could not measure satisfactory sex, or healthy children, or good community relations. Neither could he measure the utility of all the hours you might put into community, political or recreational activity.

What the economist could measure in your household would be the amount you consume and the amount of money you bring in. He could measure these statistics against other homes, and he could develop totals for communities and neighbourhoods. But he would have no idea at all what really went on in the home. A healthy household, to him, would be one where income exceeded expenditure.

A group of us in Sudbury who had been involved in a lengthy battle over jobs and housing with the various levels of government decided to form an organization called the Sudbury Citizens' Movement. Over the period of a year, we developed an idea for an abandoned prison farm thirty minutes drive from the city on the Trans-Canada highway. The prison farm had over 26,000 acres of forest and grasslands. It was on a major canoe route and close to a provincial park of extraordinary beauty. Three thousand acres were cleared land, and in fact had once raised enough food to feed the entire prison population of 700 and a small village that was on the site. Fourteen years before it had been self-sufficient in vegetables, meat, and dairy production. The year before the provincial government closed it down in a construction boondoggle, they had put $4.5 million into renovations on the 69 houses, 38 bed single staff quarters and the 6 shops and 3 barns. There was also a gymnasium that had never been used, big enough for 2 basketball courts.

A feasibility study had been done of the site in 1975 by a large consulting firm, indicating that a number of business ideas were feasible, but would create only about 8-10 jobs each. Our group spent two entire years working out a plan for the site, and proposed that the Burwash prison farm was an ideal place for a regenerative form of agriculture and an interlocking set of worker cooperatives engaged in farming, dairy processing, construction, tourism and the establishment of a group home for kids who were presently in foster care. Our own study of the feasibility of this plan indicated it might be self-sufficient within 10 years, but that it would require about $2 million investment from the province in order to bring the housing etc., back up to standard.

We spent two years pressuring the government to take us seriously and building community support. Finally, we had reached a level of community acceptance where the government was forced to take us seriously, and they responded by hiring a consulting firm to do a feasibility study. The study cost $80,000. In the end they came to many of the same conclusions we had, but they said we were not feasible because we could only create 35 jobs in five years, and would not yet be self-sufficient.

There was no way in their conclusions for them to measure the impact of our proposal on the long-term health of the land or the forest. No way for them to measure the long-term benefits for the children that could be there instead of in a city foster home. No way for them to measure the benefits of restoring the housing instead of tearing it down. In fact the indices of "success" were such that the government could find it more feasible to sell the land to the Department of National Defense for $65 an acre for a rifle range, and destroy the houses. They could only measure social benefits by the number of people we would have been able to take off the welfare roles. And because this enormous document from an expert said that we were not "feasible," we were unable to convince the press and the public that it did not make sense.

The Institutional Church

Established Christian churches in Canada have done little to confront this worship of the economy.

Writes James Berry:

> ...Religion should be the center for explaining things that have to do with reality and the meaning of human existence, and right relationships between humans, between humans and the divine, and between humans and the non-human world...The desperately needed explanations pertain to the

human role in creation…Established religion has not identified poisoning and polluting and plundering as major sins
to be explicitly and severely condemned in the moral code.
And so the perpetrators are not sinners and they may very
well enjoy good standing in the established churches.[2]

Part of the problem in established churches is the concept that the
church is there to save the world and what the purpose of the rest of the
world is nobody has the faintest idea. Church people, like the rest of us,
like to think of themselves as helpers. But they need a helpee. And most of
us would rather die than be a "helpee," where that means dependence
and charity.

That does not mean that all people in Christian churches are doing
bad things. Most of them are worried about the environment and injustice and peace. The economic crisis does impinge on most of them: even if
they themselves are not unemployed, their children or friends may be.
They can see the young people leaving their community. But churches
require money to maintain the building and the stained glass and the
minister and all that stuff. And people who can't pay their way get
squeezed out of the congregation.

The perspective of the liturgy and activities of most churches is
that of an economically comfortable person, not of the poor or oppressed.
Although at least 25% of Canadians are desperately poor, and although
75% of the world's population are poor, the mainstream churches in
Canada continue to talk as middle-class people, even when they talk
about justice.

It is very different to tell economically secure people that justice
requires that they share what they have than it is to tell an indigenous
woman who has three relatives and two family acquaintances living in her
overcrowded flat. What she needs to hear is that she has a right to decent
housing, privacy and adequate income. She needs to hear that she can
demand justice; that there is nothing wrong with fighting for your rights.

There have always been Christians who have struggled to have
the church speak with the voice of the poor and the oppressed and not at
them. Since the late 1960's the growth of this movement has created
tension in almost all the mainline churches. As one South African friend
of mine described it, "the church, too, is a site of low intensity conflict."
On one side is "liberation theology" that has grown out of the struggles of
people's movements for justice in Latin America, Africa and Asia, on the
other is protection of the institutional church and the status quo.

At the same time that liberation theology has been growing in strength, fundamentalist right wing churches have been advancing even faster. These churches do appeal to poor people: their liturgy recognizes the misery and despair in their lives. Because many of the activities are subsidized by wealthier members, often in the United States, the poor do not have to pay to attend. But the message of these fundamentalists is either that poverty and distress are the result of sinful behaviour (on the part of the poor), or that suffering will be rewarded in heaven. Both messages keep the victims of injustice from protest. In many communities they also serve to divide the communities further against themselves because they teach that it is sinful to associate with people who are not members of that church.

Most church members in the pews, of course, are caught in the midst of this conflict. They do not experience it as a conflict between justice and the institutional church. Instead it gets played out in innumerable and tedious debates over allocation of money, appointments to committees and the hiring of staff, the wording of documents, Bibilical authority and so on.

At a convocation of the World Council of Churches in Seoul in 1990 on the subject of *Justice, Peace and the Integrity of Creation*, delegates at a Justice Forum from mainstream Protestant churches all over the world voted unanimously in favour of a statement that read:

> The central issue of justice we want to put forward during the JPIC convocation and beyond is this: *the unjust accumulation of wealth and power in our societies and in our churches.* This accumulation is based on the worship of capital and profits, at the expense of people. We use the word "worship" deliberately. It is the choice of the idols of death rather than the God of life.
>
> This unjust accumulation deprives people of land, estranges them from their labour, reinforces racism, sexism and casteism. It is maintained and defended at all costs against the poor, by the use of four types of power: political, economic, social and psychological in a strategy that is misleadingly called low-intensity conflict.
>
> People and nature are one creation: injustice to one is injustice to the other. When we destroy the environment,

we commit injustice, especially to future generations. Even when people destroy the environment because of need (and not because of greed) their need is itself the result of another injustice.

We affirm that people's movements are the primary partners. We should not look at people no matter how poor and powerless as mere victims of injustice or beneficiaries of partnership. People are the main resource for justice when they organize, engage in popular education, develop networks and coalitions and are empowered to become participating subjects in their own present and future.

The power of the people includes the power of their spirituality. The Spirit has many names and should not be understood religiously immediately in Christian terms... People draw strength from various traditions and people's movements develop a deeper sense of ecumenism as they discover their indigenous spirituality.

We realize that churches locally and internationally will not take sides as a whole. They are more likely to remain "sites of struggle."[3]

NOTES

1. I am grateful to Starhawk for her terminology and insights, especially in *Truth or Dare.* (op.cit.)
2. Berry, James F., *The Centre for Reflection on the Second Law,* Circular #116. Berry edits the newsletter of this centre, and has been very helpful to me in developing this analysis.
3. *Report of the Justice Forum,* World Council of Churches, March 1-3, 1990, Seoul, Korea.

II

FIGHTING FOR HOPE

If you read through Part I, you are probably feeling pretty depressed by now. It is always overwhelming to hear how the structures of power-over work. The next four chapters are about how we can work together to heal this broken world.

For a long time writing this book, my greatest difficulty was organizing the material in some coherent way. As my friend, Dorothy Smith, told me, "First you have to decide what it is you think about the subject, then you have to decide how to present it to others." As I struggled with presentation, I was also preparing to teach a course on community development to some indigenous people at the community college. So, of course, I read all the materials I could get written by aboriginal people about community development.

In one of these books, there was a discussion of community development in a holistic framework, using an adaptation of the sacred medicine wheel. It said that for a community to be in balance, all four directions had to be represented in the work. In community development, those four directions were cultural, social, economic and political aspects of the community.

The concept of the four directions is also part of ancient earth-centred cultures in Europe and it was familiar to me from my feminist research. When I began to think about community development in this way, the next four sections quickly took form. I am grateful to the Four Worlds Development Project in Lethbridge, Alberta, for this gift.

Too often the work activists do is not balanced. We know how to do one of cultural work, group process, political strategy or economic alternatives, but whole chunks of experience and information are missing. Like a wheel that has one or two flat sides, our plans get stuck. I would encourage you to try the aspects you are least familiar with, play with them, experiment. You may find that the wheel begins to turn again.

Each chapter in this section contains some stories, some analysis and some exercises to use in a group. I hope they are helpful.

Gardening In Sudbury

Driven by dreams of healthy food and beauty,
I began this garden.
Only dead lawn, a few bits of hardy crabgrass and dandelions.
No life in this soil, except the cutworms,
Long destroyed by Gro-green and Killex.

Day after day, pushing my pitchfork into the thatch,
Pulling out the old grass and weeds,
Adding peat moss and manure,
Imported from the countryside —
If there's no life in your soil,
Bring in some outside agitators.
Adding wood ashes from my own fireplace,
Where the winter fires had brought us warmth,
Adding the compost that let us feel
Self-righteous about leftovers.

Then letting it rest for the winter,
While we dreamed through catalogues:
In this inhospitable northern climate, what will grow?
How about Siberian grapes? Nix the luscious kiwi.
Where do we place them, so they don't crowd out the others?
Warding off insects, attracting bees, exchanging secrets?
Carrots and tomatoes, sage with cabbage, beans with corn
So they get enough sun, enough shade,
So we can get at them for the harvest?

In the spring, waiting for the frost to end,
We turn the soil again, add more nutrients, make the beds.
Holding fast to the vision of
Soil, sun, rain, seeds, insects and
Gardener producing together.
The planting itself doesn't take very long.

For a few weeks, we watch the garden.
Will it to grow.

Some seeds don't come up.
Some are lopped off by cutworms.
I turn predator, dig into the soil,
Crush them between my finger and thumb.

Where soil is saturated with past chemicals
The plants are stunted and sick.
Brown-spotted broccoli, shrivelled squash,
Maggots destroy an entire crop of onions.
Acid from the belching super-stack
Deep-sixes the irises.
The war with the earwigs over the corn crop
Finds me in the store flirting
with Roach motels and Raid cans.

But other plants thrive.
Beans inundate us with green plenty.
The kids say "catsup" means
"Catch up with the tomatoes,"
Lettuce and endive and potatoes and beets
and carrots and corn and cukes.
Jaunty marigolds and daisies.
Herbs for healing and protection.
Vagabond pumpkins in the compost.
Wood sorrel and lamb's quarters between the rows.

And this is just our first year of work.
With the same care, it will be better next year…
More poisons gone, more life-giving soil,
A more knowledgeable gardener.
More ability to sustain ourselves,
More resistance to disease and death,
And, soon, the time is coming I promise you,
We will grow our own seeds.

Joan Newman Kuyek

Chapter 8

CREATING A CULTURE OF HOPE

The process of creating social change will always alter the thinking and behaviour of people who are involved in it. As we saw in the last section, a major part of the struggle in Canada is ideological: breaking the social control and conditioning that keep us from acting for change. Often this kind of activity is dismissed as "touchy feely" stuff by the traditional left, but the organizing of aboriginal peoples and the growth of the women's movement in Canada make it clear that these methods are crucially important.

I have been teaching a class of twelve students from reserves in northern Ontario. One morning, they are presenting the "maps" they have made of their communities. The maps look at the cultural, social, political and economic realities of each community. As each reserve is discussed, it becomes very clear that in those communities where traditional ways of life and traditional rituals are now being practised by the leadership, the social, political and economic life of the community is also improved. These reserves have managed to achieve 80% or more sobriety. There are interesting social programs for the young people. Women are more active in the life of the community. Disease, violence and accidents are dramatically lower. And plans to reclaim the economy and struggle around sovereignty issues are underway.

For years, indigenous people have found themselves overwhelmed by powerlessness and despair in their attempts to bring change to their own communities. Their subjugation had been brought about by police and army interventions, by the removal of the children to residential schools, by the forced removal of peoples in the creation of villages and reserves, by the imposition of regulations and laws outlawing traditional sources of income, by the plunder of their lands and resources by corporate interests and by the outlawing of their traditional language, religion and way of life.

Aboriginal people found that this disempowerment was reflected in the lifestyles and social relations of their communities. Dependence on alcohol, horizontal violence and suicide were the most prevalent symptoms. To heal the circle of life meant reawakening their connection with the earth, and beginning once again to draw strength from traditional values and religion. Time and again, indigenous people have found that the use of the medicine wheel, the drum, sweat lodges and the sacred pipe carry with it the power to heal whole communities.

This understanding of our connection to the earth has also fired the environmental movement and the peace movement of the last ten years. James Berry writes:

> You are members of a generation which inherits a diminished earth; degraded air and water and soil and sunshine. Wind, water, earth and fire, the basic supports for life, are all badly damaged. If you carry on with the life-style and philosophy of your parents and grandparents your children will inherit an uninhabitable earth. You must live lives radically different from the lives they lived. Your principal problem is to defend the earth from further damage and to inaugurate the great healing of the earth that is so essential...the culture is brainsick as well as soul-sick... The culture made it OK to destroy the source of life, to lay waste that which the human cannot do without. A culture which allows its top soil to be washed away and blown away and paved over can only be called sick...Its thinking apparatus is diseased.[1]

If we are to help create communities where life can be sustained then we also must take this radical transformation of our culture seriously. We need to create learning and working environments where people feel safe to make these changes. For Euro-Canadians, how do we address this problem?

The leaders of the earth-centred way of life in Europe were systematically destroyed and marginalized over centuries. At first, the conquests of the Romans and Christians in many European countries, then, the burning of the witches during the period that the European empires were plundering the rest of the world, left very little intact. Parts of the women's movement are now "re-membering" the wisdom of the peasant wise women and forest dwellers. Ritual and culture that are tied to ancient earth-centred practices are becoming more and more common in Canada.[2]

This "life-way" is not to be confused with the so-called New Age spirituality that one reads and hears about in popular magazines. It is practical and solidly based in values of honesty, kindness, sharing and strength. It cares for the earth and other human beings in ways that are just, participatory and sustainable. The most well-known spokesperson for the movement in North America is Starhawk, an American psychotherapist who has been active in the grass-roots anti-nuclear movement.

The courage of the Greenham Common women in England, and the mass occupations of nuclear power plants in the United States have been sustained by this kind of culture, as is the resistance of environmentalists on remote logging roads in Canada's North. Even within the mainline churches the influence of indigenous traditions and pressures from the feminist movement are opening the liturgy and ritual to new forms and energy.

Until recently, I would have argued that we must start organizing with social, economic or political questions: getting large groups of people together. I no longer believe that is how to do it. To free ourselves from the systems that hold power, we have to start to build a culture of hope. And that begins in our own lives and the lives of our neighbours and friends.It's like gardening: if you want strong, beautiful and healthy plants, you have to build up the soil.

Community-building is an important force in our struggle to save the earth from ecological destruction, nuclear war and human misery. We have to take its power very seriously.

Many pressures work to disorganize our community-building efforts or confine our efforts to a select and tiny group of friends, or make our efforts backfire with racism and sexism. When we say that we want "people on board with our ideas," we sometimes forget that the train, in this case, is made up of people's voluntary labour and time. Unless our ideas are exciting and rewarding them, the train will evaporate.

Our lives seem to be constantly rushed and messed up: our work lives are unfulfilling, and if we stop to think about it are often downright damaging to other people. Our children seem to be growing up in a world full of fear, bad values and chaos. What we really battle when we face our powerlessness is *despair*. Asking ourselves and others to take on the work of confronting these systems of domination is asking people to take on a dangerous and difficult task.

For most of us, it is easier to learn and to take risks when we can do it with other people we trust. When we don't feel comfortable with others, we are strategizing to protect ourselves from failure or being rejected or looking foolish. Learning to work with others and to build community is a skilled trade. We have already served part of our apprenticeship.

This chapter is about building up the soil, creating a culture of hope instead of despair. I have divided it into five parts. Each part provides some ideas for our work in this area: consciousness-raising groups, building a vision, freeing the child within, telling the truth, and popular education.

Consciousness-Raising

Laurie speaks:

We separated after a year, and I became a single parent and that was my encounter with poverty. I remember that I was happy about the separation because the relationship was not working out. It wasn't a bad separation, we were very "rational" about it. Of course, in retrospect, I realize we were rational about it because I was telling him to go off and lead your life and we'll be fine, I'll take care of Jesse.

But I remember that the hardest part of that was coming face-to-face with society's attitudes towards "single parents," single mothers and children. At the time I became a single parent, there was a radio talk show host named Dave Deloye. and his favourite topic was exactly that — "single mothers on welfare and how taxpayers have to pay for this and how they go and get their case of beer on welfare day." And I remember sitting in my kitchen listening to this stuff and, of course, what he does and what people who pick on these kind of topics do is incite this kind of hatred and stuff. And so he was getting these kind of horrible phone calls. And I remember that shift happening to me and suddenly the "social consciousness," that sudden awareness of where you are in society. And it happened in my kitchen and it happened listening to this hatred and stuff against *me*. This was me they were talking about. And I cried for a week. I just broke down. "I can't cope with this, I can't"; but of course I did.

At the time there was a women's group in Sudbury, Women Helping Women, and I became involved with that, and I remember that for me, although they didn't offer me money, they offered me support and some kind of analysis about why this was happening to me, and that's when I became a feminist and started understanding why we needed to support each other and start struggling on these issues. And through it all…I remember times waiting for the mailman to come up the steps with that cheque, you know those times… it was my women friends who gave me the support that I needed to carry on.

The issues became more defined for me and I was able to act politically on these issues, but it took years of support and being able to talk these things out. It was in the days when we still had women's consciousness-raising groups.[3]

Consciousness-raising was the block on which the women's movement was built. Groups of women would get together regularly and "talk bitterness," would reveal to one another the truth of their lives. Sometimes, we became very angry, sometimes we cried, or laughed. But it was freeing and wonderful to finally be able to tell the truth to one another. From the small beginnings of these groups grew movements that have re-shaped history. As one woman at that time said to me: "Now I know the real meaning of "ignorance is bliss." I can't ever go back now that I know what's happening."

Each group had certain rules. Women spoke in protected space: they were not interrupted while they told their story. What went on in the group was private to that group. No subject was taboo, and we accepted one another and our struggles to free ourselves from our conditioning. We need to continue this practice.

In indigenous communities now, people use the "healing circle" to accomplish similar ends. As squares of felt bearing the four sacred colours are passed around the circle, each person talks about how the gifts of those colours are working in their life at that time, both the positive and the negative. The space is also "protected" as people talk.[4]

Another focus for this method are meetings of Alcoholics Anonymous or Narcotics Anonymous, where people take turns admitting their addiction and talking about their lives in an atmosphere of challenge and acceptance. These programs are dramatically successful in allowing people to support one another in conquering addictions.

The following are two methods for starting a group meeting that enable participants to relate to each other as whole people.

The Web of Influences

A technique I have often used to start meetings of any group is to divide people into groups of five and ask them to take a few minutes to draw a picture of the influences in their life at this time: historical/cultural, social/emotional, physical/economic, and political/mental. I usually use a circle divided into four quadrants to make the picture. When the individual pictures are finished, the small group discusses with each other which influences create hope and energy in their lives and which influences drain it from them. It is always effective. When people do this or something similar at the beginning of a meeting, then they bring their whole lives to it. Almost always someone says after, "I don't know why we had to do that exercise, but there sure are a lot of diverse and interesting people at this meeting." The truth is, they'd have never discovered the diversity of the participants if they hadn't taken the time to find out.

On occasion, I have also used clay to do some of this work. You sit in a circle and give each participant a piece of clay or playdough to work with. Ask them to meditate on their fears for the meeting and shape the clay as they think. When they are done they place the clay in front of them. You go around the circle and describe what the shape means. Ask participants to pick up their clay figure and shape it into a form that represents the strengths they bring to the gathering. At the end, the figures are put in the centre of the circle, and participants name their strengths to the group.

Building Visions

If we don't like the way the world is now, then we need to construct a vision of what a healthy society would look like. If you are going to spend your life working for change then you need a vision worth giving your life for. As we have seen, our ability to dream on this scale is held back by many factors.

Over the years, I have led many different groups in vision exercises. On most occasions they were energizing and exciting activities. Once it created a lot of tension and anxiety: when some middle-class church folk were working with a number of leaders of anti-poverty groups. For the poor people, talking about their dreams in front of comfortable church folk was just too difficult and painful.

Here are two ways to do "visioning" that work very well. The first is an adaptation of one of Starhawk's exercises.[5]

The Spider

The leader asks participants to sit quietly in a comfortable way and close their eyes. Read the following guided meditation. After the meditation, ask participants to turn to their neighbour and discuss their major findings. Feed the findings back to the larger group.

Meditation:

Think about where you are now. (Adapt this for the part of the country you are in: this is for Vancouver)

Think first of the east, of the mountains rising into the clouds, of the foothills and the grasslands where those farmers who have not been driven from the land look to the sky and pray for rain, of the pre-Cambrian shield, of the forests and rivers and teeming cities of Ontario and Québec — women scrambling to find housing — and of the woods and farms and fisherpeople of the Maritimes and Newfoundland, and then the ocean thundering in on the rocks of Cape Spear and on into the light of the rising sun...In earth-centred cultures east is the direction of clarity of thought, inspiration, new beginnings and intellectual knowledge.

Now think of the south. We are always so close to the United States. At first their geography is the same as ours. We move down the coast of the Pacific Ocean following sand and rock and mountains through to California and the coast of Mexico, rocks and mountains full of military installations and various instruments of war. Then we can curve eastward and come to Guatemala, a land torn by war and destruction…a hidden war fought on the backs of native people, and to the western coast of Nicaragua, a place where people have dared to dream, to create their own future. What do we draw from the strength and energy of these southern lands? The south is the home of rage and passion…Those things which fire growth and change, those primal movers.

Now push your thoughts further to the West, into the enormity of the Pacific ocean, and the continents and atolls that lie beyond. The west is the home of intuition, of self-knowledge and of love. It is also the place of the setting sun, and in cultures that are not afraid of death, but see it as the other side of life, the home of death. Let us think for a moment of the cycle of life and of the way that all soil is made from decaying life forms, and we are all nourished by those that have gone before. Think of the long tradition of women that have preceded us, and the energy and experience they bequeath us in our struggle for change.

And now to the North. The North is the place of healing and physical power. Think of rocks and snow and the colours of the earth. Think of the power of the northern wind to blow everything away before it and the solidity of mountains and the frankness of the Arctic tundra. Reflect on the pioneering struggles for survival of the Gitskan people of the Dene and the Inuit people. The symbol for the North is rock in some cultures, the pentacle in aboriginal European culture. But reflect also on the role that European people have played in the shaping of the world: patriarchy, industrialization and the modern state. The power of rock and pentacles gone mad.

Now, centred, think of yourself in the middle of these four directions, and feel your place on the surface of the earth. Imagine that from your body, your legs extend like roots, going down into the soil under this place, down through the gravel and the bedrock, and into the slowly warming core of the earth. Breath deep and feel the heat of that core rising in you and then exhale and feel your connection also with the universe and all the stars above us. Sit and feel this connection for a moment.

Now imagine that from this centre there are many paths leading out in every direction. You are a spider waiting to spring. Each of the paths leads to a possible future. Think about where they might lead (pause for a few minutes). Now imagine that you are spinning a thread to tie you to this time and place, and then you choose a path you want to follow and leap off into one of those futures. You leap fifty years into the future. Now, in that future, pause and look around you. What do you see to the east, to the south, to the west, to the north? Who is there with you? What does the environment look like? Are there other people there? How do they live? What is their relationship to the earth? To each other? To their children? How do they feed themselves? Get shelter? Travel? How are they educated? How do they make decisions?

Now find your thread and pull yourself back till you are just twenty five years in the future on this path. Look around you: (ask the same questions).

Now find your thread and pull yourself back to ten years: (ask the same questions).

Now just five years in the future. What are you doing? What do things look like around you? Who is with you? Now pull yourself back to this place and time. Take a deep breath. Feel the ground under your feet. Say good-bye to the four directions. Open your eyes. Look around you. Welcome.

This exercise is very powerful. An interesting outcome of the exercise is that most Canadians actually have the same vision of what they would like life to be like, and it is in the sharing of these visions that we realize we have a common understanding of how the earth and human relationships can be healed. When we share these dreams, we are bonded to each other in some new and important ways.

Talking the Future

This exercise is done in small groups. Ask participants to sit with people they are comfortable with. Imagine that you could redesign your community in a very basic way. Discuss the following questions as specifically as you can.

- What is your relationship to the natural world? How do you ensure that the environment is protected?
- How do people get food? What do they eat? How is it distributed? How is it produced?
- How are people sheltered? How do they live with one another? Of what materials are their shelters built? What do you do about the old-style buildings? What are the sources of heat and light?
- How are children educated? What do they learn?
- How are decisions made? Do some people control others? How are deviants or violent persons dealt with?

- How do people travel? How do they share information?

When groups have spent an hour or more discussing these questions, ask them to feed the information back to the larger group. They will probably be surprised at how similarly they think.

Visions are born out of struggle; they will change and shift as people work for change. None of us know what the world will be like in fifty years. It will be a product of our work for co-operative, just and earth-centred ways of living as much as it will be a product of the continuing attempts for control by the power-structures. In Marge Piercy's wonderful novel *Woman on the Edge of Time,* she has her central character, Consuelo, end up in two possible futures: one is all that is just, kind and ecologically right; the other is run by the "Multis," where most people live as slaves in a poisoned environment and the rulers live in environment-controlled buildings with every conceivable technological toy and a number of women to serve them who are kept perfect by plastic surgery and mind-altering drugs. Like Consuelo, we can choose a vision of life.[6]

Freeing the Child Within: Ritual and Play

In the culture of death, it is very hard to be creative or to have real fun. Adults who live with scientific management at work or the nightmare of welfare become bitter and angry. Most Euro-Canadians are taught that adult behaviour is humourless and "responsible." In activist groups we tend to be overwhelmed by how awful things are and to trudge drearily through life and our meetings.

Meetings for activists in the Third World are different. For them the challenge is not to convince themselves how bad things are, but to retain their courage, love of life and sense of humour. They *know* the situation they are in is grim — they work to keep the flame of life alive.

In my experience, people really want to laugh and to play with one another. Every time I'm going to try one of the following exercises with a group, I find that I'm nervous and worried that it won't succeed. It *always* does, and the effect it has on participants afterwards is to make them more relaxed, more creative and committed in their strategy planning.

This was a hard lesson for me to learn. In 1983, I applied for and got funding to start a Neighbourhood Action Project in Sudbury. It was to hire five people to do neighbourhood organizing in my own part of the city. The five who were hired had a long history of activism in the area. I thought they would go door-to-door and look for issues, then bring people together and confront city hall, or landlords or whatever.

They did some of that, but what happened when they were together was something quite different. They started looking for ways to stimulate new ideas and community in the neighbourhood. They got involved in starting a popular theatre troop; they took workshops in how to be clowns and the clowns were suddenly everywhere; they put out a little newsletter that celebrated the victories of ordinary folk in the area; and they insisted that all of us take time to play together and laugh. At first I resisted, thought they were not serious enough. In fact, it was the energy they generated amongst women in the neighbourhood that made all sorts of other tough things possible. Their learnings are published in a little booklet called *Neighbourhood Action: Recipes for Change.*[7]

We then took these ideas and used them in many different ways. In workshops and conferences, we now make sure that some of the activities at least involve physical movement, or drawing, or music. We often end a tough working session by playing a co-operative game or playing charades with each other. We try everything we can to keep all the participants involved and thinking all the time.

In organizations, we take time to plan social and cultural events where people can actually play with one another: potluck suppers and picnics and dances. But we make these events for the whole family and include making up songs or playing silly games or doing dances in a round. We find when we don't do this, people start bickering with each other and a lot of others vote with their feet.

Our strategies try to include activities which are outside the experience of the bureaucrats or corporate types we have to deal with: masks, clowns, displays, parades, guerrilla theatre or other tactics.

For the membership of our groups, we also have begun to introduce rituals of our own. We all need ritual celebrations I think. Opportunities to mark the seasons and the phases of the moon. Ways to connect with the power and sanity of the earth herself. Last summer, I had the honour to be part of a gathering of aboriginal people on an island near here. The occasion was the making of a film entitled *Get Real or Get Lost: The Original Peoples Speak to the Human Family* by some German filmmakers.[8] The gathering was organized by an Anishinabai elder to provide a setting for elders to share the prophecies and for people to spend a week living and working together outdoors. One evening we sat around the fire under the stars while one elder made a drum for Leonard Peltier, and stories were shared from the past and prophecies from the future: the Hopi Prophecy, the story of the Seventh Fire and so on. It was a moving and important moment in my life and this is as close as I get to understanding the power of the "sacred." Not as something separate from the troubles of our daily lives, but as an intrinsic part of it.

In the last three years, a few of my friends and I take time to mark the turning of the seasons with a small and unpretentious ritual, usually structured so that it won't embarrass my son and daughter (who are both teenagers and very aware of pretention). At the winter solstice for example, we each choose a symbol of something we want to have pass in our lives and another symbol of something we would like to have born in them. We go into the woods and toboggan and play in the snow. We build a fire (usually with great difficulty) and then burn the symbols of that which we want finished and then bury the things we want to grow in our lives. We eat hotdogs and hot chocolate and go home. For all of us, this is really Christmas, the time when light returns after the longest night of the year.

We practice many rituals all the time, you know, we just don't recognize them as such. Some of these are life-giving and good. Some are expropriated by the culture of death. What about baby-showers, weddings, funerals, holidays, setting the table, singing the national anthem, going to church?

Speaking Truth

Public opinion and what is acceptable to the public is manipulated by media images and slogans. The meaning of words is affected by the images we associate with them. "Right to Life" has come to mean being against abortion. "Democracy" is taken to be the same thing as capitalism. The stereotypes called up by words like "feminist," "anarchist," "environmentalist" are all negative for large parts of the population.

Community groups also have to learn how to shape public opinion. We need to use images and slogans to speak truth: to reclaim this territory for the culture of hope. We need to have public relations campaigns for what we stand for and what we do. Our public image is important, but it doesn't have to be a phony one. As a group, choose the image you want to project and then look for opportunities to develop it.

When End Legislated Poverty was looking for a way to raise the issue of the poor in British Columbia at a time when the media generally appeared to have little interest in these issues, they decided to focus on a school lunch program for children, because it would have more media appeal. It worked.

When we were trying to persuade the Ontario government to take the Burwash Community Co-operative Project seriously, we paid for a four-page centre spread in the weekly paper. The centre spread looked very professional, explained what co-operatives were and included a very spiffy picture of our board of directors. Overnight, we became a respectable group to be reckoned with instead of a bunch of flaky romantics.

We Interrupt this Program: A Citizen's Guide to Using the Media for Social Change writes:

> How the media reacts to your group and its concerns rests largely on how much you've thought through your media efforts — how steady an eye you can keep on your goals and at the same time, how well you understand and respect the role, function and purpose of the media (even though, sometimes, it appears as though the media does not really understand or respect its own role, function and purpose).
>
> If for example one of your overall goals is to get fair coverage of your group's action, you will need to spend a number of months laying the groundwork: slowly building good personal relations with reporters and assignment editors, establishing credibility, reliability and a reputation for being concerned, honest and interested in the public good. Prepare extensive press packets with adequate information for reporters, being sure reporters get enough information and get an interview with the necessary persons. Releasing information to certain sources could also help those relations."[9]

Too often our groups don't understand that what is news to us may not be news to the media. Success in using the media depends on our ability to translate our group's information and activities into news. What are the characteristics of *news*? *Making the News: A Guide to Using the Media* says that all news stories have to have at least some of the following elements: conflict, immediacy, novelty, peril, locality , human interest. The story has to have some "hook" in it that makes it appear sensational.

Generally, media will not report ongoing activities or situations, unless they can focus on a particular person or event. Creating these events is one way to get and hold their attention.[10]

For example, groups have held attention on the housing issue in their neighbourhood with stories of individual problems and victories, with demonstrations, pickets, parades. Often the media find demonstrations and pickets boring, unless you give them a "photo opportunity": dress up a pet, give a child a sign, make a presentation, use a huge banner. At one point in Sudbury we called attention to the lack of emergency shelter by inviting the media to the official opening of The Tom Davies Emergency Shelter for Families (Davies was the regional chairman). The "Shelter" was a cardboard shack we had thrown up overnight on a major intersection where we served bannock and hot chocolate.

Community groups use a number of different strategies for getting public attention:

- News releases based on an event of some kind
- Public Service Announcements, community events listings
- Interview shows
- Press coverage of an event or meeting
- Press conference
- Columns, articles and commentary shows
- Photos and artwork
- Handouts and brochures
- Direct mail and invitations to events
- Posters, banners, buttons and bumper stickers
- Bus advertising, billboards
- Press packets (which can accompany all the above)
- Slide shows and videos

The Pro-Canada Network campaign against Free Trade became a movement as different interest groups were urged to find their own ways of opposing the Free Trade deal. Many different sectors and groups sponsored debates, benefits, picnics, videos. Every avenue for press coverage was explored. Music, art, drama, photography brought the message home. The "NO, EH?" button and bumper sticker and the Free trade comic book were brilliant strokes. We can be just as inventive at a neighbourhood level.

Our Own Media

There are times when we need to consider creating our own media to get information across. Many community groups have started their own newspapers, made their own videos and slide shows, and done community theatre. This can have the added advantage of training local people in a variety of new skills.

Newspapers

Over the years, I have been involved with four community newspapers: *This Paper Belongs to the People* in Kingston, *The Mucker, The Strike Support News* and *Le Nouvel Ontarien* in Sudbury. In all cases the papers were fun to work on and well received by the people, but they were a nightmare to distribute. Most local newspapers are supported by advertising revenues. We weren't. Because of the content of the paper, we had trouble getting advertisers, and we were dependent on sales of the paper. This took hours of time, almost entirely volunteer. And it wasn't rewarding.

Successful local papers are possible in neighbourhoods in larger cities where there is a more established counter-culture. *The Inner City Voice* in Winnipeg struggles along on donations, sales and some advertising, and provides relevant and exciting information to downtown residents. They also hold regular public forums to involve the community in the content of the paper.

There have been a number of very effective publications by indigenous peoples in Canada: *Akwesasne Notes, Kainai News* and *Micmac News* are just three of about fifteen aboriginal newspapers in Canada. Organizations like the Wahwahtay Native Communications Society, and the Woodland Indian Cultural Education Centre have newspapers as one of their many activities to promote native culture and heritage. Most of these have been possible because of federal subsidy, which was wiped out in 1990. Continuing without the subsidy will be very difficult.

Videos

Getting members of your community involved in making a video about themselves and their issue is probably worth it even if no one except the local neighbourhood sees the final product. People love the opportunity to talk for a camera and to analyze their community together. You can call a community meeting later to review the results and get diverse groups really discussing the issues. Everyone will come. In Sioux Lookout, Ontario, a video about the industrial and racial shifts in the community was used to focus a community development strategy. A video about a community garden in Regent Park in Toronto created a number of local heras.

The equipment available to us (through unions, community channels, schools and churches) is rarely good quality. As a result, the finished product is not often good enough to be shown on television. Videos are a lot of work, and do require some skills in filming, scripting, editing and organizing. Help in making them may be available from local community colleges or community channels. We made a video twice in partnership with a commercial station that needed to fulfill its community programming requirements.

In Newfoundland, Memorial University Extension Department ran one of the most exciting community television experiments in Canada. They had a portable transmitter on the back of a truck that they took to different communities. They would be in a community for five days. Each day at about four o'clock, a village could tune in to films about their part of the island. High school students interspersed the film with announcements. In the evening there would be a panel discussion and then there would be phone-in questions for the panel. The last part of each show was live local entertainment. The low power transmitter used in this way was a valuable tool for community analysis and education. Last year, provincial cutbacks for "financial reasons" killed it.

Radio

A number of community groups have established radio stations either as co-operatives or non-profits. They require a long-term commitment of volunteer energy and time. The major expense to run them is salaries. All radio stations have to be approved by the CRTC, the Canadian Radio and Television Commission.

Co-op Radio in Vancouver is one of the longest running community-based radio stations. Other alternative radio stations are sponsored by universities and colleges. CKLN in Toronto is the radio station of Ryerson Polytechnical Institute. Radio Wahwahtay in northern Ontario has been broadcasting in Cree for indigenous people for over a decade.

Community organizations can also access programs on regular radio. There are resource groups that provide tapes and assistance: Ecomedia in Toronto, El Salvador News Service, Ground Zero Productions, the Multicultural Association of Nova Scotia are a few.

Popular Theatre

Like videos, live theatre is used very effectively to create new culture and to involve the community. In West Bay, Ontario, the native community organized a theatre group that writes plays about their lives as collective creations with the people. A number of the local people who got involved in these plays now work with Native Earth Theatre in Toronto. End Legislated Poverty in Vancouver helped found the Dignity Players, a theatre troupe made up of people in the food bank line-ups. In Winnipeg, the No Name Brand Clan did plays about living on welfare. In Edmonton, Catalyst Theatre worked with unemployed youth to write and perform a play about being jobless in Alberta. The Gitksan Wet'suwet'en play, *No Xha*, documents their sovereignty struggle.

Essentially popular theatre is a tool that brings oppressed peoples together and uses some techniques to help them relax with one another. Then they work together on the development of a script out of their own realities. The script is agreed upon by the whole group, they learn the parts and perform it. Sometimes these groups work with highly professional theatre people, sometimes they just do it on their own. If they have the opportunity to work with professionals, they can learn new skills in the process. If, however, the professionals do not respect the knowledge and experience of the participants then they are destructive.

Annually the Canadian Popular Theatre Alliance holds a theatre festival where people engaged in this kind of work can get together and learn. They have provincial contact people in every part of Canada.[11]

Popular Education

Although there is only one reality, we all look at it through different windows. Creating an environment in which we can look through each other's windows helps us all to see and act more holistically. Most formal education situations give value only to the teacher's experience, and devalue the perceptions and life experience of the learners. Since most teachers come from the privileged classes in society, what is taught is the perspective of the privileged. 'Popular education' turns this process upside down, and starts with the experience of the participants.[12]

Popular education is education for empowerment. It brings people together so that they can be better equipped to change the world.

It asks them to decide what they want to learn and what is relevant to their lives, and helps them organize with one another. It moves through five distinct phases: the participant's own experience, naming the experience, analysis of the experience (perhaps with inputs from people outside their experience), planning action to be taken from this learning and doing.[13]

This kind of learning involves some risks, because it challenges people to change their roles in society. We have found that some situations are more conducive to learning and participation than others. Some conditions for creating an environment where people are ready to risk and learn with one another are:

- Getting past the roles we create for ourselves or that are created for us. Not being "the professional," "the welfare recipient," "the victim."
- Feeling that our ideas are equally valid with everyone else's and that we won't be laughed at if we are shown to be wrong.
- Getting past private property in ideas. Not feeling that because you said the idea, you have to defend it to the death or your personhood is at stake.
- Having the totality of our lives present at the meeting; taking time to care for one another as people with full agendas and concerns outside the meeting.
- Equality and willingness to give to one another in need. So, for example, if I tell you that I need material help, you will share with me; or if I tell you I need time, you will find it for me.
- Opening up our spirit of creativity and play, getting away from verbal knowledge. Too much of our activity is ruled by articulate people. We need the wisdom and experience of people who express themselves differently. When we take time to work in clay together, or to cook together, or to draw, we develop new lines of trust and communication.
- Being able to confront and deal with issues of racism, sexism and homophobia. These never go away because you ignore them, they only get worse.
- Working together on a common project. There is nothing like 'doing' together to learn to work together. The sooner the better.
- Valuing leadership as distinct from authority. We are talking about "power-with" not "power-over." We need leaders, they provide example, experience and wisdom. We should value the effort people put into improving these skills. But this is very different from authority, which carries the power to compel with it.

- Development of activities together which help to develop the group's security in economic and political terms. A group that helps me gain a living or have political power will get more of my allegiance in terms of time and energy than one that is purely social.
- Doing something of great significance will attract more energy than something with little significance. We all want to be part of making history if we only knew how.
- Celebrating our achievements and our heroes and heras. When we do something good, we need people to acknowledge it, and to acknowledge it publicly.

* * *

Following are a few examples of exercises that can make groups "safe" for participants.

Community Mapping

A wonderful exercise for beginning a workshop. It can be done by two to any number of people, but small groups should be used if there are more than five people. It takes about thirty minutes to play.

Supplies: A pencil, crayon or marker and a piece of paper for each participant.

Method: Ask participants to take ten-fifteen minutes to draw a picture of the communities they are part of. It is easier if you suggest at the beginning that everyone draws at a Grade 5 level and this is not a drawing contest. You can also suggest that they might see their community geographically or in terms of friends, work, organizations, etc.

Then ask them to discuss with each other what the major issues in those communities are, and what are the sources of hope and despair for them.

The drawings can then be put around the room for further discussion.

Media Theatre: Discovering Social Control

The purpose of this workshop is to look at what is left out of media reporting on events and activities, or what is left out in advertisements.[14] You can do it with groups from five to fifteen. If you have more people than that, divide into two or three groups. Each group, however, should have a lot of room to move about.

Before the workshop, choose a short article or ad from a newspaper or magazine. Make copies of it for the group, so that each person will have a copy. Hand it out at the beginning of the workshop.

Begin the workshop with the community mapping activity above. Take a coffee break.

Now sit in a circle and take turns reading the article out loud, playing with rhythm and tone. Encourage the group to make it as melodramatic or silly as possible. Do this for about ten minutes.

Now you are going to use a technique known as body sculpture to depict the characters in the article and their relationship to one another (as the article says it is).

Body sculpture means positioning each others bodies like clay to show relationships, power, etc. (See drawing). Participants take turns building the sculpture one piece at a time. It works best if they talk as little as possible while doing it.

Explain the sculpturing method to participants and make a few yourself. Now ask them to make a body sculpture showing exactly what the article says. They are not to add in anything that is not there.

Once they are satisfied with the sculpture, ask them to add those things that are missing from the article: the impacts of the event on the larger community and so on.

As an example, an article about a cutback in social services would not talk about the effects on the children of welfare recipients, on corner grocery stores and on the health care system. Nor would it talk about the beneficiaries of the cuts: the owners of large construction companies that will continue to receive tax exemptions, etc. Nor will it talk about the lives of the government officials and bureaucrats who are involved in the decisions. Nor would it show welfare recipients and church people organizing to protest the cuts. These are the kinds of things you should encourage the group to show in their second sculpture.

Now ask the group, again taking turns, to show how they could transform these relationships to solve the problem. As they move each part they should explain what they are doing and why. They should not debate with one another, but can rearrange any part of the sculpture they want.

When the energy begins to diminish, stop sculpturing and discuss how it felt and what participants want to say about the experience. What does it suggest to them in terms of follow-up activities?

Story-Telling

Perhaps the simplest format for any educational setting. Start with the community mapping exercise above. Take a break.

Give each participant ten minutes to tell a story from their life experience about the theme of the workshop (which can be almost anything).

Ask participants to discuss what they think are the common themes in the stories? what do they tell us about our reality?

Divide into small groups and come up with two ideas about what can be done to change some of these common problems. After fifteen minutes, write the ideas on flip chart paper.

In the larger group, discuss which ideas seem most effective in the long term and in the short term. Decide how you will carry them out. (The plan may only be to get more information next time.)

There are a number of excellent resources for popular education methods: Basics and Tools, Neighbourhood Action, the Learning Loom, The Moment, Managing the Household, Training for Transformation, the North Island Women's Book. Addresses for these resources are in the resource section at the back of the book.

In the Schools

"La Maitresse d'école" is the name of a progressive collective of teachers in Montréal that have for thirteen years been at the forefront of progressive ideas and work in education in Québec. In 1989, they published a book describing their work and some samples of their writing, called *Toward a Peoples' Curriculum.* They work in collaboration with teachers' unions in Québec, and try to bring into the schools some of the transformative methods of popular education.

One of the most interesting projects in which they collaborated was developed by an anti-war toy collective called Pacijou. The theme of the October 1988 Peace March in Montréal was "War is not a Game." Children from all over the city brought their favourite war toys to be incorporated into a peace sculpture. The children participated in press conferences, debates and talk shows.[15]

Progressive teachers in other parts of Canada have found many ways to help children learn despite the school system. In Alberta, 1982 marked the year that the Alexander Band assumed local control of its education system and introduced a curriculum at the Kipohtakaw school that is based in traditional aboriginal values of the inter-relatedness of living and non-living things in the universe. Bands have also taken over post-secondary education in the province. In the rest of Canada, aboriginal communities are quickly assuming control of post-secondary education for band members. Survival schools exist in many reserves and cities.

The magazine *Our Schools, Ourselves* published by long-time education activists is an invaluable resource for anyone interested in taking on the education system.

NOTES

1. Berry, James, *The Center for Reflection on the Second Law*, Circular #110, 1989.
2. cf. *Women of Power*, Issue fifteen, Fall/winter 1990, and Starhawk, *Truth or Dare*, Harper and Row Publishers, New York, 1987.
3. Interview with a member of Women Helping Women, Sudbury, June, 1989.
4. I am indebted to Barbara Riley for explaining this to me. Doing it properly requires teaching from someone who knows how to do it. I'm not one of those people.
5. Starhawk, *op.cit.* pages 338-340.
6. Piercy, Marge, *Woman on the Edge of Time*, Knopf, New York, 1976.
7. Neighbourhood Action Project and Sticks and Stones. *Neighbourhood Action: Recipes for Change*, Sudbury, 1983.
8. Faust Films, *Get Real or Get Lost: The Original Peoples Speak to the Human Family*, available from Native Social Work Program, Laurentian University, Sudbury, Ontario.
9. Gordon, Robbie. *We Interrupt this Program: A Citizen's Guide to Using the Media*, University of Massachusetts, 1978, p.13.
10. Ura, Michael, *Making the News: A Guide to Using the Media*, West Coast Environmental Law Research Foundation, 1989.
11. The Canadian Popular Theatre Alliance may be contacted at 413 Selkirk Avenue, Winnipeg, Manitoba R2W 0M4.
12. The term "popular education" is attributed to Paulo Friere, a Brazilian educator who developed and popularized the methodology. His most well-known book is *Pedagogy of the Oppressed.*
    In Canada, there a number of popular educators. The Doris Marshall Institute for Education and Action, 818 College Street, #3, Toronto, Ontario M6G 1C8 is a collective of competent and innovative educators.
13. Arnold, Rick Deborah Barndt and Bev Burke, *A New Weave: Popular Education in Canada and Central America*, a joint publication of CUSO Development Education and Ontario Institute for Studies in Education, Toronto.
14. This is an adaptation of a workshop developed by Augusto Boal, the father of popular theatre. The original can be found in *Theatre d'Opprime.*
15. La Maitresse d'ecole. *Building a Peoples' Curriculum*. Our Schools/ Our Selves monograph series , No.2, 1989.

Chapter 9

WORKING TOGETHER

What a community organizer really does:

I'm to spend a few days working with Mary to plan and carry out some workshops on economic justice. We had agreed a few months before, that I'd stay at her home. So on Saturday at 11 a.m., Mary meets me at the bus station. She looks drawn and tired. We take the local bus to her home — a pleasant apartment in north end of town, full of the chaos of small children. Anna (almost 4 1/2) and John (almost 7) — smart independent children — very demanding. Mary is still recovering from two weeks of flu and depression. Her husband is in Africa for 6 months with a student project and she is on the verge of desperation: malnourished, hard on herself, overworked. The children quite out of control, refusing to go to sleep at night, rebellious. On Saturday, Mary and I talk and look after children: I babysit while she does groceries, do the dishes, help cook supper. Next day, we go to church together and to the potluck lunch there afterwards. That afternoon, we take the neighbour's disabled son swimming at the local pool to give his parents a break. Later I help with kids and dishes while we try to talk around it all...

* * *

Transforming the world into something better means organizing. We have to learn to trust and work together in groups. More attempts at change and community-building fail because we can't get along with one another than for any other reason. Our organizations should reflect the kind of world we want to create: co-operative, honest, caring and exciting places. Because we do not have access to a lot of money, we have to depend on the enthusiasm and commitment of volunteers. We can go nowhere without it.

People get involved in and stay committed to change organizations for a variety of reasons: they share their goals; they learn new things; they enjoy the company of other members; they feel respected and liked by the other members and/or the rest of society. If the organization does not satisfy some or all these needs, then they leave. The key to commitment in change organizations is participation: if people feel their ideas and labour is essential to the group, they are more likely to stay involved.

Unfortunately, we too often model our groups on the structures of the larger society. We saw in Chapter 1, the effect this can have on collective, participatory work. It is the purpose of this chapter to provide you with some tools for creating alternative organizational forms.

Getting along with each other, when we have been trained from infancy to be competitive and individualistic, takes hard work, but gatherings and actions where people truly co-operate and work together for a common purpose can be so exciting that they give me shivers.

Watching a program last night broadcast from a Salvadorian refugee camp, I was struck once again by the spirit of co-operation and the celebration of life that makes even the most unimaginable material misery endurable. People in these camps get along together and collectively organize for all their needs.

Organizing in this manner is not a mystery, it is a skilled and creative process that can be learned by others. This chapter is an attempt to make visible some of those methods. It is divided into separate sections:

- leadership and the core group
- things to know about groups
- structure and membership
- meetings
- planning
- research
- fund-raising

Leadership and the Core Group

Basically, there are two places to start organizing: one starts with people we already know well; the other is a deliberate choice of key individuals from different sectors of the community.

You can start organizing with people you know, where you are and where the people you know are. You don't have to organize people different from yourself. Look for the place of least resistance, where your friends are talking about a problem, or experiencing one. Legitimize their worries and fears about the world around them. Some people are particularly prone to down-playing their own concerns. "So many people are worse off than me, I have no right to feel bad," is a pretty common response. On the other hand, if we can't deal with our own powerlessness, what makes us think we have anything to offer or teach anyone else?

Or you can start with a core group: a few people who are deeply committed to working for the community or the issue and who come from the different parts of the community whom you hope will assume leadership on the issue. These don't have to be the big names from those sectors, but they should be potential leaders. Make sure they bring a friend or colleague with whom they feel comfortable, so that they are not isolated in the group. One group started organizing with a regular Wednesday night potluck supper for about twelve people who wanted to work together.

If you are serious about having this group really inspire community change, it is important that you choose these people for their "good example": that is their openness, honesty, kindness and strength. We all slip up from time to time, but any group that is going to work for basic change together has to try to live the change it is working for. One of the functions of the core group should be to support one another emotionally and morally. "Solidarity is based on the principle that we are willing to put ourselves at risk to protect one another."[1]

Nurturing and developing this core is extremely important. You need to have not only political experiences together but cultural or social ones as well. This time, make planning a part of your agenda together.

Leaders can be anyone. Si Kahn says, "Good leaders are willing to step outside themselves into peoples lives."[2] Leaders like people, are good listeners, make friends easily, are comfortable with their own ideas, work hard, don't discourage easily, ask questions, have vision and a sense of humour.

They also have specific skills. But these are *learned*, through reading, experience and apprenticeship. The only dangerous leadership is authoritarian or hidden, so that it does not operate with the consent of the group. Leaders are not necessarily talkative people, and they frequently are *not* the spokespersons of an organization.

Leadership is distinct from authority. We are talking about "power-with" not "power-over." We need leaders. They provide example, experience and wisdom. We should value the effort people put into improving these skills. This is very different from authority, which carries with it the power to compel.

There are many unsung heros and heras in our neighbourhoods, doing work to bind them together. Who is it you go to when you need advice about choices in your life? For comfort when things don't work out? Think for a moment of who those people are? Are you one of those people yourself?

In any group there is always someone that others respect for his/her experience, wisdom or comfort. She may be a grandmother, or the local hairdresser or the coach of little league team. He may just be the old man who sits in the lobby of the apartment building. Being a trusted friend is not a position you design for yourself, it is an honour given to you by the people who come to respect your judgment. In traditional indigenous culture, people of wisdom, honesty and experience were asked to be "elders," a position that carried with it grave responsibility for guiding the community.

These are people with a real following, that is, they are respected and chosen by their peers and they serve without the rewards of the system. Their only claim is the continuing respect of others for their integrity and wisdom. Because they listen, they are knowledgeable about the state of the community they know as few others can.

Effective community organizing means finding out who the real leaders are and strengthening them. How?

- Recognition. Letting them know that they are recognized as leaders by others in the community, seeking their advice, honouring them.
- Information about the outside world. Providing opportunities, however informal, for them to be better educated about the national and global causes and solutions to the problems they work with every day.
- Information about what others do in similar situations. Setting up opportunities for them to talk over situations with their peers; to share stories and ideas from their locality and to hear others.
- Rest. Providing breaks and respite from the daily tasks from time to time so they have time to reflect or to play or to learn.
- Meeting like people and being appreciated for their knowledge and strength. This does not mean pulling them out of the local situation, but strengthening their effectiveness in it.

How do we find them? Look at our own circle and neighbourhood: who would we identify? How about other circles we know about?

In groups we belong to, who do people name when asked to think about it? If I went door-to-door in my neighbourhood talking to people, who would they name? What happens if we get these people together to talk about how they see the world and the community? What do they say? How do they get along with one another?

What do you say to them in the first place to get them to this gathering? Or do you bring them together by twos in their own kitchens? There are many older women who won't even speak in front of their husbands. Many will claim they have nothing to say. Sometimes putting together a project for children will entice the real leaders to a gathering.

In the world of power-over, instead of examining our lived experience we tend to imbue certain occupations with leadership roles: lawyers, social workers, doctors, priests, successful business men and women, politicians. Although these people have technical competence in their field, that does not mean that they have any credentials to advise on other matters in life.

More publicly-recognized leaders have different uses in organizations: to legitimize a campaign, for short-cuts in organizing. For example, "the president of so-and-so supports our cause." Quite frequently, the president couldn't mobilize anyone in his organization. Although he/she may want to support the work, it is unlikely that the membership of the organization have even thought about the issue, let alone discussed basic questions of life-style and values.

Thinking About Race and Class

Race and class differences do not go away just because we pretend they are not there. They get worse. This section of the book is written specifically for activists who come out of the dominant culture like myself: white and from a middle-class childhood.

We did not choose our parents, and it is not our fault that we are white. However, being born Euro-Canadian means that we fall into cultural patterns and expectations that shape our behaviour even when we wish they didn't. Europeans have a long ancestral history of hierarchical and highly structured government and legal systems. We are very verbal people. We move quickly. We are trained to be linear in our thinking. We are obsessive about cleanliness, order and material security. We have been taught nature is either something to be subdued or romanticized.

I am always shocked at how deeply these cultural patterns are ingrained in me. When we work with people of other races, we have to be aware that these cultural patterns can be oppressive to others; that they are only cultural attributes and not universal values. In fact, some of them are dangerous and misguided. There are many other ways to view reality, and the more windows we can look through, the closer we are to understanding its true nature.

Stereotypes about other races, cultures and classes are not only the property of white, middle-class folk. Other races have stereotypes about whites, and we have to prove ourselves over and over again. There is no quick fix, no absolution. When we work with other races, we need to be rigorously honest with ourselves, having a sense of humour about our "white mistakes," working hard to unlearn the oppressive parts of our acculturation, sharing the worthwhile parts of our training and privilege where it is requested.

Precisely because Western European culture is the predominant one in Canada, our work for change should try where-ever possible to accept leadership from other racial and cultural groups. Other races and cultures are organizing themselves in the ways that they find appropriate. We have a lot to learn. This does not mean glorifying the cultures of others. It does mean allowing the space for other cultural forms to emerge and take power. We are always in such a hurry to "get things done"; but the question is *what do we accomplish with all this rushing around?* If our goal is building a movement or a group from the bottom up, maybe we need to take the time to do it right first.

Class and race are closely related. In Canada, most non-whites have less access to economic privilege than whites. So many of the following points apply both to issues of race and class. Class is not just an economic system, it carries with it patterns of behaviour that are just as oppressive to poor people.

Some of these are:

- Too often we turn non-white, poor people into professional victims: we only want to hear about their suffering. This is using them to educate ourselves about how bad things are. But what they need to build their own struggle is to know and celebrate their own strength, courage and successes as survivors who are part of a world struggle for change.
- Glorifying the hard lives of working class and non-white people instead of recognizing them as equals comes from a particular kind of

self-hatred that afflicts whites who work with non-whites. Equality means valuing yourself, and working side-by-side. Putting people on pedestals keeps them from acting.

- Economically secure people are constantly preoccupied with their feelings, health, appearance and psychology. These are luxuries, and although all these are concerns of poor people, they do not have the same significance for them. This does not mean that they only want to talk about social change and politics either.
- Many of us act and speak as though poor and non-white people are not as "developed" because they don't talk the same way that formally educated people do. Their approach usually has less abstract theory, more concrete images and more anger.
- Hanging on to middle-class privilege instead of sharing the benefits with working class people: education, skills, money.
- When whites from middle-class backgrounds speak as though hard work has brought them skills, education, possessions and position, they ignore the fact that most poor people work just as hard, but do not get these rewards.
- The success that middle-class whites enjoy for following the rules and being reasonable often leads them to think that these are also good strategies for non-white/poor people to follow. In fact, most non-white/poor people can only use these tactics if they have "acceptable" white, educated people to do it for them.
- Because middle-class whites are rewarded with success for being nice and following the rules, they describe people who did not get this kind of positive reinforcement as "pushy, dogmatic, hostile, or intolerant."
- Not having to worry about eating or knowing where the next dollar will come from, enables middle-class white activists to take chances that are much more dangerous for non-white poor people (civil disobedience, voluntary poverty, for example).

Things to Know About Groups

Groups of people have their own personalities, internal conflicts, ways of behaving in the world. The study of group behaviour is called "group dynamics." It has a questionable history: most of it was a product of U.S. Defence Department Research during the Second World War when they were trying to help soldiers get along and co-operate under stressful conditions. There is no reason not to appropriate these learnings for our own purposes.

Looking at group process from different angles can provide some clues for making our own groups work better.[3]

Group Participation

Group interaction falls into one of three patterns: a leader talking at the members (one-directional), a leader talking and the members answering him/her (two-directional), or everyone talking to one another (multi-dimensional). Studies have established that the more interaction there is between all the members, the more sustained interest there is likely to be in the group. Although groups that are dominated by one or two people can be very productive in the short term, they tend to lose membership and energy over time. (It is worth remembering that people communicate not only with words but with body language.) How do you ensure effective participation in a group?

- The group has to perceive itself as important, both for themselves and the outside community.
- Groups that allow conflict and open discussion have higher participation levels than groups that demand homogeneity.
- Taking on tasks that are suited to the interests and abilities of participants. Too many groups depend on articulate, formally educated people with a good knowledge of the predominant language. Groups that use domestic skills, artistic skills, manual skills, etc. allow for more diverse participation.
- Groups with a facilitating leadership generally have more participation in the long run than groups with an authoritarian leadership. It is the responsibility of those who are feeling oppressed in a group to confront the authoritarian leader. In groups where "power" cannot be discussed openly, then leadership cannot be challenged.
- The more democratic the group, the more the group will thrive. The need for clear rules and avenues for decision-making is even greater in groups that are hierarchical in structure, in order to protect individual rights. In smaller groups, consensus is usually the best method of decision-making. This is discussed in more detail below.

Building a Feeling of "We"

You can judge the cohesion of a group by the number of times people say "you" instead of "we," and by the numbers of people who keep on talking in two's while the larger meeting is going on. Groups have a social climate: some groups feel nasty, some feel warm, etc. Participants usually express this in terms of who is in the group, saying things like "everyone here is so picky/ so uptight/ so wonderful/ so committed." However, I have seen many situations where the same people who were jerks in one setting are kind and co-operative in another. How we organize our groups will shape the way people relate to each other in them.

It is easy to create a feeling of "we" if the group comes together and identifies a common enemy. At the beginning of the 1978-9 INCO strike, the Wives organization had spent a great deal of effort creating a float for the Santa Claus parade. On the day of the parade, the diesel truck that was to pull it ran out of gas while it was idling waiting for the parade to begin, and the float didn't get in the parade. As you can imagine, everyone was very upset, and they all began to blame each other. It was only when they decided that it was an INCO plot to keep them out of the parade that they managed to pull themselves back together as a group. Although this provided a convenient short-cut to solidarity, it would not have been enough to hold a group together in the long haul.

As we saw in the Chapter 1, the "enemy" is structural. It is a product of human labour, and we all collude in creating it. One of the forms of collusion is giving it more power than it has: building strategies that are organized around our perception of the "enemy" instead of around our own collective strength. As it turned out the most effective group process in the Wives was around the clothing depots, bean suppers, and Christmas parties they held to keep the community together. They were visible achievements; they provided immediate help to those who needed it; they could be organized co-operatively.

The "we" feeling in a group is also a product of its common values and standards. Some of these are immediately visible in the stated purposes and goals of the group, but there are also unspecified values which can create difficulties, especially for new members, unless they are named. What do you think these are in your group? They can be dress codes, expectations of time and commitment, political beliefs, and so on. You don't all have to agree, as long as it is understood what your differences are.

Cohesion in a group is really a product of the trust people have in one another, and trust is built on honesty and respect. It can only develop through experience, and it is only possible where members of a group feel safe to express opposition or differences. If I feel I have to hide my innermost thoughts from the rest of the group, I will never feel safe. Boredom is often a clue that people are hiding feelings of anger or frustration. Get it out in the open. Take time in groups to check in with each other personally.

Cliques, Scapegoats, and Trouble-Makers

Most groups have an invisible organization as well as a visible one. The invisible organization can be made up of friendships, people who see each other frequently at work or other places, the influences of social class, race, gender, skills and so on. The larger the organization the more likely it is to develop these groupings. If the visible structure of the organization does not recognize and correspond to the invisible structures then there is going to be serious trouble.

First, there is no reason to assume that your group should include everyone. The group should be clear about who it wants to participate and what the terms of membership are: those who agree with the goals of ABC, those who are invited to join, anyone at all?

Next, if a group pretends it has no leaders, or its real leaders do not correspond to the elected ones, then it cannot hold them accountable for their behaviour. Further, it is hard on the un-named leaders, because they are afraid to exercise their leadership with any consistency. Everyone feels insecure.

In groups where an elite is developing through personal friendship, unless it corresponds to the formal structure of the organization, it is very difficult for the others to control. Quite often, the elite is defined by class, race or gender. In larger organizations it may be necessary to have formal caucuses of non-white or women's sections of the group to empower others. In many groups, the smokers become such a caucus, meeting outside or in the hallway.

It is normal for some people to like each other more; for some people to not get along. Although people don't have to always be nice to each other to have a group work, they do have to respect other members' feelings. In fact, being nice to each other all the time eventually makes a group feel dishonest. People need to feel safe to express their true feelings and worries in a group: taking time to talk personally, to check in with each other.

Sometimes groups that are stymied in their progress try to avoid their own responsibility by picking on one member (often the staff person). In social change organizations, the scapegoat will usually quit when this happens. In situations where a series of people have quit an organization, it is useful to ask ourselves if we create scapegoats for our own failings and then drive them out. I have been part of groups where the leadership consistently forced the resignation of any person who stood up to them. We were only able to change it by setting up confrontation that included all the people who had been forced to resign during the discussion.

There are, however, some people who are so dysfunctional in groups that people begin to think they are agents. In fact it doesn't matter if they are or not, the effect is the same. If there is someone in a group that is consistently disruptive, and damaging to group process, then that person should be asked to leave. It does no one any good to keep pretending. We, on occasion, would send a few people from the group to talk privately with the person about their behaviour. If it did not improve then the group would discuss it again and ask them to leave. Perhaps, also, the group would benefit from some training in group dynamics, or listening skills, or other interpersonal development.

Group Growth and Change

The kind of groups we build are very different from the institutions that enshrine power-over. In most cases we do not have access to large and consistent sources of income, so we cannot maintain a staff. The people who are members are changed by the group and by the other things that happen in their lives. Some of the people go on to organize around other issues and with other people. Some move away. Some of them just return to their old lives. Some became drunks.

Even when we do establish permanent organizations they look different from the original activist bunch and different from the dreams we had. We may mobilize people around an issue, or run an election campaign, or win a strike, with enormous outputs of personal energy and commitment, but setting up a long-term organization with no paid staff is a different matter. You cannot exact as much from the members. We look for places where funding is available, and that is for service-oriented or very limited advocacy work. We take the road of least resistance.

Low-income teenagers in downtown Kingston fought for and ran no less than three youth drop-in centres between 1966 and 1971. The authorities would close them down on some pretext or another and the kids would mobilize and get another one. Eventually the young people who were part of this struggle grew up. The men who were part of the centres originally did not stay involved in social change, but the same women who had been girls in the drop-in centres went on to organize a women's centre, a transition house, and a locally owned clothing operation.

It is the norm of organizations to shift and change. They go through different stages, and like our children, what they become when they grow up is often very different from what we had anticipated. When we formed Women Helping Women in 1979, I had visions that one day it would come to represent women in block organizations throughout the city...the group exhausted itself organizing the Wives Supporting the Strike. When the strike ended, a number of the activists from that group joined some women new to the struggle and went on to organize the Women's Centre.

I love the excitement of getting things started: pushing ourselves really hard to be relevant, to get involved in big issues. The groups do great things for two or three years and then they transform themselves as some of the members move away, drop out, go on to other activities. I always feel a terrible loss and a lot of guilt when this happens. As though there was a way to continue to build the group so that it would keep on pushing for dramatic shifts in power.

In fact, this process is a result of the dance between the forces for liberation and hope and the systems of domination and control. We push for change; they shift enough to accommodate some of our demands, but they still retain control. We push for an end to violence against women in their homes, they offer us transition houses and minimum wages to staff them. We push for neighbourhood control over health care; they give us a walk-in clinic. We push for better working conditions; they give us stress workshops.

I believe the 'product' of our groups should be to sustain the effort to effect shifts in power, to build a culture of resistance, to strengthen community leaders, and to redistribute wealth, not to build institutions for their own sake. For my work, this means moving on when the group begins to institutionalize, often working with the same people, on the same issues, under a new name or umbrella.

Different Kinds of Groups for Different Purposes

There are a lot of different kinds of organizations and they all need different structures and procedures. What distinguishes groups from one another is the amount of time and energy members are willing to commit to the group, their size, whether their focus is single-issue or multi-issue, and whether members are individuals or organizational representatives. I have briefly described a few variations here, along with a few warning lights that go with those structures.

Small Groups of People with Little Time or Energy Commitment Around Specific Issues

Often job-related, members meet once a month to share information, or to share information about an activity, a political concern or something. An example might be a Co-ordinating Committee Against Wife Assault. Most participants are not willing to put a lot of time into the work of the group, although a few often expect a great deal from it. There are often serious differences in values and methods within the group. To function effectively, the group should be very clear about its goals and expectations from the membership.

Collectives of Eight to Fifteen People

A group of this size offers the greatest possibility for truly sharing decision-making and building commitment. Depending on the amount of time and energy people are willing to commit to the group, it can accomplish a great deal. Consensus is the most effective form of decision-making in a group of this size. Some collectives take on very intense projects: theatre, civil disobedience and so on.

According to an article in *Worker Co-op*,[4] the average feminist collective in Canada has been around for 9.5 years. Most of them are formed because of women's involvement in the feminist movement. They emphasize sharing of skills, knowledge and information, participatory decision-making, and the value of personal experience. Some of the oldest are the Vancouver Women's Health Collective, Nellie's Hostel in Toronto, and the North Bay Women's Centre. Many collectives have to rely on a mixture of paid staff and volunteers to carry out their services. Often their funding is from government, and they require a board of directors separate from paid staff.[5]

Another kind of collective is known as 'self-help groups'. Organizations like Alcoholics Anonymous made up of people who identify themselves as having a common problem and who provide mutual support and encouragement to one another. These groups are therapeutic in nature. Although many of their members go on to get involved in social change work, the group itself exists for support and encouragement of the individual.[6]

Mass Organizing With a Single Issue Focus

This kind of group forms around something like a rent increase in a building, or an attempt to stop a nuclear dump in the neighbourhood, or a strike support activity. Large numbers of people from differing backgrounds are brought together for a short-term, powerful action or series of actions. They are characterized by a strong leadership that is very committed to the issue. Organizing can provide opportunities for education on the issue and related issues, for leadership development and for the building of networks outside the community. In fact the leadership often feels it cannot take the time to do this work with the membership. As a result, although people stay on board for the duration of the struggle, they then leave feeling used and burned out.

An alternative to the hierarchical structure that characterizes most mass mobilizations is a model developed by the Clamshell Alliance in the United States. They developed a structure called the 'affinity group' to sustain non-violent civil disobedience actions around a single issue. They pulled off one of the most dramatic occupations in recent history.

With age and experience, affinity groups may evolve into collectives which provide opportunities for in-depth analysis and long-term commitment to the radical project. However, this is not automatically the case.

The Clam's principles for structure were:

- New members who wanted to join the Clam were required to take an intensive training in non-violent action and the issues. Those 10-15 people who took the training together formed an "affinity group" in a local area, elected a "spoke," to sit on the co-ordinating committee.
- A co-ordinating committee was established to co-ordinate the decisions of local groups, not to make them.
- All action was to be non-violent direct action.
- All action was to have the same specific focus.

- Each local group would maintain its own existence.
- The local group most directly affected had "blackball rights" on any action. If other groups didn't agree they just didn't participate in the action.
- Affinity groups were the vehicle of decision-making and training.
- Spokes bring ideas, decisions and proposals to a larger group of spokes, but all decisions are made in affinity groups.

This method built security, community, ownership of the action, good training, and allowed decisions on the spot. The original group of people who started the Clam took responsibility for setting up the training workshops and recruiting membership, and later became accountable to the co-ordinating committee.

Multi-Issue Organization.

Residents' associations and citizens' groups fall under this category. Church organizations like Development and Peace are also multi-issue. They require the negotiation of different interests and concerns in a group in order to build a power base to achieve an agreed-upon end. It is important to be very clear about your goals. Goals for the group may be as vague as neighbourhood improvement, or welfare rights.

These groups are very hard to hold together. There is a tendency for everyone to be running off in a different direction. The work of multi-issue organizations can be facilitated by the use of autonomous task groups for different activities.

Meetings need to be carefully structured so that they provide opportunity for lots of participation from the membership. Otherwise, people will feel that their issues are not being looked after, and nasty power struggles can ensue. Annual General Meetings can easily become nightmares. These kinds of organizations cannot operate by consensus. They need room for people to disagree and fight with one another. They need at least one activity in which they all participate. They need lots of opportunities for leadership development and education.

Sometimes it is useful for special interests within the organization to form *caucuses* — groupings of people within an organization who share a commitment to that organization but want to see it be more responsive to their needs. Often the caucuses are based on gender, race or class differences within the organization. They should be democratically constituted.

As multi-issue organizations often have a paid staff, they run into problems with funders trying to dictate their issues and structure. Nevertheless when they do succeed in truly representing grassroots interests, or in uniting diverse interests in a common cause, they present a real threat to the status quo.

Coalitions

These are composed of a number of organizations which agree to work together and agree to a common position around an issue. They need to be very clear on the purpose and statement of the coalition, and working this out can be very time consuming. Representatives to the coalition have to deal with the internal politics of their own organizations, and this can be extremely difficult, especially if the coalition has to move quickly. Representatives need to be sure they can bring their organization along with the coalition. They might find that the target of their pressure calls their bluff, and they can't organize their way out of a paper bag. Being able to mobilize support for a coalition position is facilitated if the representative has a structure for accountability in her own organization and if the coalition has a very clear process for decision-making.

Because of the diversity of interests, personal networks can create jealousies and power struggles. Broad-based coalitions that include organizations of different races, genders and classes, have to be very careful not to tokenize participants, and have to be willing to accept and work with criticism from these groups.[7]

Holding Successful Meetings

Meetings are the occasions for democratic process to happen. They are the place where members of a group meet each other face to face to learn, make decisions, ruminate. In these meetings we expect to come to agreement. Another kind of meeting takes place when we negotiate, get information, or confront structures from whom we want to take power. In these we want to clarify areas of disagreement, and make a show of our strength and unity. Meetings can be of any number of people. Their size varies with their purpose and, of course, with how many people you can attract! This discussion of meetings is divided into two parts: meetings where one of the objectives is to build unity, and meetings where the objective is to show strength.

Meetings to Build Unity

Success in a meeting can mean different things to different people. For community organizers who are interested in a movement for social change, one yard stick should be that people at the meeting felt good enough about it to come to another. For me, other measures would be lots of participation from members, and accomplishing the task of the meeting (even if the task were to decide on a task).

There are some fairly simple guidelines for interesting and democratic meetings. If the rules are followed, the meeting should go well. There are a number of resources to help you run more effective meetings. *A Manual for Group Facilitators, Building United Judgment, Working Together,* are some of the best. They are listed in the Resource section of this book.

Before the Meeting:

The first rule of successful meetings is: be sure about the meeting's purpose before you start, and then confirm with the whole group that they are agreed on the purpose.

Meetings have to be at convenient times and places. Only people with university educations are comfortable meeting in universities, and middle-class people may be uncomfortable in a drop-in centre. Choose the meeting place and time that will attract the kind of people you want to have in the group.

Make sure that participants can get to the meeting: what about obstructive husbands, wives, parents, bosses? What about childcare arrangements, availability of transport? If this is the first meeting for some people, it might be a good idea to arrange for someone to bring them: it can be pretty scary going to your first meeting.

Arrange to have some food during the meeting. There is something about the sharing of food together that creates unity. What about potluck dinners, or taking turns making coffee?

Arrange the chairs and tables (if there are any), to maximize participation. Sitting people in a circle equalizes power in a group. If the circle gets too big, however, and you cannot hear each other speak, then it is oppressive. Microphones make it easier for people to hear, but they restrict participation. For large groups concentric semi-circles with a facilitator are often best.

Make sure you have all the equipment you will need for the meeting: films, flip-charts, markers, projectors, etc. Make up a list and check it off.

The Facilitator:

Any meeting with more than five people needs a facilitator/chair. Someone who will be responsible for process, and making sure that no one dominates and everyone gets a chance to participate. The facilitator can be chosen by the group at a previous meeting, or chosen as the first item on an agenda. If it is your first meeting together, ask someone to facilitate the meeting.[8]

The facilitator/chair should not actively contribute to discussion, especially if the matters are contentious. He/she is to act as a referee for the conversation to keep it on track and make sure all get a chance to express their opinion.

Occasionally, when a meeting is full of conflict, the facilitator may have to make judgement calls about what has been said, who has talked too much, and when people want to decide something. You will take flak for this, so turn it back to the participants, asking for a straw vote for or against your decision.

Rotating the chair is not always a good idea: this is a skilled trade. We should train facilitators and secretaries, etc. so that more people can do it, but not at the expense of messing up a very difficult meeting.

The spokesperson and the chair of a meeting should never be the same people. Neither should the person with the most information chair a meeting.

Outside facilitators can often be asked in to help move a group along. Make sure, however, that the group has approved this process before the facilitator takes the chair.

Taking time to laugh and play together is always worth it, and a break to go for a walk, play a co-operative game, or tell some jokes. Even in a tense meeting this can change the atmosphere very quickly.

Silence can be an important part of decision-making, as can well-timed breaks, which give people time to informally caucus together.

Getting away from private property in ideas will help people deal with real issues. Numbering off and using buzz groups can be used to break up a structured opposition and force people to act with more responsibility to the whole group.

The Conduct of the Meeting:

Meetings should not be too long, and the beginning and ending time should be adhered to unless the group decides differently.

Meetings have to have a sense of creative play, of learning and of purpose. People get bored if they can't participate or if they are holding in their anger and frustration. We all have lives that are too busy to waste time in irrelevant or boring meetings.

At the beginning of a meeting (if the group is not too large), it is often a good idea to have a check-in, where people talk a little bit about how they are feeling and what baggage they are bringing to the meeting. In a larger group this can be done in three's or four's.

The agenda for the evening should be OK'd by the people there. If there is too much to cover in one evening, make sure that people know when their pet issue will be dealt with. If there are strong divisions in the group, acknowledge them and make sure all sides are comfortable with the agenda.

Make sure that the results of the meeting are recorded, so that everyone can see what happened. This job can be rotated as long as the records are kept in a convenient place. In asking for volunteers for this, remember that many people are illiterate, or don't know how to take minutes.

Pretending that differences — race, sex, class, sexual orientation, handicaps — are not there, will not make them go away. Groups that have a very diverse membership need to be careful to balance power within the group, and not to "tokenize" anyone. Differences need to be discussed and struggled with: there are stereotypes on all sides. An excellent resource for dealing with these differences is *Building United Judgement* from the Centre for Conflict Resolution.

In their important book on feminist process, Linda Briskin and her co-authors write:

> Conflict and disagreement are necessary and healthy signs that a group is functioning well. Conflict generates creativity, especially in the context of decision-making by consensus, and the resolution of conflicts can be energizing and empowering for the group. When groups create norms that discourage conflict, and when disagreement is seen as destructive to the groups unity, those members who have questions or who disagree with the generally accepted position, silence themselves, usually by leaving.[9]

Consensus decision-making is OK when everyone agrees on the basic principles, or when the group is small. Where the group is very task-oriented and there is not agreement on basic principle, it is death. The discussion can drag on forever. It can also encourage an elite leadership who manipulate the minority, making real debate very difficult. Where time is limited and there is an entrenched opposition, it may be necessary to hold a vote on the issue.

Setting up task groups, or block groups, or committees to report back to the larger group can move a big agenda along quickly. These groups should be as autonomous as possible, so that everyone has a share in decision making. Where non-violent direct action, or other high-risk activities are planned, people on the firing line need to control the decisions that affect them.

Take time to celebrate our victories and each other. We all need recognition, and lots of it. People need time to report in on their achievements.

Meetings to Show Strength

In this category are meetings that are set up by others, and meetings where we are negotiating with representatives of a power structure. As in "meetings to build unity" there are a few basic rules.[10]

The first rule is to be very clear about what your group wants from the meeting. Is it just information? Or do you expect to get a decision? Or do you just want to show the structure your strength? Be sure that what you want from the people you are meeting with is within their power to give. If you are only meeting with them to test their response, be clear about that too.

NEVER argue amongst yourselves in their presence, unless your purpose is to show them how democratically your group operates. If you need to discuss something with each other, leave the meeting to talk, or ask them to leave while you talk, or save your disagreement for later.

Where possible decide on spokespeople before the meeting and support them. You can be sure that the efforts of the other side will be directed at dividing you. Don't allow your spokespeople to leave the group to talk with the other side. If they have something to discuss it should be done in front of the whole group.

In some situations, like a government sponsored meeting on a toxic waste site, you may want all your members to speak at the meeting. That's OK as long as you understand beforehand why you are doing it, and what you will say.

Debrief as soon as possible with the whole group after the meeting to evaluate what you achieved and how people felt about it.

Research

How do we get the information we require? Organizers and groups need lots of information of all different kinds to do their work effectively. Think with your group about the information you need in order to go forward. It may be very specific or very general.

The best kind of research for community groups is something called "participatory research": investigations that work from people's own experience. People who are oppressed by a reality need to discover for themselves the causes of and solutions to their oppression themselves.

When groups decide to do a survey of the community to get information, it helps to remember that different kinds of surveys produce different results. If the group wants to get to know people in the community and have them get involved, then it is counter-productive to treat the survey subjects like statistics. You will *want* to get back to them after the study, and you will want them to talk about other issues and matters. On the other hand, if the group is just interested in verifiable data, it will have to do an anonymous, random-sample, highly-structured survey.

Exercise:

The following exercise is an example of a participatory research approach to understanding your community. It can be used at any time in a group's life together: either to test the relevance of what you are doing at the present time, or to make plans for the future. It reveals information about the community you live in so that the flow of money, the kinds of work people do, the power relationships and the possibilities for change are visible to every one in the group. Often members of the community themselves hold more information collectively than they think. Participants would be local community people.

The exercise takes about two-three hours to do. Begin with a large blackboard and chalk or magic markers and a huge sheet of newsprint. Then ask questions similar to the following and "diagram" the participants answers accordingly:

What are the major roads?

What is the most important building in the community? The other important buildings? Where are they? (Make sure they tell you about both public and private buildings.)

Where do people congregate?

Where do people work? What do they do in a day? (If they are unemployed, find out what they do.) How many people work at each kind of work (both paid and unpaid). You can use percentages and just write them down the side. What about men's and women's work?

Make sure you include bootlegging, prostitution and drug trafficking as work. Who owns/runs the workplaces — do they live in the area?

What are the conditions of work in the major employers? Are there unions?

Where do people live? Where are the most people? What are their racial differences? Do they eat at home? Where else? Who owns the housing? Where do the owners live? What is the quality of the housing? Who holds the mortgages? Is there land speculation going on? How much of the money in housing stays in the community?

Where do the people get food? How many people have gardens? Hunt? Forage? Trap? (Ask this even in cities.) Do they buy food in the community? If not, who owns the major stores? Where do the profits go?

Where do the people get clothing? Do they make their own? If not, where does the clothing come from?

What do the people do for entertainment? Who owns the places of entertainment? Include sports in this question and look at the purchase of equipment.

What about schools? Are the teachers from the community? Do they live in the community? How do the parents, the kids, relate to the school? What are the problems? Who makes the money from the purchase of school materials and construction? Does the curriculum have anything to do with the kids real lives?

What do the young people do when they are not in school? Where do they hang out? Do they need more? What?

Where are the churches? What churches are there? How many active members do they have? Is there conflict between them? Over what issues? How much influence do they have? How would you describe the religious/cultural life of the community?

What money comes into the community? Do some people have more money than others? How can you tell? What are the class differences in the community? What do the rich do that the poor don't do and vice-versa?

What are the main sources of information in the community? Does the community control any of these (include gossip)? Who are the community opinion leaders? Who do people trust for advice and information (emphasize informal leadership)? Who do they trust the least?

Are there community organizations at the grass roots level? What are they? How much support do they have? Who are their leaders? What is your relationship to them? (Don't forget that there may be distinct ethnic and gender divisions here.)

If the group does not have answers to these questions, they may want to find out the answers by talking to others or by observation. A lot of information is available at public libraries, and the librarians are often very willing to help. Some of the information can be found in the city files or the economic development office. It is your right as a citizen to know this information, so make it a political point to ask for it.

Where Else to Get Information:

Land Ownership: registry office files. This costs money to research and a small amount of expertise. Try to find a lawyer or law clerk who will help you decipher the records. A lot of land is held by corporations. The owners of the corporations are usually required to register with the Companies Branch of the provincial government, and you can request this information.

Government Policies: regulations and laws are all public information and available in libraries and from government departments.

Historical Information: Libraries, interviews, newspaper files, company archives.

Information On Corporate Structures, Behaviour, Policies: Some corporations have archives that you can access by pretending you are a student researcher. Some corporate information has to be registered. Some is available to shareholders, and it is worthwhile buying a share to get access to the information. Sometimes you need a "mole": someone who will leak information to you from inside the structure. Newspaper clippings from financial papers carry a surprising amount of information. Research these at your local library. There are a number of public advocacy organizations that have extensive files on corporations:

- Nutrition Policy Institute
- Energy Probe, Pollution Probe, Greenpeace,
- OXFAM-Canada

Information on Toxics, Pollution, etc.: A number of organizations specialize in researching these areas and making the information available to the public. There are also corporate-sponsored groups that exist to hide the truth from the public. Always get information from more than one source where possible. Keeping a clippings file for your own area is also a useful activity.

Peoples' History/Social Activism: Doing a research project to record the history of people's struggles in your area is a valuable and interesting activity. There are also a large number of theses and books written by university researchers on social change that never get out of the library. One of the best sources of information on activism in the country is the *Connexions Annual: A Social Change Sourcebook.*

Community Information: Knowing about a particular landlord, or a road development or an expropriation case may be very valuable to planning strategy for your group. This information is collected by asking lots of questions of the people most affected, and by demanding information from public officials and businesspeople.

Research is something that should involve as many members of the group as possible, and it should be disseminated to every one. Knowledge is power, and knowledge about the organizing context will shape strategy and tactics. Find ways to share information creatively with other members of the group.

For example: if the problem you decide to take on is welfare cutbacks...you can get information from many sources. From a survey of recipients themselves — looking at effects, budgets, how much it will exhaust them, what organizations do they know that will fight it with them. You can get information from government statistics and surveys. You can get information from legal clinics and poor people's organizations. You can get it from the national church and other national organizations like the Canadian Council on Social Development. And you can get it from Schools of Social Work and other sociologists. You can also read the financial pages of the paper to see what government *is* spending its money on instead.

Another example: if the problem you decide to tackle is toxic wastes in your neighbourhood...you can interview your neighbours to see what effect it is having on them and how they feel about it, and if they would like to organize. You can talk to the municipal government and the department of public health. You can get information on toxic wastes from organizations like Pollution Probe, Greenpeace, the Clearing House for Toxic Waste or the Canadian Environmental Law Association. There are a lot of documented stories in books and films of citizens groups that have taken on the toxic waste issue, and you can see how they fought back. Libraries and government offices and United Nations publications all deal with these issues, as do academics in many parts of Canada.

In both these examples, you can see that there is a range of ways to get information. The trick is to make this information accessible to different classes and groups of people, and to put it all together. Use mapping, drawings and models (like developers use) to work it out and make it visible.

Paying the Bills for Social Change

All groups have expenses. Where we get our money is, therefore, a crucial matter. Groups can get money from membership, community fund-raising activities, grants, loans and government programs. The source of funds will certainly influence the direction that the organization takes. Very few organizations that are engaged in radical social change are eligible for government grants and corporate help, unless they find a way to design and phrase their application to suit the program available.

Since the sixties, the Canadian government has been extremely good at finding ways to manipulate social change groups through funding. As we saw in Chapter 1, a minimum wage salary is offered to a radical tenants group in return for their incorporating. Or a women's centre gets funding for special projects but not for work on reproductive rights. Or a group wants to hire staff for an unemployed help centre but can only do so on Section 38 dollars.

The intelligent use of government funding means being very clear about our own agenda and finding ways to use a variety of sources for money.

Getting funds from corporations and foundations requires similar skill at adapting our real agenda to their funding requirements. Large foundations like Rockefeller and Ford were set up specifically to gather information on and propose alternatives to socialist programs. They serve as tax shelters for the very rich. There are however, some foundations that are accessible to radical groups and do support innovative community work. In Canada, Laidlaw, Donner, Kellogg and Bronfman Foundations have quite often funded parts of our work. Information about foundations and corporate sources of funds is available in your public library or from the Canadian Centre for Philanthropy.

Applying effectively to private funding source has become a sophisticated trade. Applicants need an attractively prepared presentation of their organization, audited financial statements, and members who are able and willing to spend time cultivating staff of the foundations. Your group will also have to have charitable status with Revenue Canada.

One of the disadvantages of government and corporate funding is that it comes in large chunks and increases your expectations of what you will be able to accomplish. For example,you start to rely on staffing and lose your volunteer base. The mountains of paperwork required for the proposal and the reporting for the project exclude semi-literate people from positions of power within an organization. It encourages you to organize on a multiplicity of issues with separate organizations for each one, instead of trying to form a more broadly-based community group where you might decide that these issues have your powerlessness in common, and you need to be more strategic in tackling them.

Funding from churches can be another possibility. The structure of most Protestant churches is such that it is easier to get money from local churches and presbyteries than from the national or provincial body. This is because the broader levels are funded by allocations from local congregations. Funds may be requested from operating budgets and from bequests and trust funds. Often the trusts (money left to congregations or presbyteries by deceased members) are quite substantial, but information about them is not generally known. The Catholic churches also have money in different pockets: Development and Peace, local parishes, the bishop's fund and so on.

Direct mail is another form of fund-raising that is increasingly popular with national organizations. It is expensive and requires skilled and experienced people to work well. For most community groups it is not a viable option.

Increasingly in Canada, government cutbacks have meant that more of our energy goes into fund-raising for human and social services that should be supported by government funding: cancer treatment centres, transition houses, food banks, and school recreation programs. This means that social change groups compete with other more socially-acceptable causes for the same public dollars.

However, organizing bake sales and rummage sales and benefits not only raises money for day to day operations but has important spinoff effects in the community. There is often money even in poor communities that can be used if the people feel that the activity is important enough to their own self-interest (or their children's) to support it. A lot of things can be done by local people with "in kind" donations if they feel the organization is relevant to them.

Local fund-raising ideas include many things:

- memberships, donations, subscriptions
- rummage sales, bake sales, auctions, box socials
- bingos, casino nights, raffles
- benefit concerts, plays
- walk-athons, marches, telethons
- bottle drives, car washes
- charging the well-to-do for workshops and seminars to subsidize other activities
- community economic development activities (see Chapter 4)

There are a few excellent resources on fund-raising: Ken Wyman's *Guide to Special Events Fund-raising,* and Jeffrey Lant's *Development Today: A Fundraising Guide for Non-profit Organizations.* They are listed in the Resource section of this book.

Planning For a Change

First, get an idea of what you want things to look like if the problem is solved. Now, there will be two things you want to accomplish with your strategy. One may be solving the particular immediate problem of an individual: getting a house, getting a job, etc. but as important for the future of your committee and other people in the long-run, is going after the root causes of the individual's problem. It *is* true that the squeaky wheel gets the grease, and the system can usually respond to individual cases if enough noise is made. The difficulty is to develop strategies that go after the root causes.

No matter how fancy a strategy is, if it doesn't excite you and your members, forget it. A good strategy is one that makes you all go, 'yeah!' and has you all enthusiastic and thinking about it day and night and wanting to *go*. Play around with all sorts of ideas till you find some that fit. Brainstorm, discuss, try out different games.

Second, do some planning. What needs to be changed for you to get what you need accomplished? What rules, what laws, what systems are in the way? How do you change them and in what order. How much people power do you need to persuade those with institutionalized power to change their minds? What makes them tick? Why are they in your way? Do they really disagree, or are they trapped too? What would unstick them? If they really disagree, is there a way around them? Can they be removed from the way?

Most bureaucracies operate very smoothly as long as nothing disrupts their usual functioning. For them any hot political issue means that phones ring and people need to be pacified and things have to be explained to superiors. Then they panic, because they don't have time or systems to deal with the disruption. Sometimes they will give in to you just because it will take less time and hassle to give in than to fight. Even your children know this strategy!

Think about all the things you would like to do to solve the problem. Use buzz groups and brainstorming. Now pick those things that everyone feels the most excited about. Do you have the energy to do it? Who will do it? By when? How will they be accountable to the larger group? Beware of taking on too much yourself. If the group isn't excited enough to take things on, scale down the plan. Do you need more people? Who would be excited by this idea and work with you? Who is going to contact them? How?

Who else is working on this issue in your community? What do you know about them? Who is going to find out more? Can you work with them? What will be the problems for maintaining your own group if you work together? How do you keep a few of your people who will be on the coalition or do the liaison from having too much power to make decisions, without hamstringing their effectiveness?

Make a chart: It looks like this:

The Problem	Steps			The Vision
	May 1991	*Dec 1991*	*May 1992*	
1				
2				
3				
4				
5				

State the problem in as specific terms as possible at one side, and the goal (in a specific terms as possible) on the other side. List the steps you need to take to get from A to Z, as you know them, working both backwards and forward. Remember that there will almost always be new steps that crop up along the way, so try to anticipate them. Take each of the steps and brainstorm all the possible problems and information you need to carry them out. Try small buzz groups to work on this. List everything on separate sheets of flip chart paper as people talk.

Who is going to be responsible for keeping the group informed. Building trust and learning to work together have to be important parts of any strategy. You need to take time to celebrate your victories and your hard work, and to have some fun or to reflect together. The kind of camaraderie that gets people through crises like floods and wars is essential, and time and space need to be made for it in your strategy.

Nurture the group itself. Ask yourselves how the group is developing? Who talks with whom? How can you expand these networks? What inspired you to join? What will inspire others? What isn't being said? What hidden agendas do you have? Are people really tired? Are you excited? What can you celebrate together? Plan a social event to go with the political strategy. Figure out how to get training. Sit in silence for a while.

Think about cultural and class differences in the group. What kind of things do you know how to do now? What skills do you bring to the group? How can you use those skills in developing the strategy? Where do people want to learn new skills? How do you learn to do them? How do you provide honest feedback if people aren't doing something well enough? How do you provide apprenticeships? How do you develop a strategy that uses your skills to the maximum. For example:

In an organization of wives of strikers that formed during an eight month strike in Sudbury, the women set up an organization that used all their skills to the maximum, because of its diversity. Some women ran clothing depots, toy drives and put on bean suppers to build morale and to look after material needs. Some women organized picnics on the picket line and put on a play "INCO vs. The People." Some women sang in the Wives Chorus and set up photo displays and decorated a float for the Santa Claus parade. Some women put out a newsletter, chaired meetings and ran a crisis line. Some women made speeches. Everyone learned new skills doing it, and there was a free flow of members from one subgroup to another. The thrust of all the work was to help win the strike. The end result for the women (besides winning the strike) was tremendous personal growth and sense of purpose in their lives.

In deciding strategy, work these questions through in the larger group with discussion and small groups. Try role playing the other actors in the community and seeing where there will be conflict, or compromise. Spend time making wall sized charts of where you are in your strategy, and what remains to be done. It'll make you feel well organized and terrific.

NOTES

1. Starhawk, *Truth or Dare*, Harper and Row Publishers, New York, 1987.
2. Kahn, Si, *Organizing*, McGraw-Hill, 1982. This is an excellent resource for community organizers. This section is strongly influenced by his work.
3. There are a number of resources on group process, and I am indebted to all of them; specifically:

    Adamson, Nancy, Linda Briskin and Margaret McPhail, *Feminist Organizing for Change*, Oxford University Press, Toronto, 1988.

    Coover, Virginia, Ellen Deacon, C. Esser, and C. Moore, *Resource Manual for a Living Revolution: A Handbook of Skills and Tools for Social Change Activists*, New Society Publishers, 1985.

    Centre for Conflict Resolution, *Building United Judgement: A Handbook for Consensus Decision-Making*, Madison, 1985.

    Biagi, Bob, *Working Together: A Handbook to Help Groups Work More Effectively*, University of Massachusetts, 1978.

    Knowles, Malcolm and Hulda, *Introduction to Group Dynamics*, Association Press, 1972.

    Centre for Conflict Resolution, *A Manual for Group Facilitators*, Wisconsin, 1978.

    Lee, Bill, *Pragmatics of Community Organization*, Commonact Press, 1986.
4. *Worker Co-op*, volume 8, No.3.
5. The Women's Self-Help Network, *Working Collectively*, Ptarmigan Press, Campbell River, 1984.
6. Hill, Karen, *Helping You Helps Me: A Guide for Self-Help Groups*, Canadian Council on Social Development, 1984. More information about self-help groups.
7. Urban Core Support Network, 147 Queen Street West, Toronto, Ontario. Good help with networking.
8. Centre for Conflict Resolution, *Manual for Group Facilitators*, op.cit. For more help.
9. Adamson, Nancy, Linda Briskin, and Margaret McPhail, *op.cit.*, page 243.
10. There is a wonderful video tape called I Never Did It With a Banker Before, that was produced by the Parallel Institute in Montréal, which heavily influenced this short section. Unfortunately, it is out of print and I have no idea where to get it now.

Chapter 10

RECLAIMING ECONOMICS

I'm at a workshop on an island where I have been told there are many eagles. I haven't seen one yet. I climb the craggy hillside to look for an eagle; I sit and will it to come. But I am visited instead by hundreds of chickadees, flitting from the branches of the pine trees, chattering to one another. An hour later, disappointed, I return to the lodge where the meeting is taking place. "Oh," says Ariel, "did you see the eagle? It was circling over the lodge for most of the time you were gone."

* * *

Reclaiming economics is about rebuilding our physical relationship to the earth: clean air, water, soil, decent shelter, nourishing food in adequate supply, warmth, medicines. How do we create these things in equality, with good work and without depleting the world for our grandchildren? How do we live and work together? How do we create this physical environment for millions of people in the midst of a world already poisoned and plundered?

The seeds exist for reclaiming the economy. Although they do not by themselves provide the answers, they are important components of the transformation. There are a number of community problems we can work on ourselves within the parameters of the existing system. They include cooperatives, self-reliant agriculture, renewable energy sources, community gardens, alternative schools.

This economics is not new. Since the beginning of the industrial revolution, alternatives to capitalism have been explored through co-operatives, utopian communities, and worker control of the places of production.

Taking this approach does change the quality of life for a number of people. There can be no doubt that living in social housing beats being on the street. Or having a youth managed drop-in is better than nothing. Or going to a transition house for battered women is better than continuing to be assaulted at home. It provides the organizers and other volunteers with a tremendous sense of accomplishment.

However, it can take a lot of money to pull it off. Funding this work adequately would require a major shift in political power, since only governments, corporations, financial institutions, and a few individuals have accumulated this much capital. At the present time, when we try to access this money, we have to find ways to describe our projects that are acceptable to the economists and bureaucrats with whom we negotiate for survival. They want to know that they are "economically feasible." We have to translate our dreams into the language of business plans and feasibility studies.

Alternative economics builds on a vision of hope. When we undertake it knowing we need to ask the ecological, cultural and social questions at the same time, it can be empowering.

This section is organized into three parts:

- a discussion of the concept of community economic development with some examples,
- a catalogue of ideas for alternative economic work with examples and a few resources if you want to explore them further; and
- a chapter on grassroots organizing for community economic development.

Community Economic Development (CED)

Community economic development starts the process of returning control and ownership of economic decisions to the people most affected by those decisions...Starting locally means recognizing that there is such a thing as community economics. It means we have to take our personal economic decisions seriously: are we putting money and resources into the local cooking pot to nourish the neighbourhood, or are we sending our best resources elsewhere?...Starting locally, finally, means linking the local community to the world at large...But a better and more secure future will ultimately rest on the building blocks of strengthened, independent and interdependent communities. The challenge is to think globally, to keep the Big Picture in focus, and to act locally, because at that level every individual can make a real contribution.[1]

These days, all Canadian communities are worried about retaining jobs and attracting money. Conventional economic practice is to seek to bring investment and industry to a community with a variety of tax incentives and benefits. These benefits may include anti-union sentiment, low wages, overlooking environmental problems and pleasant facilities for visiting executives or tourists. In Sudbury recently, a social worker who told the press that there were hungry children in the city was reprimanded by the City Council, who said it was "irresponsible" to talk about child poverty because it hurt our public image.

Community economic development is a radical departure from this approach. It is about creating self-reliant communities, that are not as dependent on outside investment. As we saw in Chapter 5, however, CED means different things to different interest groups. I am talking about it here as though community organizers like myself controlled the name.

Community economic development has some special characteristics:

- It values the informal economy: the work and production that goes on that does not show up in the gross national product: child care, gardening, volunteer work, doing our own repairs, driving each other around, looking after the sick, the aged, the young, and so on.
- It is concerned about retaining wealth in a community: CED asks "where does the money go" as much as "where does it come from."
- CED is as concerned about creating viable communities for our grandchildren as it is for ourselves. Because we and they will have to live with environmental effects and social spinoffs, we want to do things right now.
- CED is concerned about getting local control over business, not trying to get another branch plant or franchise established.
- CED is about producing socially-useful products, like housing and food, not just more consumer junk, or harmful products (like military equipment).
- CED is about development that does not displace the poor or depopulate rural communities.

- CED is about redistributing the wealth and services in a community so that they may be more equally shared by all.
- CED is about creating good work: work that is healthy, satisfying and secure. It is about improving and diversifying the skills of community members.

However, CED in Canada is a kind of business and it exists within the market economy. That means that it must compete with other businesses in order to survive. It is under many of the same pressures to pay low wages, to cut back on quality and to ignore environmental concerns as any other business. Building a climate of strong community support for the CED project is essential so that people will be willing to pay a little higher price for quality or ecological soundness or justice.

A very interesting example of community economic development is to be found in Uniacke Square, a public housing development in Halifax. Here a group of low-income women got together first to transform a proposal to gentrify their neighbourhood from one that would evict many of the residents to one that improved the buildings but allowed them to stay. This tenants' association then organized a Parent Resource Centre that has provided support to low income black women since 1986. Its goal is to promote a healthier community for women. They sponsor parenting skills programs, leadership skills, confidence workshops, bringing women together to focus on issues that concern them. They established an organizing committee against violence in the North End and wrote a proposal for a researcher on safe house networks. A resource person in popular theatre did a workshop on family violence. They have held workshops and exchanges with Third World women organizers including Sistern from Jamaica.

A food co-op grew out of the women coming to the Centre hungry because they fed the kids first and it grew into a catering worker co-operative. They started with six members, and now have thirteen. They set up a worker co-operative with adolescents in the square to do maintenance and repair. The dollars go to the co-op because welfare would deduct wages, so the money is used to buy food, christmas trees, etc. Joan Mendes of the group says: "It isn't easy because of family commitments and problems, special needs, racism, isolation, poverty, minimum wage jobs, and lack of proper health care. But more groups are organizing all the time. There have been definite changes in the women."

The Calgary Immigrant Women's Centre helped establish an ethnic catering company to overcome language and job opportunity barriers that create isolation and employment barriers for immigrant women. They set up a training program at the local community college to train women who were employed as domestics, so that they could establish a seamstress business. The benefits for the women in self-respect and new skills may not be measurable, but they are as important as the jobs created.

The Meadow Lake Tribal Council established the Meadow Lake District Chiefs Joint Venture in 1981. It now owns or holds shares in several businesses and organizations. It has launched many training programs, and has had greater success in getting credit. Money that used to go to white companies in the south, now stay in the communities. They are partners in a consulting firm. They established the National Indian Forestry Institute. They provide training on forestry management, policy-making, planning, budgeting and other matters. They have organized joint purchase of supplies for housing and other band construction projects.

In the Pointe-St.Charles area of Montréal, community organizations have set up a community economic development project called PEP which has created or helped over 75 businesses, and created or maintained 300 jobs. Through previous community action, people in the Pointe have also established a daycare centre, anti-poverty groups, housing co-ops, a community health clinic, a legal clinic, emergency shelters for the homeless and women in crisis, and other social services. Although PEP has not been able to make up for the destruction of the local economy by outside forces over the last thirty years, they have taken significant steps to reclaim their own economy.

In an Acadien area of Prince Edward Island, the Evangeline Credit Union is the centre of "the co-operative capital of North America."[2] Fifteen co-operatives provide a community of about 2500 people with services ranging from banking to handicrafts to funerals. In 1988, these co-operatives provided 324 jobs, 48 full-time and the rest seasonal or part-time. There is a fish plant that buys fish for canning and processing, and supplies boats and supplies to its members. There are two consumer co-ops selling groceries and hardware. There is a pioneer village museum which is a full-fledged tourist attraction. There is a potato chip factory (Olde Barrel), a handicrafts co-op, a children's clothes manufacturing co-operative, a funeral co-op, and a forestry co-op. A community health clinic employs five doctors and a dentist.

A Catalogue of Ideas For the Alternate Economy

Social Accounting:

This is the development of ledgers for economic projects that measure the real impacts of the activity on the individual, the household and the community. For example, in the construction of a new highway, it might look at:

- Present uses of the land surrounding the site, and the benefits to the community from them: children's informal recreation area, wildlife habitat, oxygen production, informal pathways from one area to another, soil, marshlands, alternative possibilities for the land.
- Costs in terms of: greenhouse effect, accidents, stress, changes in driving patterns for users (will their factory be located further from their home), loss of arable land, oxygen, disruption of community around the highway, injury to wildlife, effect on house prices both around the highway and in the area bypassed by it, occupational hazards and costs of production, local retention of profits from production, costs of future maintenance.
- Comparative social/environmental and extrapolated economic costs for alternative transportation systems like rail or other routes.

As one indigenous man said to me "When a scaler looks at a large cedar tree he sees $40 a board foot; I see $4000, because I know the value of the tree to the forest, to the atmosphere and to my people, but I also know what the tiny carvings made from every twig of that tree can sell for."

Groups that want to have this kind of accounting recognized have to fight for it: it is becoming the touchstone of environmental assessment hearings in forestry and energy production. A new book by Lester Milbraith, *Envisioning a Sustainable Society* (Suny Press 1989), provides some guidelines.

Co-operative Living

When five of us (plus our children) decided to buy an enormous old house ten years ago, it cost us $47,000 plus the lawyer's fees. When we had to renegotiate the mortgage a year later, however, the interest rates had sky-rocketed to 22 and 3/4%. The credit union re-evaluated the house lower than the purchase price, so we had to take out a loan for the balance at an even higher rate of interest. To pay the doubled costs of living there we took in more people. Suddenly there were twelve people living and eating and sleeping in that house instead of seven. The emotional intensity increased exponentially.

On the other hand, while everyone else we knew was losing their homes, we kept ours because we were willing to share it. When the willow tree ate the sewer line, and the roof started to leak like a sieve, we had a lot more hands to repair it. The kids grew up with an extended family, even if I did scream like a fishwife at them all every morning as they poked around getting ready for school.

And now although many of us have moved out and on, it is still home for six people…a beautiful home with a garden and a swing and a crab-apple tree that blooms every spring. And my children and I have an extended family that enriches our lives. All for a shelter cost of less than $200 a month each. How do you beat that?

In Canada there are many examples of collective houses (like ours), co-operative and non-profit housing developments. In November 1987 a Co-operative Housing Federation of Canada survey found there were 40,000 non-profit co-operative housing units owned by 1,249 housing co-operatives with an additional 4,600 units under development and another 5,500 units in the planning stage. There are over 60 resource groups in this sector providing expertise and help in setting up and obtaining mortgages for co-ops and non-profits.

Most co-operatives and non-profits have support from the federal and provincial government through provincial housing programs. They vary greatly from province to province, but one thing they do have in common is an enormous and complex amount of paperwork to get off the ground. If you are interested in pursuing this area, you would be well-advised to seek the help of a resource group. Their fees are part of the loan package you get from the provincial government.

You can also seek private funding to establish co-operative housing from regular financial institutions, alternative investment funds and many churches. Provided your proposition is viable, this may be an easier route to go than the government one.

Co-operatives are individual housing units that are owned in common by all the occupants, and managed by an elected board. The rents are determined by the costs, although most co-operatives can subsidize some units for members who cannot afford full market rent. One Charlottetown co-operative purchased an entire block of older row housing and rehabilitated it. They turned the centre of the block into a beautiful and useful landscaped common space. Other co-operatives build new units.

Non-profit housing has the same range of options, but it is owned by a non-share capital corporation. Although tenants can have representation on the board or have a tenant management committee, the board of the corporation is legally responsible for all contracts and so on. If most of the units are to be rent-geared-to-income, or occupants don't want to be owners, this may be the only way to get funding. Some church properties have even been converted to non-profit housing for the elderly or low-income people.

Homes First Society in Toronto, Communitas in Edmonton and the Downtown Eastside Residents Association in Vancouver are organizations that have been very successful, not only in building housing for homeless people, but in influencing government policy to be more responsive.

Other options open to church groups interested in helping with housing are financing through remortgaging church property, selling air rights, and providing office and administrative help. There is a network of activists in Canada that provides support and information for groups and people who want to get involved in this area. They are the Urban Core Support Network (UCSN), 147 Queen Street West, Toronto, Ontario, M5H 2N8.

Land Trusts

Land trusts are democratic corporations that hold land in the public interest. They can be non-profits or co-operatives. The land cannot be sold for private profit, but can be used by renters for private advantage, so long as they do not violate the purposes of the land trust. Land trusts can stop land speculation and other types of profiteering and can provide guidelines for land use within their territory.

In Canada, most land trusts are formed in order to accumulate land for housing in city core areas. The government of Saskatchewan had a land banking scheme established in 1972. It purchased land at market value from current owners and leased it back to them or to others. The lease could be passed on to dependents. There are also religious communities like the Hutterites who remove agricultural land from the market and hold it for later development by themselves.

In the United States there are many examples of successful community land trusts. Common Ground in Dallas has received donations of land and deteriorated housing plus loans and cash. It holds title to all the land, but makes it available for low income housing and community space.

Co-operative land trusts may provide a vehicle for farmers in crisis to retain occupancy of their land; for example, a municipality or a church might buy land from a credit union that has had to foreclose on a number of farmers and is unable to sell, and then either lease it or resell it to a co-operative land trust of farmers.

There is also some history of co-operative farms in Canada.

In 1945, the Saskatchewan government encouraged the establishment of co-operative farms for returning war veterans. They were run democratically by their members just like any worker co-operative. One of these was the Matador co-operative, which has been in existence for 42 years.

Worker Co-operatives

A worker co-operative is an enterprise that is owned and controlled by the workers. Decision-making is on a one member-one vote basis. No outside investors are permitted and no exploitation of capital over labour is tolerated.

Worker co-operatives provide an opportunity for workplace democracy. The only bosses are those chosen by and responsible to the workers in the enterprise.

Worker co-operatives have a better survival rate than other forms of business organization, and higher productivity than traditional forms of business organization.[3] They make a valuable contribution to increased democracy at work and to the democratic structure of the country as a whole. They tend to be more responsive to the needs of the community in which they operate and to job satisfaction for the member-workers.

Worker co-operatives are frequently considered by workers as an alternative to plant closure. One of the most renowned of these was the attempt to buy back Hamilton Porcelain in 1985.

In 1989 there were over 350 worker co-operatives in Canada and a great deal more in the rest of the world. In Canada, the majority of worker co-operatives are in the forestry sector in Québec. The first forestry co-operative was started in 1938; by 1970, there were 166.[4]

The Big Carrot (a health food retailer in Toronto), and CRS Worker Co-operative in Vancouver, are two of the larger enterprises. The Big

Carrot, opened in 1983, after the workers in a health food store decided to become a worker co-operative instead of being laid off. They now have 30 staff and have recently opened a 14 store mall on the Danforth in Toronto, called Carrot Common. CRS worker co-op in Vancouver is the largest wholesaler of natural foods in Western Canada. It was started in 1973 as a resource group for buyers clubs: it now has 37 members.

A magazine, *Worker Co-ops*, regularly gives information about the state of the movement in Canada.

Perhaps the most sophisticated worker co-operatives in the world are in the Basque Region of Spain, where the Mondragon Co-operative has been in existence since 1946. An interlocking set of worker co-operatives engaged in plastics, food production, training, medical care, and a credit union now employ more that 25,000 people in over 150 enterprises. There are a number of films and books on the Mondragon experiment.

Worker co-operatives in and of themselves do not guarantee social transformation: if the co-operative members are fascists, you will have a fascist co-operative. On the other hand, for those of us who want to do "good work" together this is an ideal model.

There are now resource groups in Canada that assist community groups in establishing worker Co-operatives. Co-operative Work in Toronto and Community Economic Options in Vancouver are two of the most experienced and approachable. Co-operative Work has also published a manual called *Starting a Worker Co-operative*, which is very useful. Information about worker co-operatives and resources is available from the Worker Ownership Development Foundation, 212-348 Danforth Avenue, Toronto, Ontario M4K 1N8.

Buyers' Clubs and Food Co-operatives

We all spend lots of money on food. In most Canadian cities, that money goes to a few large food giants: Weston, Steinbergs, Oshawa Group and A&P. They own the "independents" too, although it may appear that we are shopping somewhere else. Every middleman in the food industry increases the price to the consumer.

Buyers' clubs and food co-operatives attempt to eliminate the middleman and cut down on the amount of the food dollar that goes toward packaging and advertising. In Pine House, Saskatchewan, the reserve kicked the Bay (a multi-national retail enterprise that has a monopoly on many reserves in western Canada) off their reserve, and set up their own highly successful co-operative store.

There are two kinds of consumer co-operatives: one sells the products at the regular market price, but it is owned by members who receive dividends on the sales. The other, a service co-operative or buyer's club, sells only to members, at the wholesale price, and members pay the servicing charges separately.

Buyers' clubs can be very productive ways of building relationships between people, and getting less expensive and better quality food.

Once a week, or less often, members get together to agree on an order...so many pounds of flour, sugar, so many tins of tomatoes. One of the members takes responsibility for purchasing these goods at bulk rates from the wholesalers, and then he/she brings them back home and people come to the house to pay for the goods and pick them up. There are fairly simple book-keeping systems to facilitate this. Members may agree to rotate the purchasing task, or they may pay someone to do it for them. More sophisticated buyers' clubs have refrigerators, and lists of good sources of organic produce and so on. In some areas, they may even purchase direct from the producer in some areas.

Food co-operatives are big buyers' clubs. Many of them find themselves in competition with supermarkets, and unless there is real member loyalty, they are unable to compete. Some of them, trying to cut costs for their members, end up exploiting their labour.

Alternative Investment Funds

Many useful community projects suffer from their inability to raise sufficient capital to get going. Recently a number of organizations and individuals have been setting up funds that will make loans to "high risk-low return" ventures out of their regular investment portfolios.

In Montréal, the Third Avenue Resource Centre spearheaded a project to establish a Community Development Corporation in the impoverished Grand Plateau area of the city. They quickly discovered that they needed capital to assist small businesses to get started. In a few years they had formed an investment fund and begun to make loans at low interest to local individuals so that they could help make the Grand Plateau more self-reliant. Capital for the fund came from the City of Montréal, churches, community groups, foundations and individual donations.

The Calmeadow Foundation supports another kind of community economic development called micro-enterprise. Assisting people to expand the tiny businesses they run out of their homes: making bread, and pizzas on an Indian reserve for example, or putting a snow plow on a local truck. The fund is modelled on the highly successful Grameen Bank in Bangladesh. A community, like the Wekwemikong Reserve in Ontario, applies to Calmeadow for assistance. Calmeadow guarantees loans from a nearby regular lending institution like a bank. The people in the community organize a borrowers' circle: up to 6 people who are willing to guarantee small loans for each other's business ideas. The first loans are very small, under $500. When they are repaid, the circle can ask for other loans. The loans actually come from the bank. As the circle establishes its reliability, they can slowly increase the amount of borrowing. Other circles are also encouraged to form. The first circle has to be largely women.

In Vancouver, a fund called Womenfutures guarantees loans for women who want to establish small businesses but cannot get credit from traditional lending institutions. Organizing this fund, which is supported by individual donations from hundreds of women, was an incredible learning experience for the women who started it.

Credit unions like Bread and Roses in Toronto, CCEC in Vancouver and the Ottawa Women's Credit Union specialize in helping community enterprises get loans. They are very willing to share their experience with others.

The Solidarity Fund in Québec is established and maintained with deductions from the wages of workers in the major unions in Québec. It has assisted in rescue operations of companies that were being closed by multinationals and some community economic development projects like the Project Economique du Pointe St. Charles (P.E.P).

The United Church has established two sources of this money. Loans can be made to non-profit and co-operatively owned community economic development ventures at a reduced rate of interest. Also, $1.7 million of the stabilization fund has been set aside for loans of this nature. Local church congregations could set up similar funds to assist their community: using equity financing on their building or selling air-rights for example.

CommunitiWorks in Ottawa assists community employment initiatives, worker co-operatives, and affordable housing construction in the Ottawa area. The fund became possible after the profitable sale of a college residence in the downtown area.

Short-term Sharing Activities

Undertaking activities that share living and working experiences but do not require setting up an entire institution can be empowering and economically important. Some examples of these are:

- Group-living experiences: camping, retreats, shared parenting, training sessions;
- Sharing meals on a regular or occasional basis, including preparation, cleanup and planning;
- Setting up a childcare exchange;
- Building bees, cleaning bees, quilting, etc.

A wonderful story from a friend of mine:

Her husband bought a car. But it cost him too much to operate because he insisted on parking it on the street and got fines — lots of them. He decided to sell the car and one of her friends bought it for $300. She took it to get estimates on repairs and it came to $900. When she told X she couldn't afford it, X got two of her friends to go in with her and now 4 of them own it co-operatively. It is used to drive women and children around, to get groceries, to go to the park and so on. The car is parked in X's driveway. Her husband can't figure out how she did it.

Regeneration Projects, Sustainable Agriculture and Forestry

Some alternatives to the destruction of the environment, and the corporate practices which cause it are quite simple to initiate, others require considerable research, shifts in technology and capital. I list some possibilities here to help you get more information:

- Sustainable agriculture that does not depend on an export market, and that returns to the soil what it takes for production. The most sophisticated analysis of the food system in Canada is available from the Nutrition Policy Institute, 125 Highfield Road, Toronto, Ontario M4L 2V4. Resource: Canadian Organic Growers, 46 Lorindale Avenue, Toronto, Ontario, M5M 3C2. (416)484-9345.
- Organic gardening, urban gardens. In the downtown East side of Vancouver, a beautiful urban garden shows off the ethnic diversity of the neighbourhood and allows even the poorest street person to garden if they wish. Many municipalities have composting programs; in

some cities this is being extended to create garden plots. Wild flowers and wild spaces are more ecologically sound than lawns and grassy parks.

Resource: *Green Cities: Ecologically Sound Approaches to Urban Space,* edited by David Gordon, Black Rose Books, Montréal, 1990. A project of the Pollution Probe Foundation, 53 Queen Street, Ottawa, Ontario K1P 5C5. (613) 235-9266.

- Forestry practices are being challenged by aboriginal people, environmental groups and the Canadian Paperworkers Union. Timber management plans that include selective cutting, proper reforestation, the preservation of old growth areas and wetlands, and biological diversity are possible and available.

Resource: The best information is available from regional groups like Forests for Tomorrow in Ontario. For information about the groups in your region: Canadian Environmental Network, P.O. Box 1289, Station B, Ottawa, Ontario K1P 5R3 (613)563-2078, and Friends of the Earth, #701-251 Laurier Avenue West, Ottawa, Ontario K1P 5J6. (613)230-3352.

- Tree planting projects in rural and urban areas: wind breaks, reforestation, green spaces. Cleaning up streams and river beds.

Alternative Transportation Systems

The Green Consumer Guide says: "Second only to industry in its consumption of energy, transportation accounts for more than one quarter of all energy used in the country, with road vehicles responsible for 83% of that share. It is also the country's largest source of air pollution, every year spewing into the atmosphere some 13.6 million tonnes of noxious fumes that poison forests, lakes, and marine life, contribute to global warming and endanger human health... A Swiss study found that, compared with trains, motor vehicles account for 3 times as much land use, 3.5(cars) and 8.7 (trucks) times the energy consumed, 9 times the pollution, and 24 times the accident rate." [5]

There are a number of ways to tackle this problem: increased use of trains and street cars in urban centres, and improved and extended public transport — a small car with two passengers uses 2570 BTUs/passenger kilogram; a bus, 285; and a subway or LRT 1750. We can design our urban spaces so we can walk more safely and pleasantly. We can fight urban sprawl. We can increase the number of bicycle paths and walkways. We can fight for reinstituted and improved inter-city rail transportation. Resource: Transport 2000 Canada, P.O. Box

858, Station B, Ottawa, Ontario, K1P 5P9 (613)594-3290. A national federation of consumers of public transportation involved in research, education and consumer advocacy.

Bingos and Lotteries

In most poor communities people spend a lot of money on the bingo and the lottery. Canadian society is based on gambling: the wealthy gamble on the stock market and the poor have bingo. Bingos and lotteries are very destructive to poor communities when the money spent on them leaves the community. Most bingos are run by private operators and "charitable" organizations, not by the poor. In Akwesasne, Ontario and New York, the bingo and lottery operations are controlled by organized crime and have had very serious consequences for the local people.

Recently a number of aboriginal communities have been taking control of this source of funds. The money gambled in the bingos is spent on recreation, economic development and alcohol treatment programs. In a community where everyone is poor, it is a way to redistribute the wealth, certainly fairer than the class system. The provincial governments have been fighting this tooth and nail, because the bingos are such a lucrative source of revenue. In Shawanaga reserve in Ontario, the band has had all grants cut off until they stop running their "illegal" bingo. It has become their only source of revenue.

Alternative Health Care

Most of admissions to hospital are not bacterial diseases, but are the result of accidents, heart attacks, cancer and alcohol. Doing something about our transportation systems, environmental pollution, level of exercise and stress and the sale of alcohol would go a long way to change our health care system. Community groups have undertaken a number of interesting projects in this line:

- Magazines like *Healthsharing,* bring news about health to women
- Community health clinics and dental clinics, like the North End Community clinic in Halifax, provide support to low income persons, and advocate social changes that improve health.
- Advocates in the Public Health Department in the City of Toronto organize seniors activities and other recreational programs, developed

a Healthy Cities Project, and fund workshops on understanding the political economy of health care.

- The South Riverdale Community Clinic takes initiative in providing aid to new immigrants, and helps organize a coalition against violence against women.
- Organizations like the La Leche League and midwives associations push for the de-medicalization of birthing.
- People Living With Aids organizations work for medical care, hospices, legal protection, public education and acceptance.

Waste Recycling Projects

In the last decade, waste recycling has become imperative. According to the *New Internationalist,* (Jan/90) Canadians produce 1.496 lbs of waste per person per year.

There are an almost endless number of projects that are available to community groups:

- Flea markets, rummage sales, second hand stores;
- Automobile recycling. Although this has gone on informally in poor communities since the invention of the automobile, a group of laid-off mechanics in Lethbridge are trying to turn it into a business. Old cars are taken apart and completely rebuilt, and then resold to the public at considerably less than the cost of a new car;
- Composting;
- Paper, glass, rubber and plastic recycling. (Excellent resources are *Work From Waste* available from OXFAM Canada, 1011 Bloor Street West, Toronto, Ontario, M6H 1M1, and Friends of the Earth, #701, 251 Laurier Avenue West, Ottawa, Ontario K1P 5J6.)
- Some other ideas: tool loan, toy libraries, bicycle libraries. In Sudbury, the teenage street kids who ran the Do-Drop-Inn went to the police and asked them to give them the bicycles that they were going to auction off that spring. With these bicycles, they ran a "bicycle library" for the summer. Bikes were loaned out to kids, and kept in repair by the teenagers.

Economic Conversion Projects

Military spending creates severe economic and technological distortion. In the U.S., prolonged dependence on military spending has drawn 50% of scientists and engineers into this work, when their talents could be used for peacetime purposes.

The diversion of only 10% of world military spending into development projects would yield $42 billion for peacetime work. The tax burden would be reduced. We would have cleaner air and water; there would be more jobs and food, benign energy sources and better health and education. Safe water for all within a decade would only cost $4 billion.

One Trident submarine would buy $1.6 billion in food programs; one navy jet fighter would buy over 3000 teachers' salaries for one year; 100 B-16 bombers would buy a ten year commitment to renewable energy.[6]

Conversion projects attempt to switch a specific company's military capacity or environmentally destructive production to the meeting of serious human needs: low-cost housing, solar and wind power, mass transit, agricultural sustainability, soil regeneration.

Economic conversion is undertaken all the time by corporations: it is part of their search for greater profits. The term, however, has a more specialized meaning among environmentalists, peace activists, community organizers and trade unionists. Here it is seen as the solution to the tension between the need to bring an end to destructive production practices and the need to save jobs that will be lost in these cuts. Conversion planning can enable workers in vulnerable occupations to support disarmament and environmental initiatives.

European countries have been involved in conversion projects of this sort for two decades. The best known is the experience of British workers in the late 1970's at Lucas Aerospace, a producer of military aircraft equipment. Hearing that there were to be massive layoffs, the Lucas shop stewards surveyed their co-workers for alternative production ideas and came up with a list of 150 products in six major areas: remote control systems, alterative energy systems, medical equipment and so on. They called it "The Corporate Plan."

The Corporate Plan was presented to management and government (the Labour Party was in power at the time). Mobilization in support of the plan prevented one plant closing, and stimulated the Greater London Council to set up other publicly funded conversion projects. With the rise, however, of Thatcher, trade unions were forced to worry first about fighting anti-union legislation and the Greater London Council was destroyed. The Corporate Plan was blocked completely by Lucas management, and increasing military contracts removed the threat of layoffs. Although Lucas provides important lessons, it was not a success.

There is also considerable U.S. experience in conversion projects. Some of these are listed in the resource directory at the back. A Canadian example is the Cruise Missile Conversion Project, and the best source of information is Project Ploughshares.

Because conversion plans are for specific factories and other centres of production, the plan must come from the workers in the industry, or at least be substantially supported by them.

If the workers are not organized into a union, their jobs are too vulnerable to get involved. Many trade unions already have committees looking into conversion to more environmentally acceptable production methods, and to the phasing out of military production by management. The Canadian Paperworkers Union, for example, has hired consultants to help them develop a plan for sustainable forestry.

The European and American experiences with economic conversion make it clear that the process is only possible when community and union activists work together on the plan. It requires considerable political mobilization to move management and government to make the plan a reality.

Organizing For Community Economic Development

To begin with, the process is not really different from any other organizing described elsewhere in this book — all the same principles apply. However, because it is economics that is the focus of your strategy, you will come smack up against the jargon and mystification that keep us all powerless when dealing with the "experts." So one of your first tasks is to help everyone you want to involve in the project to value their own economic experience.

Introducing Economics

Valuing shadow work: Participants are asked each to draw a circle and number it off into 24 hours. Around the edge of the circle, they write down or draw pictures of all the different tasks they do in a day, from dressing, to soothing a relative on the phone, to driving to work and so on. They discuss with one another who benefits from each aspect of this work: themselves, the community, corporate power?

They circle work for which they are paid with blue, work that benefits their employer but is not paid with red, work that benefits the community in green and work that benefits themselves in yellow.Discuss the implications of this.

The Ah-hah workshop: This excellent tool was developed by GATT-FLY and is described in detail in a booklet called the *Ah-Hah Seminar.*[8] You can do a modified version of it with any group struggling to understand their community using questions like those on the chart below. This will help people see where the leakages of money are in their community, and how they are disorganized by corporate interests.

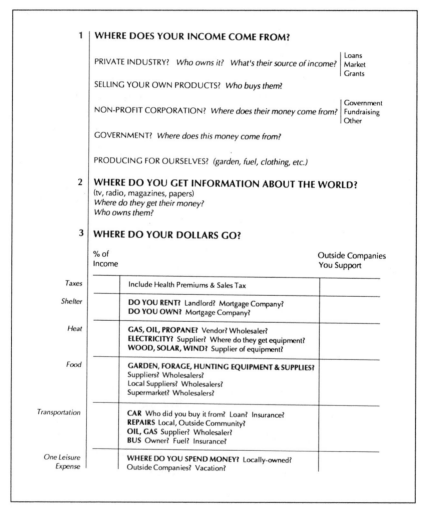

1 | WHERE DOES YOUR INCOME COME FROM?

PRIVATE INDUSTRY? *Who owns it? What's their source of income?* | Loans / Market / Grants

SELLING YOUR OWN PRODUCTS? *Who buys them?*

NON-PROFIT CORPORATION? *Where does their money come from?* | Government / Fundraising / Other

GOVERNMENT? *Where does this money come from?*

PRODUCING FOR OURSELVES? *(garden, fuel, clothing, etc.)*

2 | WHERE DO YOU GET INFORMATION ABOUT THE WORLD?
(tv, radio, magazines, papers)
Where do they get their money?
Who owns them?

3 | WHERE DO YOUR DOLLARS GO?

	% of Income		Outside Companies You Support
Taxes		Include Health Premiums & Sales Tax	
Shelter		**DO YOU RENT?** Landlord? Mortgage Company? **DO YOU OWN?** Mortgage Company?	
Heat		**GAS, OIL, PROPANE?** Vendor? Wholesaler? **ELECTRICITY?** Supplier? Where do they get equipment? **WOOD, SOLAR, WIND?** Supplier of equipment?	
Food		**GARDEN, FORAGE, HUNTING EQUIPMENT & SUPPLIES?** Suppliers? Wholesalers? Local Suppliers? Wholesalers? Supermarket? Wholesalers?	
Transportation		**CAR** Who did you buy it from? Loan? Insurance? **REPAIRS** Local, Outside Community? **OIL, GAS** Supplier? Wholesaler? **BUS** Owner? Fuel? Insurance?	
One Leisure Expense		**WHERE DO YOU SPEND MONEY?** Locally-owned? Outside Companies? Vacation?	

See endnote 7

One thing you would like to change: I owe this exercise to Melanie Conn of Community Economic Options. At the beginning of a large conference, participants were divided into small groups with a facilitator. They were each given a paper and pencil and asked to draw a picture of their community, and then draw in one thing they would like to change. They took turns describing this to the other people in their small group. Then they worked together to brainstorm those things that would help this goal, and those things that held it back. At the end, all the factors were listed together on flip charts.

Explaining corporate decisions: Present the group with the following scenario:

Mary Jane's husband was laid off by Via Rail five months ago. They have three small children and live about a thirty minute drive out of town. Between his unemployment insurance and her part-time work at a donut shop in town they barely manage to make their monthly expenses. Yesterday, the clutch on their car went, and now Mary Jane has no way to get to work, and Bob can't get into town to look for work. This morning the telephone company called and said they were disconnecting the telephone service, because they owed a three month bill (not long distance, just local service). Despite her protests that the telephone is their only hope of getting out of this mess, the service representative said that the phone was going to be disconnected and they would have to pay the full bill as well as a $500 deposit to get it reconnected.

Now ask the group to discuss how the following people would see the problem:

- Mary Jane and Bob
- The service representative
- A telephone company shareholder
- The public relations director for the company
- The supervisor in the accounts department
- The unemployment insurance officer that handles their case
- A bank manager

Ask the group to think about where the differences in these viewpoints are reconcilable and where they are not. Discuss possibilities for change.

Stimulating Ideas for Economic Activities

Coming up with ideas for what the group is going to do can be very difficult. Here are a few suggestions for getting started:

The micro-enterprise brainstorm

This exercise helps people value the production they do in their home as a kind of economic activity, and look at its potential for growth. Since it is a "brainstorm" the facilitator only notes the ideas on flip chart paper or a blackboard. Ideas are not criticized or challenged by participants.

Ask participants to list any services or products they do or make for the rest of the community. Some of these will likely be knitting, car repair, snow plowing, baking, pet care, child care, working rummage sales, growing herbs, making chutney.

Discuss possibilities for expansion (however minor) of some of these ideas.

What skills do we have?

Ask participants to think very carefully about skills that they have developed over the years. Write a bit about each of these on separate file cards. Participants tape the file cards on a wall under the following headings: 1) teaching 2) clerical and book-keeping skills, 3) house construction, repair and maintenance, 4) agriculture, 5) fishing, trapping and hunting, 6) automobiles, 7) working with children and youth, 8) health and social services, 9) artistic, 10) other.

Read the cards out loud to the group. Brainstorm how you would put these skills together in a project (any silly idea goes).

What do I want to learn to do?

Have participants think carefully about what they would really like to learn to do. In small groups discuss how these ideas might become possible.

What things do we put our money on that we could repatriate?

Use the exercise for community economic development, and then brainstorm which items our community could supply for itself. (See page 135)

Deepening Our Knowledge

Showing films, bringing in speakers, resources

There are an enormous range of speakers, films and resources to choose from, depending on the groups area(s) of interest at this point. Make sure you have the equipment you need on hand. After the showing or talk, it is often wise to break the participants into small groups to discuss the film or talk, and ask them to come up with ideas about how this might be used in the community. Be sure to keep the names of people who attended, and contact them as soon as possible after the event to get them more involved. There is a list of some available resources at the end of this section.

Ideas for businesses can also be generated from looking through information from your local economic development office, reading the Canadian Import Opportunities Import Profile, and from talking to community business leaders.

Building the vision.

Use a vision exercise to stimulate a dream of what the neighbourhood or community could look like, then choose the ideas that excite people the most and brainstorm ways to achieve them.

Getting Comfortable With a Strategy

From the ideas that have been generated in the previous workshops, make up a few scenarios: For example, you are a group of tenants in the local public housing development, and your kids have been complaining that they want jeans like the other kids wear to school, not those available from the clothing depot. Make up a plan for some way to solve this problem. You can pretend that some things assist you: the church may donate space, or whatever.

Or, you want to get better quality and cheaper food and also find some way to support some local farmers. Come up with a strategy to do this.

Give the problems to small groups to work on. It is often a good idea to give the same problem to three or more different groups. After a half hour or so, have the groups share their solutions. Then try another scenario, and work out solutions. Share them. After a few practice runs, people will begin to feel comfortable with their own ability to take this on. Try a real one.

Will It Work? Feasibility Studies and Business Plans

Once you have agreed on an idea for your project, then you take a look at whether it is feasible to do it or not. All funders and most businesses use the "feasibility study" and the "business plan" to make this decision. Before you approach them for help, your idea should be written up in that format and preferably in that language. The process, however, is not very difficult for a group to do itself. If you do it yourself, have a business consultant or someone else who is trained to write business proposals, go over it with you before you see a funder. Your initial credibility with them is very important.

The following questions will take you through the major questions that feasibility studies and business plans require.

Preliminary steps

Catalogue your own skills and experience. The group making the proposal will have to show how responsible and innovative they are.

Who will this project benefit? You'd be surprised how many people take on a project expecting housing or employment for themselves or their neighbours, only to discover that they don't fit into the criteria. Although there is nothing wrong with doing a project for others, it is better to understand that from the beginning.

Describe similar projects in other areas: what problems and successes have they had? Magazines like *Worker Co-op,* and the *Journal of Community Development* are good sources for this information. So are government small business programsand some community colleges. The Canadian Co-operative Association, 400-275 Bank Street, Ottawa, K2P 2L6, may also be able to steer you in the right direction. For environmental projects, the Canadian Environmental Network can direct you to organizations in your area.

Government regulation

Find out what laws, regulations and bylaws apply to your project. What government programs regulate it or fund it? What will you need to do to meet these criteria?

Check patents.

Technical expertise

Your project will require technical and financial skills of some sort to proceed. If you don't have access to this expertise, find it. Double-check everything you hear: experts often have strong opinions, but they may not be the only ones.

Set up a training plan, so that as many members of your group as possible understand the technical aspects of the project. It is very easy to leave people behind at this stage, and you will pay for that later. Technical expertise includes all the machinery and design considerations, as well as administration, marketing and bookkeeping.

Training for members can be done through your own programs, through community colleges and secondary schools, or through other means. The co-operative sector has a number of training modules which can be purchased or led by co-op groups. Many environmental groups do also. A number of publications and videos can also be used for training. Community colleges and distance education programs are often eager to provide skills training to your members. Check it out.

If you need to hire outside experts, find out if they are available. The employment office is a good place to ask this question.

Is there a market?

Is there a market for your product (whether it is housing or recycled newspapers or daycare)? Will you have competitors? What makes you think you can do better? At what price will you have to sell your product in order to get people to spend money on it? How much can you sell in each of the first five years?

Is this project environmentally safe?

Some of this information may be available from your "experts" or from the government legislation you have studied. However, it is wise to consult a body like Probe International or Friends of the Earth, or some local environmentalists before proceeding.

What will it cost to start this project?

There are two kinds of costs: start-up costs and operating costs. It is usual to project these costs over five years.

Start-up costs:
– purchasing land, a building, or bringing one up to standard;
– any equipment or machinery you require, including office;
– installing sewer, water, hydro, roads, telephone;
– pollution controls;
– legal and business services;

– labour necessary to start-up;
– market research and establishing it.

Operating Costs:
– purchase of materials (inc. shipping);
– interest on any loans;
– labour;
– advertising;
– taxes;
– insurance;
– waste disposal;
– heat, hydro, water, telephone;
– distribution costs (inc.transportation);
– repairs to building, machinery and equipment;
– reserves for replacement of machinery;
– legal services, banking charges;
– office expenses.

What sources of funds are available to you for start-up?

At a workshop on worker co-ops at Grindstone Island (a co-operatively owned retreat centre in Ontario), the following were listed as sources: members (shares, memberships, loans, donations, sweat-equity, in-kind donations, family, friends, and benefits and fundraisers); lending institutions:(banks, trust companies, credit unions); alternative investment funds; pension funds, unions, insurance companies, lotteries, government programs at all levels (vary from place to place); foundations (see Canadian Centre of Philanthropy publications); churches and non-governmental organizations.

Some Words to the Wise

Although it is an exciting way to do social change, there are a number of pitfalls on the way to establishing an economic alternative. I want to mention a few of them here...you'll probably discover your own.

• Most of the skills required to satisfy funders and to write up a feasibility study are middle-class skills. Funders tend to prefer people like themselves. Within a community group, this means that frequently the people who set up the project are from a different class, race and gender than the people who will eventually live or work in it. It has destroyed many community organizations. If the working class people, or non-Caucasians, or women are marginalized during the lengthy start-up process, they will vote with their feet.

- Getting start-up funding can take so long that the market has dried up, your prospective tenants have all moved, and the potential workers have all got other jobs or left town.
- Start small. Start with the woman who makes great chokecherry jam in her kitchen. Get experience and immediate feedback before you tackle anything big. In a lot of community groups, starting big just scares people off, and no one benefits in the end.
- Beware of *tourism*. In many parts of Canada, this is being sold as the panacea for all community economic development. It has a serious downside however:

   It sends land values soaring, with it property taxes. For poor people, this is disastrous. It can squeeze out low-income tenants and rooming houses.

   Politicians at all levels will pay more attention to the tourist operators and developers needs. Voting patterns can shift dramatically. There will be battles over schools, roads, new developments, water and sewer rates and so on.

   It can destroy a distinctive way of life, as fishing and agriculture are destroyed and an influx of wealthy tourists from other places demand an atmosphere of leisure and entertainment. These same people rewrite history to get rid of the "unpleasant parts." Complaints about injustice will be suppressed in the interests of public relations.

   The jobs it does create are low-paying, part-time jobs like cook, chambermaid, guide, waiter. Many of them are seasonal.

- Any economic activity has to compete in the "free market." that means that your organization is under tremendous pressure to be just as tight on wages and as dishonest on quality and environmental issues as any other business. Keep your vision very clear.

NOTES

1. Zalent, Kim, *Economic Home Cooking*, Chicago, 1987 page 5.
2. *Worker Co-op* Vol.3, No.3.
3. Axworthy, C., *Worker Co-operatives*, April 4, 1986, Sudbury, Ontario.
4. *Worker Co-op*, Vol.9, No.1.
5. Pollution Probe Foundation. *The Canadian Green Consumer Guide*, McClelland and Stewart, 1989.

6.   *ICCR Brief,* Vol 17, no.1, 1988.
7.   Kuyek, Joan, Managing the Household, United Church of Canada, Toronto, 1990, p. 24.
8.   GATT-Fly, *Ah-Hah! New Approach to Popular Education,* Between the Lines, 1983.

Chapter 11

REPOSSESSING POLITICAL POWER

A Long Story

In 1983, there was a terrible housing crisis in Sudbury. INCO, the major employer, had shut down for six months to try to save themselves some money. So there was a whole lot of people losing their homes. In 1982, the interest rates had also gone way up, and this made it worse.

I was working in the Sudbury Community Legal Clinic. Day after day more INCO workers were coming in who had lost their houses to the Canada Mortgage and Housing Corporation through power of sale and foreclosure and were looking for some place to live. Their vacant houses would sit there empty while they were homeless. At the same time, landlords were finding excuses to evict single parent mums and kids to rent to the "more desirable tenants" — an INCO worker with a family. The real meaning of "trickle down"!

Even the Sudbury Housing Authority was doing what they called "preventive maintenance checks." They would go into the home of a woman who had been living there for sixteen years, and find every little thing that was wrong with the house — a lot of it was Sudbury Housing's neglect — and say if she didn't pay $2000 damages, she would be evicted. So the impact of these layoffs from the company was really on single parent women and kids.

A group of us had been doing a lot of work together over the years around housing, and we started to talk about what we could do. We did two things. First, some of us began to call ourselves United Tenants. UT were mostly single parent women that I had met when they had organized their building, or confronted their slum landlord. There were also a few staff people from the Neighbourhood Action Project. When we did get together we decided to do whatever needed to be done to get more affordable housing and to prevent evictions and so on. We met in the tiny office that belonged to NAP, where there weren't enough chairs and we'd talk about things and laugh with each other and plan. It was exciting.

At the same time, there was another group of people called the HELP committee that the regional government had got together. It was an ad hoc committee of human services managers, church leaders, a representative from INCO and Falconbridge (the mining companies) and a union representative from the USWA. They were expected to find ways of dealing with the crisis. I was able to get appointed to it after the USWA representative pushed the issue with the regional chairman.

Although a lot of the committee were window-dressing, a few people on it were very humane. This small group used the HELP committee to establish a hot-line phone-in show giving information about welfare, landlord problems, foreclosures and so on. One morning a man called in. He and his family had been living with his parents for a month. They were all going crazy, because the place was so small and they thought it was going to get violent because everyone was so angry at each other.

With me on the show that day was the public relations man from INCO, Ernie Hedigan, and Ernie St. Jean from Local 6500 USWA. Hedigan simply couldn't believe that this family was unable to find housing. St.Jean and I told him about how serious the housing crisis had become even while there were 120 houses sitting vacant that belonged to CMHC, a crown corporation. "Why can't we get those houses rented to the homeless?" we asked. And he said, "Well, of course we can. We'll just go to the Canada Mortgage and Housing Corporation and say, rent them."

So a little delegation from the group went to CMHC and asked. Well, they couldn't do it because the policy said they had to be sold, not rented. The man from INCO simply couldn't believe it. He was having a lot of trouble because it was his company's shut down that was creating the problem, and he was the public relations man, and here was this government organization that wouldn't do what he wanted. He was very upset. I laughed and said, "Maybe if we sat in at INCO, CMHC would be made to move." He looked embarrassed.

Practically every time someone new was going to be homeless, I would find out at the Legal Clinic because the victim would come to us for help to fight the eviction or to get welfare, or to get a hydro deposit and whatever. Day after day, they came.

I made it my job to involve the HELP Committee members in looking for housing for each and every one of these families. Soon there was no doubt in any of their minds of the severity of the crisis. For the first time in their lives they realized how terrible it was not to have much money, to have children and no place to live. Most of them had never had this experience. They always thought that if you wanted something bad enough you could somehow get it.

They wrote letters and presented briefs to the provincial and federal governments. They pressured the regional government. At one point we even held a meeting of all the levels of government that were involved in housing to try and get an agreement worked out. Nothing happened.

United Tenants realized they had to do something to increase the pressure. That summer Tom Rummel and his wife and two kids had no place to live. The Rummels were the kind of family that the whole community could sympathize with: a laid-off miner, a hard worker, a good marriage, cute children, the whole bit. As usual, the HELP committee tried to persuade CMHC to rent them a home. Then we begged the regional government for emergency housing. When this got nowhere, United Tenants helped the family put up a tent at Memorial Park in downtown Sudbury.

UT sent out press releases and press packets. They arranged with the mayor to keep the pressure on CMHC and the province, if he'd keep the police off the family. They even arranged for round the clock support, food, tents and heat. They organized clowns and music and theatre. It took two days before the Rummels were housed: and it was a private citizen who offered them a place. CMHC still wouldn't budge, and we kept sending deputations to them.

Then in August, another friend of ours, a single parent, had no place to go. Every day, she was walking past a house on Melvin Street, which was for sale, empty, owned by CMHC. "I want that house," Paulette said. So once again the HELP committee started going to CMHC and asking for it. We intimated to them that she was angry enough to just move in if they didn't agree. Within a day, CMHC suddenly had a vacancy in a regular rental unit in Apollo Terrace. I still don't know how they found it. She moved in.

Of course, a few weeks later there was another family with no place to go. There were always lots of families in this position, but most of them were too afraid to fight back. This family was ready. UT had a meeting with the family, and they wanted to move into the Melvin Street house. "That house is sitting there empty. These people need a place to live. Which is the more important right, private property or shelter?"

It was agreed that unless the Landrys were housed within a week, we would occupy the house. We sent a delegation to tell the HELP committee of our decision. Because the HELP committee membership were people with "clout," with titles and positions, we felt we needed them to give strength to our situation. By now they were just as frustrated and angry as anybody else, and they agreed that we should go ahead. The HELP committee sent a delegation to the regional chairman, and said that unless the family was housed in 24 hours, they could not be responsible for what might happen. The regional chairman sent a telegram to the premier of the province and to CMHC asking them to intervene. Like us, he hoped that the pressure tactic would free up money or policies to help the crisis. But nothing happened.

So the day that the Landry family moved into 370 Melvin Street, there were 100 people including representatives of the bishop and the head of the Ministers Association, to help them. (The INCO guy said that although he supported us, he'd better not be seen there.) The MPP, Floyd Laughren, was the first to cross the threshold. There were twenty women with their kids from United Tenants and they moved into the house. Because we had warned the press, they were all there too. Hydro and heat were on in the house, but there was no water. After a phone conversation with the union representing regional workers, they drove up and turned the water on.

The Landrys and their supporters stayed in the house for a week. We couldn't ever leave them alone, because we didn't know when the police were going to come to evict us. We had wonderful press; they loved it.

The time in the house was exhausting. No one got enough sleep. You had to worry about how you would feed all these people, women worried about the CAS taking their kids. Also, the house became a centre for helping others. A woman would come in and say "My refrigerator isn't working," and people would go off and fix it. It was a most exciting time. It became a place where, when things needed to be done you did them. When CMHC officials went through on inspections, we would all gather in the living room and sing.

Meanwhile, the negotiations with CMHC and the province appeared to be going nowhere. We were all getting quite nervous.

Then our lawyer called and said that the Crown had decided on charges. We had all thought they would only charge us with mischief as a summary offence. But they had decided to charge us with mischief as an indictable offence, which can carry up to 14 years in prison. The squatters had a meeting right away to talk about it. Mrs. Landry was too exhausted to continue; her husband wanted to be a hero and go to jail. The group felt that they didn't have the energy to sustain a legal defense over a long period of time. We debated whether to move the pressure to the INCO offices or the region. Finally, we came to an agreement to move the demonstration to the regional council offices the next day.

The next morning we cleaned the house, and then marched to the regional offices. We sat in the big foyer there and sang songs, while members of the HELP committee negotiated with the regional chairman about his responsibility to find this family emergency shelter. Later that day, one of the civil servants succeeded in talking a slumlord into renting them a place. Within four months the Landrys got public housing.

It is almost impossible to believe that it took so much effort just to get one family a home. How much we had really won didn't show up until later, when the public no longer made a connection between our action and the results. We continued to pressure the levels of government and eventually we got some results. The region established an emergency housing agreement. CMHC subsequently rented vacant houses to any homeless families that we told them about. That year, Sudbury received far more than its share of non-profit and co-operative housing money. We were able to make our new non-profits 85% rent-geared to-income instead of the usual 45%. Funding was also received for a Crisis Housing organization.

Repossessing Political Power

Most political action for change looks a little like this: a strategy that escalates as you go along. Exhausting proper channels first. Then a militant statement of position. Negotiating with people who hold power and having to prove you are not bluffing. A dramatic action to attract public attention. Support of the public and the press are possible when you have the support of known community leaders. Lots of detail work to sustain the action itself. Then the cycle begins again. Stonewalling and delays by bureaucrats. Taking care of the individual and not the problem. Attempts to evade responsibility. A bigger action. Major actors (like INCO) moving behind the scenes. The power structure moves to prevent this happening again. You get some concessions. Moves are made to disorganize you. Victory at a time where it does not legitimize the pressure tactics that you organized; or your group falls apart.

In the last analysis, all organizing efforts mean that you are going to confront a "power structure" — those people who perceive themselves as benefiting from the way things are now and who control dollars, resources and labour that could solve the problem.[1]

Organizing is Like Making Soup Out of Left-overs

You may be dreaming of bouillabaisse, but when you open the fridge and find some beans, a potato and an onion, you use your imagination and creativity to make the best soup you can.

When you counter injustice effectively, you organize together. You decide not only what you want to do, but how you are going to do it.

- Work with an issue or situation for which you and your group feel real passion, preferably one where you have first-hand knowledge, and that affects you or your family personally. Any situation exists in a web of relationships and is part of a history. Just by choosing this focus, you are making a statement. Sometimes the issue or situation chooses you.
- Ask yourselves what do you really want? What would the ideal situation look like? What would have to happen to achieve the ideal situation? What is in the way? Is there a reason why you should not ask for the ideal solution? What would happen if you did?
- Ask yourself who is with us? Who is against us? What can we realistically ask for? (Chances are you won't really know what you can ask for until you ask a lot more questions.) The possibilities and boundaries will expand and contract throughout a struggle.

For example, I may feel that every tenant in this city is getting ripped off, and should have the right to shelter; that everyone is entitled to enough space and comfort to live decently; and that his/her income should have nothing to do with its accessibility. To take action, my group needs to decide on a way to focus this dream. It may be presented to us: some people with no place to live, no emergency shelter, an unconscionable rent increase in an apartment building, a slum landlord who doesn't do repairs, a series of illegal evictions. We can take on a single issue and still tell the truth about what we really want. The bigger dream weaves the individual issues together.

Maybe I live on an Indian reserve, where my desire to reclaim my land for my people is webbed to: 150 years of white settlement, the reduced numbers of my people, our inability with these numbers to prevent trespass, the white control of our economy, deep divisions within my own community after years of struggling over too little money and too few jobs, a white controlled court system and police, the desires of lumber companies to log it out, white environmentalists who want to turn the area into a national park, a provincial environmental minister who is on our side and a federal environment minister who has good rhetoric, but lousy politics and so on.

This means that my community and I have to struggle with all these problems if we want a realistic strategy. We can say what we really want, and make that known. We can begin to rebuild the fabric of the community. And then we have to figure out a strategy to protect the resource as much as possible and to get as much self-determination as possible without jeopardizing our ability to make more demands later when we are stronger as a community.

These questions — What do you really want? What can you realistically expect to get? Where do you start? — are the crucial questions in planning strategy. Too often we limit our demands to what the power structures allow us to have.

Political Strategy

Once you know what your goal is, you can start to plan strategy. Who do you want to make do what? Why aren't they doing it already? The answer to this question might be simple like "so far they haven't had to" or, "maybe they don't know what hardship the present situation is causing." I believe firmly that it is a good idea to see if this is the reason before you do anything else. Document the need, and bring it to the attention of the person or people who need to make the changes. Even if they don't do anything, you will know their response, and you will have put them on notice that you are concerned about this situation.

In many groups, there is one person who says, "Well, did you tell the bank president/ the mayor/ the corporate CEO about this problem?" I think it is important to be able to say, "Yes, we did and this is what they said."

Once you know that these are not the reasons, then you need to do some research about what might make them change their mind. *Remember that government is usually acting for interests other than the average voter's.* Most new construction projects, like roads and buildings, are not about building hospitals closer to home, or increasing jobs in an area or anything like that. They are about providing contracts to construction companies. Most changes in deficit financing are about helping banks. Most hydro projects are about helping industrial consumers, providing contracts to construction and electrical companies, and paying interest and dividends to financiers.

Who do they listen to? What are they afraid of? What do their close contacts, workers, other committee members, family, think about this issue? Is there any chance to bring them on side and have them work on the people whose minds you have to change? If you are talking about a cabinet minister or a senior bureaucrat, where are the contradictions within their own departments? Where is there space to manoeuvre?

There is a difference between the power people have because of the job they do, and the power they have because of their personal wealth, connections, etc. If you can't get the person with the title to move, what about finding people with personal power to influence them?

You may simply be unable to get this kind of information about the people you have to change which means assuming that they will respond to strong expressions of public opinion in support of your cause. Your actions will now be geared to educating, informing and mobilizing the public or specific sectors of it.

At a certain point, you will want to tell the target that a lot of people now agree with your position, and maybe they would like an opportunity to review the situation. You can imply that you have the power to embarrass them publicly if they do not shift.

Remember that the threat of an action is often more powerful than the action itself. An experienced power structure will know that the press will cover an action only for a very brief period of time, and that there are other ways to disorganize you. Also, if this is the first time you have tangled with each other, they will call your bluff, assuming you cannot pull off a very good action anyway.

You should never threaten to carry out an action unless you can carry it off, and you should never exaggerate your strength. One of the biggest mistakes inexperienced organizers make is to call demonstrations, rallies and marches to which very small numbers of people show up. Unless you know you can mobilize hundreds, take actions that are effective with smaller numbers like "family" picnics, guerilla theatre, information pickets or booths in shopping malls. Always indicate that you didn't try to get a lot of people for this activity.

By the way, people don't come to these kind of events on the strength of a leaflet or a newspaper story. They come because they have been *organized*, by you, or through their union, or through another community group.

The demonstration or other action should have a clear focus. It can state what you really want, and it should state the focus of your action. If you name your target specifically, you may find that he entrenches himself deeper. Sometimes it is better not to do this.

Politicians and the power structure never want to be seen to back down under pressure. Always offer them an out.

If this first action is not effective (and it rarely will be), then you will be engaged in an escalating pattern of pressure on the power structure. The pattern usually is as follows:

1. You ask for support with letters, briefs, delegations, etc. through the "proper channels."
2. The organization or people you approached, evade the issue in some way: "not our responsibility," "the policy says...," "not enough money," etc.
3. You make a public statement of your organization's position and begin to build support from key people, community leaders, the workers in the bureaucracy you are trying to move, unions, etc.
4. The target group/person either stonewalls, denies there is a problem, ridicules the group making the demands, or claims to be "looking into it" (giving you the run-around).
5. You continue to work through proper channels: presenting briefs, attending meetings and so on. *If continued for long, the run-around can kill enthusiasm and energy in a group: it excludes people without formal education and elevates the articulate.*
6. They continue to drag things out.
7. You call an action, like a demonstration or a picket to draw public attention to the issue, and to involve your group in an action together.
8. They will claim publicly that they are working on it, and they may begin to respond with token concessions. Alternatively, they might continue to stonewall and discredit the group.
9. Your organization calls a more dramatic action: an occupation, a blockade, a boycott of a major store. You build a coalition to support your demands and act together. You shift the focus of your action to the corporate mover behind the scenes (the construction company

that profits from the logging road instead of the Ministry of Natural Resources; the big local developer instead of the Rent Review Board, the major department store instead of the welfare office).

10. They try to intimidate you, with experts, military force, cutting grants, attacks in the paper, on television, etc. They may also offer you grants to shift the direction of your organization. (They may try any of the tactics listed in step 12.)

11. If your organization survives this onslaught, and you either continue the action or escalate it, then other people within the power structure will begin to be nervous that the structure itself is now in jeopardy. For example, there may be a number of workers in their organization that support your position and are beginning to make noises through their union, or to sabotage equipment, or there have been some major press leaks. Or perhaps they are nervous about their control over elected officials. Or maybe their power position is being attacked from outside.

12. The contradictions and competing interests within the power structure will begin to make themselves felt. One of two things can happen:
a) You will find that there has been a shift of responsibility within the structure itself, and your demands are being met (they will say that it is the previous group's fault that the matter was not addressed), or
b) the competing parts of the structure will unite to disorganize your group.

This is a crucial time in long-term political organizing. The power structure will respond with whatever means it feels are necessary to maintain itself. This may include illegal actions and violence. The level of their attack is an indication of their perception of our strength.

1. They might decide to postpone action by calling a Royal Commission, or an environmental assessment or hiring an independent consultant to recommend. Although this may offer them an out later, it will also effectively remove the action from your turf. It will once again use the skills of formally educated people and you will have to participate in this study. Find a way to keep your membership actively involved and the issue before the public.

2. They will start to use rhetoric that sounds like yours. Be prepared to translate what they are really saying to you and to the public. It will

require your best public relations work ever. Following pressure from native groups the government now talks about "self-government"; following pressure from women's groups, the government talks about "affirmative action"; following pressure from the poor, we now hear about "empowerment" everywhere.

3. They will give you token satisfaction, designed to split your group. They will find housing only for group leaders; they'll introduce a food program in one school; they'll make the trouble-maker at work a supervisor; they'll grant a couple of workers' compensation appeals. It may be impossible to ask the leaders to turn down the token offer when it is made to them, they will get caught between loyalty to their families and loyalty to the group.

4. They may claim that although they support you, they do not have the power to grant what you ask: insufficient money, not their responsibility, etc. Your position should be that if this is true then they should work actively with you to influence the body that has the power, and you will continue to fight for their active support of the cause.

5. They may claim that the only way to grant what you ask is to punish some other group, i.e., we can only grant welfare reform, if we tax homeowners more, or we can only protect your community from nuclear waste if it goes to some other community. You have to make it clear that this is unacceptable and be ready with alternatives.

6. They may try to draw you into action in another forum, like the courts. This may be a strategy you have chosen yourself, or it might be thrust upon you. Be very careful to evaluate the costs in money and time before you get into this position. It might be better to get out while the going is good.

7. They may move to disorganize your group. Suddenly there may be people who cause trouble in meetings, or who want the group to get violent, or who attack leaders who are the backbone of the group. Some of this could be a result of poor organizing on the group's part, but it could be infiltrators. There certainly is enough history of this in Canada. Whatever their motives, if the group cannot handle these people, get rid of them.

8. There may be acts of violence against members of the group: beatings, destruction of property, intimidation, arrests on unrelated charges, even "car accidents" and other very serious stuff. If your group has been built strongly enough, then these acts may serve to bring people tighter together. For women and children in the group, this may take the form of domestic violence or sexual harassment.

As the business agenda for Canada increases the gap between rich and poor and the struggle over resources and the future of this place heats up, there is a real possibility that both personal and state violence will become more prevalent. Our best protection against violence is to build a strong movement of solidarity that can speak truth and support one another. We have to work to make it clear that violence is unacceptable.

Political Organizing Within an Institution

Organizing within the major institutions of our society is not very different than within any community. They are all sites of struggle for differing values and structures.

Within workplaces, churches, unions and non-profit organizations, we need to take our organizing very seriously. The first step in organizing in these places as anywhere else, is to get a group of like-minded people together.

There are a few basic things to remember when you are organizing in any bureaucracy:

- Even though particular bureaucrats may want to help you, they may have no influence in the areas where the changes need to take place. It is important to target someone with enough power to pull these things together.
- Knowing the various pieces of the pie that have to be changed to get your demands, means that you can target each individually, or as important, avoid being nasty to someone who is really trying to help. For example, let's suppose that one member of your welfare rights group has been cut off. You need to know whether she has been cut off by family benefits or municipal welfare and for what reason. There will be a big difference in your tactics if the cut off is contrary to the regulations and law, or within it. If it is contrary to the regulations, you try to get current policy enforced. If it is contrary to the law, then you try to get either an exception to a policy, or get the law changed. Changing the law requires moving the government at the provincial level.
- All front line workers have supervisors who have more power than they do to make changes and exceptions. These supervisors also report to others who have more power and so on. As you go up the line, the employees have progressively more power and less local involvement.

They are also more likely to identify their interests with the interests of the institution itself. That is how they got to the power position they hold.

- Workers have a life outside the work place which is often very different from their job. The values they are forced to live at work may be in conflict with their personal values: ecologists in the Ministry of Natural Resources, for example. People deal with these conflicts in a variety of ways in order to maintain their self-respect: they become cynical; they blame the victim; they adopt corporate values; they look for ways to "get the system."

- Unionization at work means that employees are less likely to be fired for speaking their minds. Unionized workers take more chances. They also may have a forum for discussing the product of their work and the character of their work place. Don't count on this however. Most unions provide their members with little room for discussion and are very under-serviced. Some unions are down right repressive.

- If a buck can be passed to someone else, it will be. All workers are overworked and busy. They do not want to deal with difficult tasks or problems that will take any time. Any tactic that disrupts the working day of a worker is seen with dread. Often a bureaucrat will decide to give in to pressure rather than have to waste time fighting it. All workers fear having to explain themselves to a supervisor, and supervisors dread having to explain themselves to the public. If you have effectively messed up the life of a department once or twice, then even the threat of causing this kind of disruption again can get results. Alternatively, they might just stonewall you.

- Getting a group tied up in pursuing proper channels can kill all enthusiasm in the group. On the other hand, if you are charged with "not following proper channels" you will have a difficult time getting public support. To get around this problem, have a small group follow the proper channels, but build your pressure on the streets. For one thing, following these channels is an activity available only to people with middle class skills: brief writing, organization and presentation. At the root of it however, is power, and that is built with numbers and commitment.

- In any group, it is very easy to have the people with middle class skills take over. They are more likely to believe that the system can be made to work through persuasion and reason. In fact, the main reason things change is because those in charge are afraid of losing their position. Often when it appears that a victory is the result of reasoned argument, in the background there is a group of angry teenagers or workers raising hell. The old tactic "if you don't talk to me, you'll have to deal with the militants" works.

- Once the formally educated people take over, working people get squeezed out, and with them, their kinds of survival knowledge and expertise.

Building a Public Campaign

Building a public campaign around a systemic problem means choosing a specific, representative issue, so that your group can have some victories (however small), and so the media can focus on it. The following story is from Jean Swanson:

"I'm from Vancouver and I'm the co-ordinator of a group called End Legislated Poverty, a coalition of 22 groups that begs and badgers governments to end poverty. We think that certain things would end poverty like creating jobs, raising welfare rates, raising wages, building housing, rent control, affordable services.

"What I want to talk about is how we have used the struggle for a school lunch program to broaden the base of people that will work to end poverty. A spin-off of that is to actually feed the kids.

"We know what we want: we want a nice clean environment; we want everyone to have a decent life with enough to eat; we want everyone to love each other. But it is hard to move from what we want, to getting people to fight for that and actually implementing it. What we've found in this work for the food program is that it is a tool that can actually do this.

"It started in April 1987, when we decided to have a forum on child poverty, co-sponsored by the school board and the teachers but controlled by us. At the forum, we sent a sheet around to get the names of people who wanted to work on child poverty, and we got tons of media coverage on the forum and there was a really good report in the *Vancouver Sun*. Out of that forum came a little committee called the Child Poverty Action Committee to work for a universal food program in 12 inner-city schools.

"We went to the School Board and they said there were no hungry kids in downtown Vancouver. We said 'How do you know?' And they said, 'We asked the kids to raise their hands.'

"We had a great student panel at the first child poverty forum and they made some recommendations. Then we had a parent workshop and they made some recommendations. When the school board asked me to come and tell about our forum they expected a one shot 5 minute presentation, but we dragged it out. We had the students go and we had the parents go and we had the teachers go and we had a delegation of low income people. All in all we were there about twelve times.

"The school board set up a hungry kids committee that they wouldn't let any low income people be on. But the teachers were really good and they slipped us information about when they met. It was really fun seeing all these middle class people around this table saying things like, 'What pays the most, U.I. or welfare?' They didn't even know this stuff and there were big intellectual arguments.

"After a while, everyone on our side — the teachers and parents were on our side and they were on the committee — and I wrote out a resolution. It was passed when the trustees weren't there. The resolution was to adopt in principle a school lunch program, with three principles: that low income kids wouldn't be identified, that the food would provide one third of the daily minimum requirement, and that the food would be available to all the kids in the school in a way of ensuring that kids who didn't pay weren't stigmatized. So that passed and then we had to get the funds for it.

"Food can become an issue of the right. For example, in Calgary they have an alleged food program which costs them $25,000 a year and feeds 30 kids in 34 schools. You can imagine this is a program where when the kid slumps over his desk at ten thirty in the morning the teacher sends him down to the principal's office for a peanut butter sandwich and if the kid goes three or four times the family gets reported to social services. It is a nothing program. It is a program that is designed to keep people of our ilk from succeeding and bury the poverty issue.

"So we had to develop some principles in working for the program:

- Low income communities, not individual children, should be identified for the program and the food should go to all the kids in those schools.
- Every time we mention the need for the program we also mention the need for decent jobs, higher welfare rates and this ties this into a larger agenda.
- We stressed that people on welfare without kids also needed more money, because they are in fact worse off and we didn't want to add to that.

- We rejected charity. Whenever the issue of hungry kids come up people start showing up at the schools with boxes of oranges, pop-up tarts and stuff. Charity creates the idea that poverty is being dealt with when it isn't. It stigmatizes low-income kids and it is never enough.
- And our last principle was that low-income people should control the work, so that when you have someone at a forum pop up and say "Low-income people should just budget better" you can have six mothers on welfare say "Look, I can give you budgeting lessons and this is what I live on."

"If you go along with these principles to build the food program you can use the fight to get all these other people involved: teachers, parents, unions and churches. They would all go to the school board in delegations. We went to council and they turned us down three times. I think it was the ninth time we went to the school board, that the one COPE trustee made the motion for $200,000 to fund the program and it passed on some fluke.

"At the same time that the food program became a provincial issue, our wonderful Socred government decided it was going to save some money by taking $50 monthly from each single parent. And it did it in a really sleazy way. What happened was that all the people who were activated to fight for the food program realized that cutting back $50 a month from single parents was just obscene. The United Church had a letter writing campaign; there were resolutions, public demonstrations. We were funded by the unions and teachers etc. As a result, it took eight months but we stopped the fifty dollar cutback.

"So now we have the food in 12 schools. In March we took balloons and red apples to be delivered by little six year olds to all the trustees to thank them. We thought they would only vote for 8 schools, so we thanked them in advance for voting for 12 and it worked! They loved the program. Even those who voted against it had tears in their eyes. The image of poor people has now changed to that of a hungry child. Now the school board and city council have passed resolutions asking for an increase in welfare and wages.

"A lot of this has come from the awareness built by the food fight. It became a big issue in the civic election. Everyone was in favour of food for the kids. Now we have committees in Nanaimo, Surrey, Burnaby, Victoria and Kamloops that are working on this."

Direct Action: Some Ideas That Work

Boycotts

Boycotts mean organizing people to refuse to deal with a store, individual or government that you want to persuade. A sustained boycott is very labour intensive, and can be very effective. We are probably most familiar with national and international boycotts: California grapes, Kraft cheeses, Shell Oil, South African goods, Nestle products.

Community groups use boycotts for different reasons:

- To get one part of the power structure to pressure another part: boycotting a local stationary store over an education cutback, so that the owner will pressure his friends on the board of education to change their minds.
- To end a discriminatory practice at one institution: for example, boycotting a bar where women staff have been sexually harassed, or where they have refused to hire indigenous people.
- To indicate public outrage at the behaviour of a public body: boycotting hearings, elections and administrative tribunals. This kind of boycott is usually of short duration.
- To force a merchant or other organization to change their behaviour: for example, refusing to shop at stores that will not give credit to strikers, or refusing to shop in stores that sell war toys.
- To be in solidarity with a national or international boycott.

In undertaking a boycott, be very clear about *who* you want to have do *what*. Be careful not to overestimate the willingness of the public to support the boycott. It is very easy to have a boycott backfire, and actually increase the business of a merchant or give extra air-time to your opponents. A boycott can go on for a very long time, so often it is wise to determine a way to end it if you need to and not lose face.

Make sure you really have something significant to withdraw from the target...and that they will regret losing your support. When our women's group decided to withdraw all its money from the Toronto-Dominion bank because of its investments in South Africa, we had a demonstration at the branch as we took the money out. We sent the signing officers into the bank to get the money, only to watch as they had to pay off the overdraft to close the account. Not a disaster, but certainly embarrassing. The bank was not sorry to see us go.

A number of years ago, I watched the Dario Fo play "Il faut pas payer" in Caraquet, N.B. This extraordinary comedy, adapted to the local scene, was about the wives of striking fishermen who refuse to pay full price for their groceries at the supermarket, because the supermarket should be helping the strike. They load up their baskets, pay what they think the food is worth, and take off with the groceries.

Blockades, Occupations and Work-ins

Blockades are becoming one of the most effective and popular tools of the aboriginal struggle and of the environmental movement. In addition to, or as an alternative to strikes, workers and/or community people can choose to disrupt the functioning of a company or a government institution from the inside.

They are usually illegal, and charges can range from a summary charge of mischief or trespass, to heavier indictable offenses. There is also the possibility that your organization will be sued for damages that you have caused including loss of income to the target group and policing costs. (The costs for policing the Temagami dispute were more than $1 million.) However, because this kind of civil disobedience is so dramatic, it is a very effective way of resisting.

Blockades are a good strategy when:

- A sufficient number of local people support the action.
- You have a reason of sufficient seriousness that a good part of the public will support civil disobedience: a clear moral high ground.
- You have a large and committed enough membership to sustain the blockade, occupation or work-in. They can last a few days or years.
- You are clear about whether you intend the action to actually stop your opponents, or if it is only symbolic. Unless you were clear about your expectations at the beginning, your membership can be very divided when things get tough.
- There is a specific focus for the action: stopping a road, or timbering, or a nuclear generating station. Getting housing for the homeless, or getting a more efficient public transit system. Using the radio transmitters to educate the public about an event.
- You have enough inside information on your opponents' plans to anticipate their reactions to your action. There is nothing worse than being in an occupation, with no information about how your opponent is responding.

- You can arrange media attention (and therefore public awareness) for your action.

From looking at the experience of blockades, here are a few suggestions:

- In Canada, many blockades and occupations have to be in remote areas of the wilderness. Make sure that participants and supporters know exactly how to get there, and that there is sufficient shelter, food, warmth for everyone who comes. The magnitude of arranging for transportation and everyday life can be overwhelming for some groups. You also need a good communication system with the outside.
- Gear the extent of the blockade to a realistic assessment of support. Remember that people may be arrested and removed almost as soon as they arrive. Most people have to work at regular jobs, or have kids to look after, or have other struggles they are deeply engaged in; civil disobedience will take them away from this. Also remember that quite often the very people who need to engage in this kind of action have criminal records or are on probation or parole (often because of the class and race biases of the court system) and will face more severe repercussions than others if arrested.
- Humanize the opposition. The Teme-augama people opened their second blockade with a Remembrance Day service and invited the provincial police officers to join in the service. One of the elders then spoke about the role of the police, who had to do the "dirty work for the people who make the policies." He made an appeal to them to support the blockade. By the end of the blockade, even the construction workers were beginning to sabotage their own equipment.
- One organization suggests beginning an occupation in an office building by presenting flowers to the receptionist and apologizing for messing up her day.
- Make clear whether or not decisions about continuing the action or what to do during the action can be made by the people on the front-line. Affinity groups work best (see page ???)
- Be prepared to work through the court system after the blockade, because people are bound to be arrested. Have good legal advice lined up.
- The power structure has learned a long time ago that boredom can become as effective as fear in disorganizing as a group. Use the time during the action for educational, cultural and social group building. Use it to show the public how things could be done if it weren't for

profit. The bus drivers of Victoria and Vancouver won public support despite a thirteen week service shut down. In a two year campaign, the union emphasized service — refusing to implement service cuts, wearing costumes to work, producing "un-fare" cards and so on.

Strike and Strike Support

Many legal strikes at the workplace are like going in to a formal battle and giving the opposition the time, date and method of attack. Strikes have become ritualized showings of support for bargaining demands, where the workers agree to withhold their labour from an employer until they get a decent contract. Although workers pay themselves strike pay out of their accumulated strike fund, they face serious financial hardship on a long strike. Much of this hardship is born by women, as they are usually responsible for trying to manage a reduced household budget, and suffer the ire of creditors and the tensions of the family.

Successful strikes behave in ways that have not been anticipated by the employer:

- Whenever the strike costs the employer substantially more than he saves on unpaid wages.
- They last longer than the employer expected: the stockpile is used up, the competition starts to take over the market and so on.
- When the employer thought the workers would not strike and they did. "Wildcat" strikes are illegal in Canada. If the union leadership does not discipline the workers they can be held liable for damages to the company. However, because they are so rarely anticipated by the employer, they can be very effective.
- When the strike creates secondary pressure on the employer: from the community, its customers, or its shareholders.
- When the strike starts to affect the value of company shares.
- Where the strike is used in conjunction with blockades, work-ins, or occupations.

Although I have been involved building community support for a number of strikes, the most effective work we did was for the INCO strike in 1978-9. Despite an enormous stockpile of nickel and other metals, a very angry membership in Local 6500 of the USWA voted to strike in September of 1978. The 12,000 INCO workers were the major source of income in our community. Our organization, Women Helping Women had a number of union wives in its membership and we decided to get the wives together to provide mutual support during the strike.

Wives Supporting the Strike developed a committee that organized a Christmas party for all the children, a bean supper in 23 different halls on one night, committees to run food depots, clothing depots and baby care depots throughout the region. They put a float in the Santa Claus parade. They collected monies at the plant gates of other unions. They put on a play called INCO vs. the People, and wrote a comic book for the children called *What's a Strike?* A Citizens Strike Support Committee worked to put out the *Strike Support News*, raised money, and organized benefits across the country.

Because of the enormous support generated for the strikers, the strike lasted for almost nine months, much longer than the company had anticipated. Their public image was in ruins and those who called for the nationalization of INCO were starting to be heard. The union won the strike. A film, called *A Wives Tale* documents this battle.

Throughout the nine months, the hardest struggles were not overtly with the company, but with the internal politics of the union and the wives and the domestic politics of strikers' families. These all got more intense as the strike continued and money both in the union and in the community got tighter.

The non-nursing staff at Windermere Central Park Lodge organized a union in 1979. Most of them were immigrant women who had been very worried about organizing a union and had struggled both at work and with their husbands and families to do it. The nursing home was owned by the Bronfmans through Trizec corporation. The workers voted 90% to strike in April 1981. The government hired scabs but when the nurses' union respected the picket line, the employer was forced to hire scabs with nursing degrees from temporary employment agencies. The strikers then picketed the employment agencies. They found out where other temporary agency nurses were located in unionized hospitals and persuaded unionists in those hospitals to refuse to work with the temps. To the hospitals, this disruption wasn't worth the fight, and they stopped using the agencies. The agencies gave into pressure and refused to send any more temps to Trizec. Trizec then had to recruit very costly out-of province help. Anxious to increase pressure on the employer, the Windermere staff turned their attention to Trizec suppliers. This too worked — one unionist by herself turned back 3 semis from Florida. The strike was won and the wages went from $4.00 an hour to $8.00.[2]

Neighbourhood Organizing "Alinsky" Style

Saul Alinsky, the author of *Reveille for Radicals,* was a famous American community organizer. Starting with the Back of the Yards, a working class neighbourhood in Chicago, Alinsky developed a style of organizing that was very similar to the trade union organizing of John L. Lewis (his hero and friend). Back of the Yards and other Alinsky organizing drives all began with a crisis in a community. The leaders of formal community institutions would get together and ask the organizer to "come into the community." They would also commit themselves to raise the money for the organizing.

The organizer hired a staff and they spent their time talking with community-based groups and going door-to-door in the neighbourhood challenging and encouraging people to get involved in the community organization. The organizers helped the people select a "winnable" issue first and then the people (now "the organization") confronted the politicians or corporate official whom they identified as having the power to change the situation. The same strategy was used again and again, building the confidence and leadership abilities of the local people who got involved.

Alinsky set up a foundation — the Industrial Areas Foundation — to train organizers and raise funds. Alinsky-trained organizers became famous for the innovative tactics that they used to intimidate power structures. One was a "shit-in" in an airport: the community organization kept all the washrooms occupied until a crisis was reached in the building. Sometimes just the threat to "bring in Alinsky" would make a corporate or municipal decision-maker cave in.

One of the most famous neighbourhood organizing projects in Canada was Riverdale Community Organization in Toronto's East End in the mid-1970's and early 1980's. Don Keating, who was the original organizer on the project, has written a book about it called *The Power to Make It Happen.*[3] The organization won over 200 issues in 4 years.

In an article written by Keating he outlines the assumptions of this kind of neighbourhood organizing:

- The underlying problem of the neighbourhood is one of powerlessness and the twin goals are to win results and build power.
- Politicians, bureaucrats and owners of companies respond to pressure, but the pressures on them from above (from organized economic interests), and from around them (from colleagues), far exceed the

pressure from below that any individuals in the neighbourhoods can exert.

- People respond best when given an opportunity to choose their own issues.
- "Those who fix problems are the ones who increase their strength. You must not give your issues away for someone else to solve ...You do your own fixing by dealing with the person causing or responsible for the problem...deal directly with your adversaries."
- "To build strong organization, the people with the problems need to be involved in winning the results...choose a method that can best be expected to produce results on the problems and involve the greatest number of people affected."
- "The problem constitutes an injustice and for every area of need there is a government responsible to see that justice is done."
- "The relationship between politicians, bureaucrats and the people is paternalistic, that is characterized by an inequality of power."
- "There are limits to the amount of pressure any powerholder can withstand even from a group of "nobodies" and none is invulnerable." [4]

Alinsky style organizing delivered. A lot of "nobodies" got a taste of leading a group, learned that sticking together could win some issues for their neighbourhood, and taught people how ineffectual and scared a lot of public leaders really were. It made immediate and concrete improvements in the lives of people in poor neighbourhoods.

What this kind of organizing did not attempt to do, and in fact attacked other styles of organizing for, was raise questions about the basic nature of our economic or political system. It didn't even question the position of women. Alinsky believed that the American democratic system and the capitalist form of economy were the "best in the world," and that all that was required was for the poor to organize for a voice in the political process. He said at one point that the real sign of victory for the poor would be when they had a poor peoples' representative on the Board of Directors of AT&T.

Although this kind of organizing was relatively common in the 1970's, there are few examples of it left.

What were the reasons for the demise of neighbourhood organizing? This particular style of community empowerment worked, but it had an Achilles heel. It was costly — it required inputs of salaries and training for full-time people over a two to five year period — and it made the people in power very angry.

In the United States, the money was put up by the national offices of mainstream churches. In Canada, some of the training money was from churches, but the ongoing salaries were obtained from different levels of government. In both Canada and the United States, as the people became more powerful, the funders were more threatened and more angry. And they got even: the source of funds dried up.

Alinsky's analysis did not go far enough. When the power structure was too weak to withstand pressure at the local level, the big boys were willing to step in to protect it. It was Alinsky's concentration on only winnable local issues that prevented him from foreseeing the extent to which the power structure was willing to go to stop the people. Because no attention had been paid in the community organizations to larger issues of culture, solidarity or analysis, the community people had no way to protect themselves when the money was withdrawn and the organizers left.

In Holmes County, Mississippi — about 85% black and the poorest county in the United States — the Rural Organizing Committee had received core funding from the United Methodist Church for almost ten years. ROC has been able to get black people into many elected and bureaucrat positions. It has changed the way the schools and court systems operate in their area. It has even run candidates for mayor. However, in the last few years, as their power has grown, they have started to threaten the local white power elite. Most of the elite are Methodists. Last year, the Methodist church cut off funding to ROC and they have had to lay off their full-time staff. Although some of them are continuing to work without money, they believe that the whole project is in serious jeopardy. They had not foreseen this coming, even when the United Methodists began to fire all the national staff that supported community organizing work.

Municipal Election Strategies

Municipalities in Canada have very little power. Almost all their decisions have to be approved by the provincial government. Their only way of raising tax revenues is through the property tax system, which is extremely unfair. However, for those of us who are anxious to see basic social transformation, we have to pay serious attention to getting control of municipal power. Municipalities can initiate decisions around alternative transportation systems, city planning, alternatives to the "social safety net," housing, recreation, and neighbourhood centres. It can determine the level of democracy at a grass roots level in the neighbourhoods and the city itself. Organizations like hydro boards and school boards, can also develop an informed public and bring about significant changes at a local level, especially if they are willing to confront the province.

There have been a number of places in Canada where activists have worked to get control of municipal councils, schools boards and so on. Usually, very few people actually vote in municipal elections, so the trick is to pull the vote. To know who your supporters are and how to get them to the polls.

The Riverdale model (three canvasses of the entire ward) has been found to be highly effective. It is labour intensive and is only possible with a lot of real community support. The first canvass is with a short leaflet when the candidate announces she/he is running. The second, in person with a more sophisticated leaflet, continues throughout the campaign. The third, a reminder to vote giving the polling station, goes to supporters and "indefinites" in the last week. The candidate calls on as many people personally as possible. On voting day, those persons who were found to be supportive, are called and reminded to vote, and offered help getting to the poll.

It becomes clear, however, looking at the histories of municipal election work that the ability to do anything once you get on council is directly proportional to the level of organization in the neighbourhoods. Having sympathetic politicians in office is of very little use unless they are one part of a much larger organization.

In 1968-70, I was the alderperson for St. Lawrence Ward in the city of Kingston. I had been elected as a part of a protracted battle over tenants rights that had been carried on by ATAK (The Association for Tenants' Action Kingston) for over two years. We ran four candidates in the municipal election, and endorsed the Labour Council candidate. I was elected and the labour council guy was elected. It was quite an experience.

My constituents would phone me at all hours of the day and night for help with problems from housing to sewer backups, and I found that there was very little I could do, except try to pressure the bureaucracy. But because the senior staff at City Hall hated ATAK for its militancy, they worked against my requests. We still had to pressure in the same ways we always did. The people in my ward would accuse me of not working on their problem. Then, within the Tenants Association itself, because the media singled me out for attention, the other members were resentful. Some of them actually believed the media hype and began to defer to me.

I had very little time left to organize or to deal with these problems. I got nowhere in council, as anything I supported was defeated 14 to 2.

The whole thing came to a head in September 1970. ATAK had been working for rent controls in the city for years: petitions, demonstrations, proper channels. You name it, we'd done it; it was clear that the majority of voters in the city supported rent controls. The night it finally came to council, it was voted down without even a debate, 14-2. The tenants in the council chambers disrupted the meeting and the mayor adjourned while the police dragged everyone out. John Meister and I were dragged out with the rest. At the request of the ATAK, I resigned from Council, and we published the reasons in a special edition of our little paper which we distributed throughout the ward.

I swore at that time that I'd only run for office again, if there was a clearer understanding by both parties of the role of the elected person and the community organization.

Elected representatives are a very small part of an overall organizing strategy, and they have to be accountable. I'm sure that the Kingston City Council was no worse than any other, but the level of stupidity and greed of those men was quite astounding. A basic part of any democracy should be recall provisions for any elected officer, and should be exercised a lot. To a very large extent, just the process of being elected changes how the candidates think about themselves. It is easy to let it go to your head: to think you know more than the people; to get wrapped up in "how complicated the whole system is"; to become a broker between the power structure and the community organization instead of their representative. Just the volume of work makes it hard to keep a radical perspective unless you have help with research and choosing priorities.

NOTES

1.   Three excellent resources on political strategy, which have influenced this chapter are:

Speeter, Greg, *Power: A Repossession Manual,* University of Massachusetts, 1978.

Kahn, Si, *Organizing,* McGraw Hill, 1982.

Kahn, Si, *How People Get Power, op.cit.*

There are also some detailed and excellent case studies of community organizing strategies in Canada that are listed in the Resources chapter at the end of the book.

2. Yandle, Sharon, From a talk to a conference on *Workers and Their Communities*, York University, Toronto, May, 1989.
3. Keating, Donald., *The Power to Make It Happen*, Greentree Press, Toronto, 1972.
4. Keating, Donald R., "The Future of Neighbourhood Organizing," in Dan A. Chekki, *Participatory Democracy in Action*. Vikas Publishing House, New Delhi, 1979, pages 228-231.

III

DOING ANALYSIS
Thinking Like an Organizer

There is only one reality, and we all see it through different windows or frames. In order to understand what is going on in that reality, or to change it, we need to know how others see it. We need to look through their window. As in the story of the blind men trying to identify the elephant, we can analyze the beast by seeing it from all sides.

You can be almost sure that if you are experiencing something as a problem, someone else thinks she/he is benefitting from the situation. This benefit may be illusory, and it may be only short-term, but your problem almost certainly stems from decisions taken in someone else's interests in some other place. For example, if you need regular bus service to get to work, your life will be considerably disrupted by a cutback in the service. The decision to make the cutback is not meant to cause you difficulty; it is meant to balance a municipal budget.

Whenever we experience something as a problem, the cause of the problem can be found by asking the question: *Who benefits from this situation?*

This chapter provides some practical exercises in doing analysis for social change.

Five situations from people's lives are presented with study guides. The first part is a *story:* it may be yours, or your neighbour's, or someone you work with. Whatever, you will probably recognize some of these situations quite well. Feel free to make up your own stories too, or to transform and play with these. Drama is just another way of looking at real life.

Following each story, the reader is challenged to look at it from different points of view, different windows. In the paragraph entitled *Ways to Describe the Problem,* some examples are given.

Then the analytic question is asked, *Who Benefits?,* and again some ideas are put forward.

Once you have figured out what the problem is, then you have to decide what to do about it. *What are our Options for Action?* Often your experience or imagination feels very limited when it comes to getting out of your difficulties. For this reason, I also propose a whole range of ideas for dealing with the problem. Some of them may seem completely off the wall to you. However, almost all of them have been tried by someone in this country at some time. Some of them were very effective. Which options you choose will depend on what you think is enough within your experience and energy to undertake. Go with the options that feel "right," but don't ignore the others. Someday, they may feel right too. Invariably, you will have other ideas for action than those listed here. Great.

I have also included a teaser: *One Vision of an Ideal Solution to the Problem* to stretch your imagination. The ideal that accompanies each story may not be your ideal. That's OK. Develop your own. Unless you take time to dream about an ideal situation, how will you know where you are going?

These exercises are meant to provide a model for doing social analysis on other issues as well as those included here. I hope they are useful.

Chapter 12

THE EXERCISES

The Social Costs of Unemployment

Story: Since you retired, you and your husband live in a two bedroom apartment in Saskatoon. Two months ago, your twenty-six year old son and his wife moved in with you "temporarily" until he could find work. He had been working for a job development program of the federal government, but was laid off almost a year ago, and his Unemployment Insurance has run out. She is working as a cashier at a nearby store, and they help with the rent. You are getting on each others nerves because you are so crowded. Your workload has been increased tremendously in terms of handling family stress.

Ways That This Problem Can Be Described

> Government cutbacks
> Extracting wealth from Saskatchewan
> Stress
> Human greed
> Your son's laziness
> Potential violence
> An unemployment statistic
> Families taking care of one another
> A saving in social expenditure
> A patient with new problems
> A consumer of pharmaceuticals
> The poor to be helped
> A neighbour in trouble

A new member of the Unemployed Organization
Lack of affordable housing
Need for emergency housing
Lack of jobs
Inadequate education
Underpaid women's work
Inadequate retirement income
Family breakdown
Forced retirement

Who Benefits in the Short-term From this Situation?

The decision to lay your son off was made in order to cut government expenditures in wages and social services and to increase it elsewhere. Who benefits from these kind of cutbacks?

Once your son moves in with you, it frees up one more housing unit in a scarce stock. This takes pressure off the government to construct or make available more affordable housing.

Your own income is too low to move to larger quarters; and your daughter-in-law's is too low to support the family. Why are these incomes so low, and who benefits from that?

Who benefits from the one-year term for Unemployment Insurance, and the inadequacy of welfare once it runs out?

Where is all the wealth in Saskatchewan going anyway, and why isn't it available in times of need like this?

How does the apparatus of social workers, psychiatrists and drug companies see this problem? What do they stand to gain?

Who benefits from the loss of talent and energy that your son's idleness is causing?

Who benefits from the construction of apartment buildings so that there is no space for workshops and common meeting areas and other public spaces that would take some of the pressure off your home?

What are the Options For Action?

Your family and your son's family could look for a slightly larger dwelling, and share the rent on a more permanent basis.

You or your son and friends could move into a tent in City Park, or sit in at a government office, or squat in a vacant building to dramatise the situation.

You could get involved in a co-operative or non-profit housing venture, and convince a church to back it, or you could pressure banks to make money available at very low interest for this kind of housing.

You could join and work with organizations like the unemployed group or the coalition against cutbacks to try to stop the government and/or change it.

You could urge your son to move to Ontario to look for work or to get retraining for other work.

You could find other families who are in the same boat and try to support and help on another.

You could organize a worker co-operative or a community economic development project to create work for your son and others like him, or for yourself and others like you (the object being to increase family income); and/or you could try to get outside funds set up.

You could organize for higher wages for your daughter-in-law, and/or more affordable housing in the city.

You could organize for better stress management for people in these situations.

You could ask your church to take up a collection to help you, or ask a fellow church member with a larger house to take your son in.

What Would the Ideal Situation Look Like?

The I Ching symbol for crisis is made up of two characters, "opportunity" and "danger." What questions does this crisis raise in terms of opportunity?

What do you and your husband want to do with your retirement anyway? Do you want to be involved in your community? Do you want to live by yourselves? Do you want to be involved in the issues of your time? How do you really want to relate to your family?

What do you have to offer from your experience that could help solve these problems for yourself and others?

There are a number of exciting possibilities in this crisis. Suppose, for example, that you and your husband and your son and his wife decided to go with the co-operative housing option. You would find other people who wanted to build together, would get to design the kind of living space you wanted (within reasonable limits), would borrow money from a church and from a government housing program, and would have the housing within a few years. The housing co-operative could set up its own maintenance and repair worker co-operative and employ your daughter-in-law or your son, and could perhaps also develop a buyers' club for getting groceries cheaper and some small businesses to look after other needs in Saskatoon (using the asset of the co-op as collateral).

The possibilities are only as limited as your imagination.

Farmers in Trouble

Story: You live on a farm in southwestern Manitoba which has been in your family for three generations now. You raise grain and have about 60 head of cattle. You are in your early forties and so is your wife. You have two young teenagers. You enjoy living in rural community and you like the work of farming, although lately it feels as if you spend all your time in a car or a truck because the population of the area is getting so sparse. You belong to a rural life committee in the nearby village, but lately no one seems to be doing anything but talking about how bad things are with the drought. There are 8 people on the committee. You all live within 60 miles of one small community. You and your wife have never been farm activists, and now you find yourselves having to be one on the committee. Personally, you think you may lose your farm this year if things don't look up, but you haven't told the group.

You are one really worried man, who is spending a lot of his time in that truck wondering how you will make it through the next year. The people leaving the rural area has made it harder for you to have social contact, and you go to the rural life meetings as much for companionship as for any hope of change.

If you do lose your farm, then the question is, what do you do next?

Different Ways to Describe This Reality

> Loss of the family farm
> Destruction of rural community
> Opportunity for corporate farms to expand
> Market for fertilizers and pesticides
> More efficient method of production
> A market for gas, oil and automobiles and farm machinery
> A result of the use of fossil fuels
> A native land claim

A boring way of life for teenagers
A market for alcohol and drugs
An uneconomical rail line/bus route/post office
A potential foreclosure
A stress management problem
An outmoded way of life
Potential trouble makers
An opportunity for setting up retraining programs
Longer and more dangerous school bus routes
Misused grasslands
Statistic in the streamlining of agricultural production
A bad investment
A drain on the public purse through subsidies
A potential contract farmer for Cargill
A result of the green house effect

Who Benefits?

The large corporations that make up "agri-business" benefit from this situation. They sell the farmer seeds, chemicals, implements, oil, gas, tractors. The banks benefit because the farmer's largest expenditures are on interest. If he goes bankrupt, the corporate farms that gobble him up will benefit. He and his family will add to the pool of cheap labour in the rural villages and, if he loses the farm, in the cities.

What are the Options For Action?

You can sell out and go bankrupt.

You can do more effective stress management workshops with the rural life committee.

You can get involved in working with one of the farmers' organizations to lobby for changes in prices and subsidies.

You can combine your farm with a few of your neighbours and share equipment and labour.

You can work to convince the municipality to purchase land that has been foreclosed on and not sold and establish a land trust.

You could work to convince a city church to mortgage its equity and set up a land trust.

You could work to establish a community economic development corporation in the small town, to prevent the leakage of dollars out of the community.

You could establish a plan for greenhousing and diversified horticulture to feed the community itself and reduce food costs.

You could lobby to convince the government to purchase supplies from the local area for the local hospitals and other institutions.

You could lobby to convince the government to relocate an office in your area, thereby providing jobs.

You could investigate and seek funding to try one of the new bio-technology options, in your area.

Your committee could decide to let all the farms except one go to grassland, then co-operatively farm the remaining one, sharing labour and equipment and emphasizing self-sufficiency for the members first. Money could be obtained for co-operative housing on the farm from the government, and production could be transformed to ecologically-sound uses.

You could organize along with displaced rural people in the cities for a massive land reform in Canada, similar to what we support in Third World countries.

You could ask urban churches to use their trust funds to pay for organizers to create this movement.

You could pressure banks, and organize urban Churches to pressure banks for a moratorium on foreclosures and forced sales. You could pressure government to make this law.

What Would the Ideal Situation Look Like?

How do you see your own life in the next twenty years? What would the problem look like if it were truly solved for you?

The answer is only limited by your own imagination or despair. Imagine, as an example, a thriving small town with a number of greenhouses around it, supplying salad stuffs and fresh vegetables all year round, heated with solar power and wind power. The town has a farm machinery and automobile recycling worker co-operative that takes old equipment and retools it from the inside out for sale all over the province. The town also has its own dairy herd and produces its own eggs, and has a cheese factory. It makes its own real ale from perennial grains and sells it to the hotels in the neighbouring city. A large part of the area is given over to grasslands and buffalo roam there, the property of the native community. There is little new housing construction, but an excellent construction co-operative has become very adept at renovating abandoned buildings and at moving them from one site to another. The population of the town is from many different races and colours, refugees from all over the world, who have been allocated small plots of land on condition that they farm by the principles of the land trust: environmentally sound, closed loop agriculture. Trees have been planted everywhere, and now forests grow along all the river banks and in all the valleys.

Education Isn't Working

Story: You are a teacher in an elementary school in Ontario and have been for about fifteen years. You went in to teaching because you love helping children learn, and you consider yourself to be very good at your job. However, in the last few years, you feel like you are less and less able to teach. The class sizes are bigger and you often have severely handicapped children in the classroom. You also seem to have to spend more time filling out forms and marking papers, and have a lot less time with the children. Also, years ago, you knew the children better. They usually lived within walking distance of the school and if someone had problems, you'd ask them to come early or stay late and help them. Or you could call their parents and chat. Now over half the children come on the bus and can be kept in only at noon. This is self-defeating because they are rangy all afternoon afterwards. Your union has expressed concern about this matter, but in the last analysis, the only changes they appear to be able to get are higher wages.

You have a very personal relationship to the problem, but the depth of your passion probably depends on how much doing your work well means to you and on your expectation of success if you tackle it. You are in the union so you do have access to others who feel as you do, and some protection if you want to organize for change.

Who Benefits From This Situation?

The major beneficiaries are those who benefit from the government spending that is no longer allocated to teachers' salaries and small neighbourhood schools. Big centralized schools benefit construction companies, raw material suppliers, energy companies and land speculators. On paper, big schools are easier to administrate. They also turn out a more standardized product, and students are less likely to expect to be upwardly mobile in socio-economic terms. A greater diversity of program can be offered, but it is taught in less depth. The increased class size cuts costs dramatically. The breakdown in parent-teacher communication has also protected the School Boards from concerted pressure on a regular basis.

Ways of Seeing the Reality

The children should learn to settle down.
Some children just don't do as well as others.
Teachers expect too much.
Teachers are overpaid.
We need to get back to "basics."
We need bigger, newer schools.
Children need to be better disciplined.
Teachers are not being trained properly for modern education.
We should stream children earlier.
Parents should discipline their children better.
Children with learning disabilities should be identified earlier.
The school day should be longer.
We need more informed school trustees.
We put too much money into a school system that doesn't work.
Parents should be helping their children at home more.
The curriculum doesn't hold children's interest.
At least we don't have violence in the schools yet.
We need to give children less freedom.
The teachers' unions are too strong.
Taxpayers are demanding more accountability from schools.
(School Board members) — I want to be re-elected.

What are the Options For Action?

You can quit and get a job somewhere else.
You can organize within the teachers' union for more control over class size and paperwork.
You could run for the school board, or run someone else.
You could begin an alternative school.
You could start a campaign to explain the social costs of under-funding education.
You can organize with the parents for smaller classes.

You could organize with the students for a critical view of the education system.

You could try to raise foundation money/church money to do a pilot project around effective education and publicize it.

You could refuse to do half the paper work, and ask a different parent each month to act as a teachers aide.

You can subscribe to *Our Schools/ Our Selves,* and hand it out to everyone you know.

You can write nasty letters to your school board trustees, and try to influence their opinions.

What Would an Ideal Situation Look Like?

What would you like your job to look like if you were successful? What is the best way to teach children? What about for example:

A school where the pupil teacher ratio is one to ten or fifteen, and children are given freedom to choose teachers they are comfortable with. Although there is some standardized educational classes, children can learn at their own pace and can pursue their particular interests. Schools are located within neighbourhoods, so the teachers know the parents and can converse with them often about the child's needs. Teachers are allowed lots of opportunities to upgrade their own knowledge and teaching skills, and to discuss students' problems with their peers on a regular basis.

Environment, Aboriginal Rights and Jobs

Story: You live in a small town in northern Ontario where there is a major battle going on over logging rights and a native land claim. The native band, which is presently confined to a very small reserve area, has made a claim to most of the area in the community and has placed a "caution" on the title of most of the property. In the white community, there is high unemployment, and the major source of income has been a company that produces wafer board and lumber to ship out of the area.

The lumber company now claims that they need access and logging roads to more forest in order to survive. A number of men in the area contract to the company to cut logs, and they insist that they need this access too. The forest in this area is extremely beautiful, and tourists come from southern Ontario to canoe and camp here every summer. A group of high-profile environmentalists from down south are now co-operating with some local people who are known to be part of the peace and environmental movements to prevent the logging roads.

The government has recently announced that it will allow an extension of the logging and will increase the size of the provincial park area. The native people last week blockaded one of the logging roads. Feelings are running very high in the area. You are a co-owner, with your husband, of a gas station and restaurant in the area. You have two teenage children, one helps you in the gas bar, the other works summers at a tourist lodge. You expect they will move to Toronto to get work when they finish high school. You enjoy the bush around the area, and have lived there all your life. Your father worked at the lumber company before the wafer board plant was built.

Different Ways of Seeing This Problem

The environmentalists are concerned about the long-term future of the forests, and claim that the ever diminishing number of trees on the globe will cause the greenhouse effect and massive erosion. They don't want to see the extinction of any more species.

The tourist industry is concerned that the appearance of the forests along canoe routes and waterways be maintained, so that the American and southern Ontario dollars will continue to come in. Most of the expensive tourist lodges are not owned in the area, neither are the outfitters'. They are very upset with the native caution on their lands, because it blocks potential sales.

The native community is concerned with regaining control over the management of the timber resource, so that trapping, hunting and fishing can again become their source of livelihood, and so that the forest can be preserved for future generations. They also feel that the land was stolen from them in the first place and that they are entitled it. This is the only economic development plan that appears possible given their small reserve.

The wafer board plant owners need access to enough acreage to feed the high technology mill. They want to be able to clear cut large sections of the forest after they remove the bigger trees for lumber. If the plant isn't used to capacity, it will lose money, and they will probably close out the operation. The plant, however, is locally owned, although it is only one operation of this diversified company (they also do road construction and concrete work). If the plant gets access, the owners can become quite wealthy. If they close it out, it will limit their personal wealth.

The employees in the wafer board plant are very nervous. Most of them cannot imagine where else they could get work if the plant closes down. The working conditions and wages there are lousy, but its better than nothing. One attempt to unionize was stopped dead in its tracks by the company.

The contract loggers are also concerned. Most of them own their trucks and pay all their own expenses. They get paid on the basis of the lumber they bring out. If they don't get access to the forest, many of them will lose their equipment to the banks. They don't know where they would earn a living if this falls through. Some of them are native people from the reserve. They find themselves in a very difficult position both at home and with the contractor.

Small business in the community is caught in the middle: they like tourist dollars, but they also need the regular incomes of towns-people.

The provincial government, which has to make the decisions, is trying to weigh the effectiveness of the environmental-tourist lobby to make trouble across the province. Until the blockade, they did not think the native people had much political weight. Now they are nervous about that.

What Are Your Options?

You can research the claims of the environmentalists and see if there is substance to their fears of the greenhouse effect and the long-range self-interest of the area.

You can work on yourself and your neighbours and your church congregation concerning the issues of racism and land claims that have been raised by the indigenous people. What would the effects of winning their claim be? What are the possibilities for negotiation over local interests? Who does benefit from the rich tourists who come in anyway…is it really local people?

You could organize kitchen table discussions around the environmental and native aspects of the problem, so that people made be better informed.

You could try and form a small group of local opinion leaders from all the groups to bring some reason to the dispute.

You could organize a local event to examine community economic development alternatives to expansion of the logging and clearcutting operations. And then follow this up with a plan to do it, asking for government investment to make it possible.

You could research other logging methods, like selective cutting, and publicize these in the community.

You could ask the wafer board plant for a full accounting of how it presently uses its profit, and seek to have it invested in some other community business.

You could work through your teenagers and others to popularize the long-range interest of the area approach: what happens after the forests are cut down? What happens when most of the tourist dollars go to Toronto?

You could join the indigenous people in their blockade, and try to persuade your friends to come.

What Would the Ideal Situation Look Like?

The ideal situation would be, obviously, to protect the forest resource, recognize the entitlement of the aboriginal people, allow some tourists access to the land, and provide wages and/or income for all the residents of the area at the same level or higher than it had been. Is there a way to make this possible?

Imagine that the town was dedicated to self-reliance and that the lumber mill was now owned by a combination of indigenous people, white residents and workers. The profits from the mill are used to develop a pre-fab log housing industry and to reforest the area. The community is working to become as self-reliant as possible. It now produces most of its own vegetables, meat and dairy products which are sold through local co-operatives. The aboriginal residents are developing a plan for the forest and fish resource and have already established a boat-building co-operative and a car and skidoo recycling plant. Every individual and business in the area has an active membership in the new credit union which loans out the money to community development projects.

Housing Crisis

Story: You are a tenant in a six-plex in downtown Halifax. You have two small children. The other tenants in the building, like you, have relatively low incomes and small kids. The landlord lives on the other side of Halifax, and works as a lawyer. You all have a number of complaints about the building, and he does almost no repairs. This month, you all received a notice of rent increase. Your neighbour says that she simply can't pay it and pay her hydro. She also does not believe that there will be any place cheaper that is vacant. She appears to be distraught and at the breaking point.

You work as a secretary for a law firm in Halifax, and are an active member of your local church. You help with the clothing depot there and teach Sunday School. The church has a lot of active young members and an enthusiastic minister. You have never been involved in anything even vaguely "political." Your family lives in Halifax, and they just wish you would move to a better neighbourhood.

Different Ways of Seeing This Problem

You could see this problem as a stress problem for your neighbour, or as a medical model (get her tranquilizers, better nutrition, exercise), or as a problem for emotional support (visitation, comfort,etc.).

You could see this problem as one for the government to deal with: is the rent increase legal? What is the landlord's legal obligation to make repairs? Can hydro disconnect your service if you don't pay?

Because the lawyer owns the building, he believes he has the right to extract a maximum profit and to leave the tenants living with poor conditions.

The tenants could see this problem as one of power. They pay the landlord's mortgage, taxes, heat and profit with their money because of their need for shelter for themselves and their children. Which need is greater, theirs or the owners? And how do they assert their power in this situation?

You could also see the problem as one of low wages for women, or inadequate support for families, or inadequate protection for the children of single parent women.

You could see your neighbour as being in need of charitable support for the church, or in need of political support from the community.

If you were the landlord's mortgage company, you would be interested in whether he makes his payments on time, whether the property maintains its value, and whether he pays his taxes.

What Are Your Options For Action?

You can spend a lot of time listening to your neighbour's worries and helping her look for more money or another job.

You can share what money you have with your neighbour.

You can go to the rent review board and fight the rent increase.

You can get the other tenants to work with you, and you can all go together to the rent review board and fight the rent increase.

You can ask the City to enforce the minimum standards by law and force the landlord to do the repairs on the building.

If the landlord responds by harassing you or the other tenants, you could tell him you are going to (a) get him charged with harassment under the Landlord and Tenants Act, (b) let it be known publicly that he is a slum landlord, through the legal community, and through your contacts in the community.

You and the other tenants could organize to build co-operative housing together or to buy the present building if it is in good enough condition, and ask a charitable organization, church or social agency to guarantee the down payment.

You could ask members of the congregation to support the tenants in the struggle over the rent increase, through the media, through attending hearings, and through finding free legal advice.

You could get involved in other work that is being done in your city around affordable housing and rent controls, by joining committees and sitting in coalitions.

You could raise the housing issue in your congregation through speakers, bulletins, posters and photo-displays. You could ask the minister to set aside a Sunday to deal with affordable housing issues...maybe the other tenants would like to prepare the presentation for the congregation and the Sunday School.

You and your congregation could use this issue to begin a discussion in the city churches around conversion of church land to socially-useful purposes.

What Would the Ideal Situation Look Like?

Imagine if we lived in a world where all housing in the city would be controlled by councils of the people who live in it, and the housing charges would be geared to one-quarter of a person's income. Standards of maintenance and repair would be strictly enforced, although the costs of doing those repairs would be considered part of the housing charges. It would be a crime to own housing for private profit, or to speculate in land. Housing would be designed for the comfort and safety of children and the infirm, and would, as a matter of course, allow for the expression of an individual's personality in the design.

CONCLUSION

GET REAL OR GET LOST

"Get real or get lost," says my friend Art Solomon. And that's what it comes down to.

"Power-over is the result of millions of human choices made again and again. It can be undone by small and repeated acts of liberation".[1] Systems of domination are maintained by human labour and with our consent and they are located in the patterns of our daily lives.

Some organizational forms bring out the co-operative, sharing, honest parts of people; others bring out the competitive, treacherous and greedy side. We have seen many examples in this book of the way people organize for truly transformative politics embodying the kind of world we want to create.

Activists in this country and throughout the world are labouring to birth a just and humane society that can live in harmony with the earth. They recognize, understand and change those systems that foster destruction and exploitation.

Here are some more creative stories from community organizing work in Canada.

"I'm talking about the staff that works at the Friendship Centre. It seems to me that most of the problems that the native people have got has to do with alcohol. Alcohol makes you do things that you don't normally do. I think it does that to everybody, it doesn't matter if you are native or non-native. But this is what happened in our community and further up north too.

"When you look at the court system and statistics, whenever someone goes to court, it always goes back that they were intoxicated. And I know that more and more people in our community now are starting to sober up. They know what is causing the problem and it takes them a long time to come around and realise that.

"We have a women's group that was started by a family court worker in Timmins. And there's a few women who went to a treatment centre here in Sudbury. They all come back and they all have hopes when they come back with their children. Most of them have families and they are broken homes. These women meet once a week at the Friendship Centre and talk about their problems and they seem to be coming back and focussing on their families and getting their lives together.

"This is one segment of the population anyway that is understanding that the problem stems back to alcohol. And the men are going to be starting to do the same thing. And there's a youth leisure time co-ordinator there that works with teenagers and high school kids too. And this is what she's been doing the last couple of years. And there's hardly any problems with the high school students any more.

"Like, the Friendship Centre is doing good, we are working very hard with the people we come in contact with every day, to make them see what the problem stems from when they have trouble. And with the women, some of them have lost their children to Children's Aid and they really have to fight to get them back. And now they're saying we're sober now, and we can go back to our children. And they're getting them back and they are struggling. But they need support and our help. This is just the story I wanted to share. I think it has a good ending."

* * *

"I'm going to tell you about a literacy project. It's called Journeys Education Association in Winnipeg. It got started when some people founded a drop-in centre for inner city youth and noticed that a lot of the kids that were coming to the drop in during the day were obviously not going to school, so that started off classes at the drop-in centre which is a lot more conducive learning environment for a lot of these kids. After a few years, the workers started to notice that family members who were not of school age were hanging around the edges of these classes. These were adults, parents, grandparents. Most of these people were unemployed, on welfare. So one of the staff started a small after hours program for adults, starting at any level up to grade 12 GED.

"At that point, Journeys moved to a house. It was on Elgin just off Salter, and that's the point where I started to find out about it. A really comfortable environment, lots of beat-up old couches. People were studying everywhere, people were helping people, so you'd have little groups of people working together, lots of chatter, lots of buzz, lots of people interested in learning. So out of that situation, a dream grew that Journeys could expand and take in more students and be open more hours. Funding was a problem all the way along. The program depended on different pockets of money, different funders with different timelines. And the money would run out, and we'd try to transfer money. And those of you who were at the North End yesterday met with some women who used popular theatre methods to tackle the problem of getting a chunk of money for day-care (the No Name Brand Clan).

"As it went along more and more needs got determined. Many of the students wanted native studies, as about 60-70% of the student population is native. So they decided who they would hire and started doing native studies. They were offered desk top publishing equipment which is great, so the students started publishing their stories, volumes of their own work. Which was really very affirming, it is just wonderful to see the effect this has on people who have just learned how to write. So we are into the third volume of published student stories now, and they are used as text books in other literacy resource centres.

"As this was happening and people were doing native studies, I think political consciousness got focussed a little bit more. It's about the time, about a year ago, when the aboriginal justice inquiry was putting out feelers to people in community organizations like myself to see who wanted to give brief to the inquiry. So I got this request at the North End community ministry and I took it (I'm on the board at Journeys) to the board. The board is very interesting in that it has 10 student members, 4 community advisor members and now a tutor representative. This was a hot struggle. Trying to decide if this was an appropriate thing for a group of adult learners to do, to take time to gather their ideas, write them down and make a presentation to the inquiry. The main opposition came from one of the teachers who felt that it would be divisive and upsetting in the class. Some of the students said they weren't good at writing but they would interview people and get the stories out, someone else was practicing public speaking so she offered to make the presentation. So all of this took about a six week period. And the students did present and did a really fine job. And I think it took a lot of courage for people to come out with their stories of how the justice system has not worked for native people in Winnipeg. Part of my intrigue with Journeys is to see how far literacy training can go, as it works with the needs that the students have identified."

* * *

"We started organizing the Canadian Farmworkers Union in 1980. In the first years we were able to certify unions with a few large growers but the B.C. governments change in labour legislation in 1986 left us with only one place certified, Fraser Valley Foods, where the inside workers are in Canadian Food and Allied Workers and therefore were able to support us. Almost 80% of our B.C. farmworkers are Punjabi speaking landed immigrants. They survive on their meager earnings by living in extended families.

"Tops, they get 17 weeks of picking, mostly berries and fruit, and then they used to get UIC, but changes in UI will mean they probably will be unable to even get that. Many are not eligible for welfare because they are sponsored immigrants for 5-10 years or life. This need for enough weeks to qualify for UI makes them dependent on labour contractors who exact a high percentage of their wages to do this.

"Many of the workers are women who have to take their children with them to the fields. We know of one child who died in a pesticide vat. Often they drink from the same stream where pesticide containers are washed. Farmworkers are not covered by the Occupational Health and Safety Act. The union has undertaken a home to home English as a second language campaign in order to organize with the farmworkers and we have a campaign against the pesticides to educate our people. It is a difficult struggle."

* * *

"This summer I moved, but I didn't move very far. I moved within the same neighbourhood, close to a complex of very old factories in the centre of the town I live in, which is St.Jean, Québec. And shortly after I moved there was a provincial election, and a report was leaked by someone in the Ministry of the Environment concerning this area. There was a factory which was engaged in recycling automobile batteries that had been functioning there since 1984. It had a huge pyramid of these batteries in its yard. People had been complaining about this. When it rained the earth around this, all the wet earth and water, bubbled. And a lot of the housing around this plant was old time workers housing that is now rental housing and the people who live there now, do so because it is cheap housing.

"The story broke right in the middle of the election campaign and it was very embarrassing to a government that was shipping PCBs to England and back and so on. And right away the DSC (the public health authority) called a series of public meetings in the community centre right across the street from where I live. What struck me about them was the controlling of information that was going on there. The cooling out of this issue...saying that 200 micrograms per litre in the blood stream was probably an acceptable level, and not to worry about anything over that. I didn't know too much about this whole issue of lead toxification at the time, but tried to learn as it went along. The control in information made me angry.

"Soon after that, about the 21 September, a citizens group called a demonstration outside the Balmet company. The Ministry of the Environment had issued an ordinance that required the company to do a number of things, one of which was to temporarily pave over this area of lead contamination. They had done soil samples and there was a highly contaminated area. There was dust from this factory yard that was getting into people's houses and kids were eating it and stuff like that. They were going to test all the kids from ten years old and down in the area. When they first did this they announced that 90% of the kids in the area were fine...But 10% were up over 200. There was one little girl with over 400. This is the level where the World Health Organization says you must take a worker off the job. I discovered, however, that in Québec, its 700 before you take a worker off the job. And this company had a bad record for people being pulled out of work.

"A small citizens' committee got busy and organized a demonstration outside the factory on the 21 of September, from 4 till about 6 o'clock in the afternoon. They advertised it just in the neighbourhood. They didn't want to get involved with any of the political parties during the election. It was well organized. They had banners, and chairs for older people and coffee and juice and balloons. There was a declaration to be read. The kids all wore the number showing their level of lead contamination. So you had little kids running around with numbers like 350 and 305 and 255 on them. It seemed to me it was good demonstration. Only one TV outlet covered it, unfortunately in English. None of the French electronic media covered it. The local paper came out the following Wednesday, the demonstration was the same day that the municipal authority had given permission to the company to dig out the contaminated soil in its yard and replace it. All this was included in the story on the demonstration and the demonstration was put on page 33 of the local paper under the headline 'Failed Demonstration' , because there were supposedly so few people, 'only 100'. I was very angry about this. I have often got angry about things that happened to other people and I have been trained not to get angry about things that happen to me. And since then I have got very involved in this issue, and we're trying to expand the citizens' committee and follow this up."

* * *

"I want to talk about the work we are presently doing in a group called the Melita Rural Life support group.It actually got started by some people who were in the United Church and lived in some charges in southwestern Manitoba. They were concerned about farmers being in financial difficulty and not having any support in the rural community. And once the group got rolling, I got involved in it and one of the beautiful things about the group was that you didn't have to be active in the church to participate. The group has been very open to allow anyone in who wanted to be.

"We are very small and informal and stayed away from structuring ourselves aside from having a chairperson and a treasurer. We've looked at several issues, and have given farmers a lot of support, even going to court appearances with them when they are fighting over possession of land.

"There are two special projects of the group that I am especially keen about. We have intentionally tried to make the group a group of husbands and wives, a joint group, and generally we have kept it that way by having things like potluck suppers instead of straight meetings. But it became clear that people had to talk about what was happening in their lives. Particularly for women to say what it has been like for them when the farm goes into financial trouble. Even though they are not equal owners they carry an equal amount of debt. Because they have been forced by lenders to sign on the debt. Lots of stories about how this happened. So Nancy Painter and I pulled together a group of women and we acted as facilitators and as documenters of their stories. We called the group the "Anonymous Womens' Group" because if we had named them they would have been very identifiable in the community. It is important to realize that when you are in financial difficulty you are very vulnerable, not only to the lenders but to the other farmers in the community, who can make gains off your failure.

"The women gave their quotes and we put together the broadsheet. We had to depersonalize the quotes to hide the identity of the women. We then did a mass distribution of the whole southwestern part of Manitoba. It was very exciting because it was the first time women had done this sort of thing, and it became something they had accomplished. I'm sure the same story could be told by the men, and we need to figure out how to do it."

* * *

"The Gitksan Wet'suwet'en people are claiming jurisdiction over the animal, vegetable and mineral resources of watershed of the upper Skeena River in the interior of British Columbia. They are an ancient people, who lived on the plateau between the glaciers during the Ice Age. They have asked the courts to declare that the provincial government has no jurisdiction in their territory. In 1927, some aboriginal people petitioned for title and the parliament responded by making it illegal for them to meet to discuss land claims and outlawed all traditional feasts.

"The court case has been going on for over two years now. In the court house, the white judge sitting there listening to the evidence. The case of the Gitksan Wet'suwet'en lies in proving that they have managed the lands in question for 20,000 years. Their elders and leaders gave evidence from their oral history. It was backed up by the evidence of anthropologists and other "acceptable" experts. The evidence of the Crown depends on proving the extent to which indigenous self-government and traditions have been destroyed. Any place or time when the indigenous people have co-operated with the federal or provincial government now becomes evidence against them.

"While this difficult and exhausting case goes on, the Gitksan-Wet'suwet'en work to involve their people in the decision-making. After every day in court, a debriefing session is held with the lawyers and the people to explain what happened that day and to discuss what will happen in the future. A play is written by the people with the help of Headlines Theatre, called *No Xha* that explains their struggle to themselves and the outside world.

"At home in their ancestral lands, the people battle the intimidation of Westar, the major logging company. They work on strategies for community economic development with the white community, so that they can become more self-reliant. Some of the women reintroduce the community feasts to teach the children their role in the society. Each child sits beside someone who explains the meaning of the feast and the clan system to him or her."

* * *

"I live in the NDG/West Haven area of Montréal. There are a lot of people on welfare here. It is a self-contained area, cut off by railroad tracks. We started an anti-poverty group a few years ago. With the help of some people from St. Columba House, we found a place to meet, and then I got together some people I knew and we started meeting. We put out a flyer downtown offering information sessions on welfare rights. At the first meeting we had 12 people, and then a few of these met three days later. At first we met two times a week. People were that excited. When we told them about the new welfare reform, it was new to them.

"NDG has a lot of ex-psychiatric people, and so in our group there are different levels of capacity. Men have particular problems identifying themselves as welfare recipients. Now we are starting to tap into our members anger and it is quite constructive.

"We choose our own issues: housing, the psychiatrized. We have made presentations to our member of the National Assembly. We attend public functions together. Our meetings are very loosely structured. When we had a speaker from Loyola College on housing, the whole group turned out. It was their first public event together. We are putting out a newsletter on a borrowed computer. We put on a picnic for the people in West Haven. Now we want to run our own food depot and a quarterly community meal. It's coming along slowly. You need to learn as you go along..."

* * *

These stories remind us of the richness and diversity of people's struggles for justice and dignity in Canada. Healing the earth will be possible as we multiply and deepen the work that is being done by very ordinary folk in theplaces they call home. We have learned a lot.

When the Work is Rooted in a Land Base It is Stronger

When the organizing is tied to a specific land base, whether that is a city neighbourhood or a rural area or ancestral lands, it creates the possibility for real community to develop among the people involved. Although we make friends with people we go to meetings with, this is not the same as the complex dynamic created by that daily sharing of a living and/or working space with people who are very different from ourselves. Being known to our neighbours and the people around us keeps us accountable to them, and builds responsibility for one another and for the place we share together.

Building a base for a long-term struggle with power-over is easier when we root ourselves firmly on this planet. We all need, literally, to know where we stand, where "home" is. Bases built on a strong foundation have the capacity to resist the agendas and demands of the state and corporations. The risks in resisting are very high, and unless people trust their neighbours and the rest of the movement to support them in *concrete* ways when the chips are down, they rarely take those risks. Sending telegrams and making speeches of solidarity is not enough for most people: we have to see sharing of privilege, money, land. Building vision and hope in people's lives is done by example; words are not enough.

Establishing our place on the planet is done in different ways. Squatters occupy vacant land and buildings. Aboriginal groups claim their ancestral lands through court challenges, negotiation, occupation. Farmers and impoverished city dwellers demand an end to foreclosures by banks on homes and agricultural lands. People establish land trusts and housing co-operatives. Tenants demand security of tenure. We can plant trees, and grasses and protect swamps and forests. We can demand public space in cities, and city gardens. We can "reclaim" soil with composting projects. We can demand that empty buildings, churches and factories become housing for the homeless.

Some of the most effective work for change in cities is the creation of secure places to stay for tenants and homeless people who are constantly being shunted from one bad housing situation to another. In Toronto, the Fred Victor Mission worked with homeless men to redesign an abandoned warehouse to provide homes, shared living rooms and kitchens, a clinic, a recreation club and a restaurant. In Montréal the Milton Park Co-operative is a model example of the redesign of a low-income area by the people who lived in it, instead of by the developers who wanted to destroy it. In Vancouver the Downtown Eastside Residents Association has created hundreds of units of housing for homeless people. Since it also has a community garden, a fine drop-in which is the Carnegie Public Library, a women's centre and an innovative daycare centre, the Downtown Eastside has been one of the most community-minded poor neighbourhoods in Canada to live in. This community is now under renewed attack by corporate interests.

Effective community organizing starts by listening and talking in the place where you choose to place your allegiance; building on the problems and strengths that people there identify: environmental, recreational, welfare battles, absentee landlords, etc. Get neighbourhood leaders together for workshops and discussions about the neighbourhood, organize potlucks, build friendships at a local level, help one another with crises as they arise. Community gardens, composting programs, emergency daycares, toy libraries are organized and run within neighbourhoods. A neighbourhood frustration over traffic patterns, or danger to seniors, or bored teenagers turns into mutual organizing.

The Systems of Power-Over are Resisted in Our Daily Life

When we care about social change, we think about how we organize our own lives to be as free as possible to do real work. Real organizing for change is a way of life, not a job. Most of the jobs we get waste our time, or use it for destructive purposes: we sell our labour to earn the means of survival for ourselves and our families. Most of us have had to sell it to large corporations or the government, where what we produce will be determined by their need for profit, control or just "measurable results".

Here are a few ways people manage to do work for change.

People who work full-time and have to, think about how to use relationships with people at work, or the job itself for the social change project. Sometimes organizing a union to protect themselves is the first step. Or getting very active in the union. Some unions and workers are gathering ideas for economic conversion, or healthier work, or more environmentally friendly workplaces. Some workers have access to information that could help the movement: statistics, documents, clients with similar problems, policies and plans that will affect your community. Sometimes just being an honest and caring person to the people you work with provides an example that is almost revolutionary.

Some activists develop lifestyles that free them from the need for full-time work. They share accommodation, appliances, child-rearing, vehicles, wine-making. They get part-time work, so they have more time to organize. They take turns working for money.

Young people find hundreds of places and ways to start organizing. They get groups together at school or with their friends, or they join an existing group that interests them. They start teen-run drop-in centres, or street theatre groups, or odd-job worker co-operatives. They are organizing around issues that affect them as youth: police harassment, homelessness, repressive and irrelevant schools, parents, tuition fees for colleges and universities. They form the backbone of a number of environmental, justice and peace groups.

People on social services or unemployment insurance or a pension sometimes have more time to lead organizations. In many groups from peace to playgrounds, they provide the hours of volunteer time that keep the group going. They organize with others in the same position, or with their neighbours around childcare, buyers' clubs, co-operative cars or community gardens, housing, alternative medical care, schools.

The issue we choose is not that important so long as it manifests our desire for justice, and the healing of the earth. It's what you *do* with the issues that counts. Try to live in a way that reflects how you want the earth to be. Try to organize in a way that treats others with respect and justice.

Activists are always seeking ways to support one another financially, but if we do find funding to begin this kind of work, it has to be on our own agenda. Central to building a neighbourhood movement is developing the willingness of participants to put their own money, time and energy into it.

Recognizing that democratic organizations like labour unions, churches and non-profit organizations are sites of struggle, we insist that they act democratically. We fight to get and maintain access to these institutions so that they are relevant to the long-term needs of people.

We pressure and campaign for changes that make life better for all people. We insist on our rights to housing, food, and protection. We establish our own organizations for self-reliance, and pressure for government support and protection for them.

We Can Collectively With-hold our Consent

Activists boycott destructive systems and refuse to supply resources to them. We make it impossible for logging to take place, or road-building, or nuclear reactors, or domed stadiums. We withhold something they need: labour, consumer dollars, smooth functioning of a system, public goodwill, votes.

We withhold our consent and withhold our labour from those who would oppress others and destroy the earth. Doing this individually is not very effective since we are so easily ignored or replaced. But, at work, we make it a union demand, or begin to talk about it, or sabotage employer's plans. We leak information, names, cases to welfare rights groups, environmental groups. We find those places where the system could be disorganized from within at crucial moments. We make sure grants get to the appropriate projects. We pressure for changes in the systems: fairer credit, better policies. We build solidarity with other workers and with consumers so that we are less afraid to fight for change.

We Are Building the Movement

Some of us have begun consciously to develop base communities: people who will stick together and support each other in the long haul. That means doing the process right the first time. Examining our own reality. Taking on tasks that benefit the victims of injustice immediately. Being within walking distance of each other. Luring with carrots not sticks. Educating ourselves. Planning events as much for ourselves as for each other. Talking honestly.

We try to tell the truth and broadcast our dreams. We name those responsible for injustice and hold them accountable. We speak out, write and demonstrate. We ask for what we really want. As Starhawk says: "We must stop obeying, stop complying. Refuse to keep silent, to lie, to not notice what is going on. We can develop a "bad attitude" one that questions authority." [2]

We all need a vision worth living our lives for, but it will develop out of the daily struggles of ordinary folk in their neighbourhoods. We are building a movement of these concrete struggles at the base, through exchanges between grassroots people, to share stories, methods and break down racial and cultural barriers.

We try to create an environment where people can feel at home with a new way of thinking. We try to meet people's needs for recognition, useful work, learning and so on. We work to pay attention to issues of language, race, class and gender, and deal with them as they arise. Since fear of shunning is so deeply imbedded in our society, we work to build self-confidence.

We develop activities together which build the group's security in economic and political terms. A group that helps me gain a living, get decent housing or have political power will get more of my allegiance in terms of time and energy than one that is purely social. Doing something of great significance attracts more energy than something with little significance. We all want to be part of making history if we only knew how.

In Canada, it is unrealistic in the extreme to believe that work for change will receive any kind of ongoing or core funding from the government, private corporations or foundations. We may be able to get bits and pieces or the occasional pilot project out of them. But that's it. The effort for this money may still be worth the proposal writing and lobbying and cajoling it takes. God knows we need all the help we can get.

We also have to support those people within institutions like the church who struggle to hold on to staff time, resources and money that can be used by the movement. It isn't any fun spending your weekends in church meetings trying to ensure that money continues to go to justice work. It doesn't always feel worth it to butt your head against a wall in the union or the service club or the office, trying to get them to free up resources for change. People who work in these places are engaged in the institutional sites of low intensity conflict. We need to support each other, sympathize, strategize and celebrate victories together.

Activists, however, have realized that if we want to create change, we have to want to do it badly enough to find the time and money ourselves, to lobby wealthy friends, to ask for bequests from the disaffected children of the rich.

We work to take over the institutions of power that are available to us: municipal councils, boards of education, hydro boards, community centres, social agencies, and make them accountable to the people and to put their resources at the service of transformation.

We persuade credit unions and pension funds that this is worth supporting. We support trade unions in major workplaces that want to act in solidarity with this kind of community initiative. We build our own bases of land, resources and production, to get the capital we need.

In June of 1990, I attended a three-day workshop for coalition activists sponsored by the Social Solidarity Working Group and what was then known as the Pro-Canada Network. Both the sponsors had organized as a response to the grossest excesses of the business agenda in Canada. They involved many of the key activists from the traditional sectoral interests in Canada: labour, church, women, some academics, and a number of non-governmental organizations in social service and development education work. They had some support from the Assembly of First Nations and some black groups. The coalitions' initial agenda had been to develop a full-employment agenda for Canada and to oppose Free Trade; they engaged in an enormous public opposition to the Goods and Services Tax. At this writing (June 1990), the workshop appears to mark an important step forward for these coalitions - which represent the "popular sector" (such as it is) in Canada and Québec at this time.

Coalition politics however does not build a grass roots movement for social change. A coalition reflects the organizations that compose it. If those organizations do not question the fundamental character of Canadian society as it is now, then the central message of the coalition will be "don't make things any worse".

These coalitions, however, are very important to the social change project. They can compare stories and social analysis, and broadcast the truth. They provide grassroots organizers with the opportunity to meet other organizers and to learn from each other. They are a place for people in local work to see the strength of opposition to the business agenda. They make it difficult for the business agenda to march ahead, and so win space and time for organizing work for all of us. They can make an alternative collective vision of the future possible.

Coalition politics do not take the place of organizing in local communities and workplaces around the issues that are important to the local people. In fact, the strength of coalitions is completely dependant on the independence and strength of local organizing work. Meeting and communicating across great distances is expensive and time-consuming. Keeping our leaders in the air flying from conference to conference has actually disorganized local work.

* * *

The end of the last decade has seen massive non-violent public uprisings in the countries of Eastern Europe, that have brought down governments entrenched since the Second World War. Other demands for democracy are growing in Asian countries: South Korea, Taiwan, China. A new spirit of rebellion is in the air.

The method used to assert people's power in these countries is the active practice of political non-co-operation and non-violence: the civilian insurrection. The Albert Einstein Institution defines it as:

> A non-violent uprising against a dictatorship, or other unpopular regime, usually involving wide-spread repudiation of the regime as illegitimate, mass strikes, massive demonstrations, an economic shut-down, and wide-spread political non-co-operation. Political non-co-operation may

include action by government employees and mutiny by police and troops. In the final stages a parallel government often emerges.

If successful, a civilian insurrection may disintegrate the established regime in days or weeks...

Although the non-violent insurrection itself only takes a short while to bring down the regime, it is possible only when citizens have been organizing themselves and educating themselves for a very long time. It requires from the people an incredible level of personal discipline and responsibility to one another.

This kind of wide-spread, orderly and non-violent resistance can only be organized from the ground up: in neighbourhoods, in industries, in government offices. It becomes possible where substantial numbers of people in the police and the army identify with the human aspirations of the insurrection.

* * *

In Canada this summer the leadership of aboriginal people in the struggle for social change is reaching a crescendo. Mohawks in Oka resisted the dismantling of a blockade to protect their lands from being eroded to build a golf course. The government responded with an unprecedented show of state violence: machine guns, tear gas, tanks, radar, razor wire and state terrorism of the grossest kind. The armed show was only exceeded by the control of media and the propaganda generated by the government. In the face of this almost surreal provocation, the Mohawks and other native people responded with superhuman self-control, peace camps, truth and non-violent civil disobedience.

In July, Elijah Harper and the Assembly of Manitoba chiefs blocked the Meech Lake accord, using the white man's own rules.

Over and over again, in their struggle which has gone on for five hundred years, aboriginal people have told us that change comes through sharing, kindness, honesty and strength -- that we have to live the society we want to create, that the four colors of humankind must work together to heal the earth. The non-violent direct action and self-control with which they lead is a model for all of us. Perhaps as their prophecies say, the time has come for the red people to tell the white people how to live.

Today, the federal government in power has the support of less than 20% of the voters. Outrage over the treatment of aboriginal people, vocal and organized opposition to privatization of crown corporations, new taxes, cutbacks to health and social services, indigenous and womens' programs, and inadequate programs to protect the environment, falls on deaf ears. This is a government that does not care if it is re-elected. It intends to implement as much of the business agenda as possible before it is defeated — an agenda that includes the destruction of the forests of northern Alberta by Mitsubishi, the James Bay II hydro project in Québec, the construction of five more nuclear power plants in Ontario. The government that follows this one will have no economic base left on which to build a program.

In fact there is a question of whether Canada as we know it will continue to exist at all. As our business elite ally themselves with the North American trade zone, they have less need to continue to support the parts of the country where the resources are mined out. They no longer want or need the east-west communications systems that have strung this country together. Provinces become more effective instruments to extract wealth for them than the federal government. From the point of view of the transnational business elite, provinces could as easily be states. The elite may opt for the slow disintegration of the federal state.

The Chinese word for "crisis" is two characters: danger and opportunity. The next decade is certainly a time of crisis. It also carries with it opportunities for us to develop plans for political, social and economic transformation through a sovereignty association of aboriginal, Québecquois and other regions: real neighbourhood-based and land-related participatory forms of self-determination and community control. We begin by building our communities from the bottom up: block by block, to provide neighbourhood, security and health and peace to one another.

NOTES

1.   Starhawk, *Truth or Dare,* Harper and Row Publishers, New York, 1987, page 314.
2.   *ibid,* page 316.

RESOURCES

POWER IN CANADA

Bird, Pat, *Of Dust and Time and Dreams and Agonies: A Short History of Canadian People,* John Deyell Co., Willowdale, Ontario, 1975.

A people's history of Canada, rich in anecdote and lived experience.

Baxter, Sheila, *No Way to Live,* New Star, Vancouver, 1986.

This is a collection of first person stories from poor women in a variety of situations offering an extremely readable and skilled analysis of Canadian social structures.

Braverman, Harry, *Labor and Monopoly Capital: The Degradation of Work in the Twentieth Century,* Modern Reader, 1974.

The most important work on the organization of the workplace in the modern industrial state.

Burstyn, Varda and Dorothy Smith, *Women, Class, Family and the State,* Garamond, Toronto, 1985.

An important study of the relationship between patriarchy and capitalism in everyday life.

Clement, Wallace, *The Canadian Corporate Elite: An Analysis of Economic Power,* McClelland and Stewart, Toronto, 1975.

An exhaustive study of the concentration and perpetuation of economic power in Canada. A solid historical analysis of the Canadian economic elite.

Kneen, Brewster, *Trading Up: How Cargill, The World's Largest Grain Company, is Changing Canadian Agriculture,* NC Press, Toronto, 1990.

An excellent case study of the role of a multinational grain company in transforming Canadian agriculture.

Laxer, Robert, *Canada's Unions,* James Lorimer and Company Publishers, Toronto, 1978.

A detailed report on the state of the trade union movement in the 1970's, with an intersting historical perspective on international unions.

Luxton, Meg. and Harriet Rosenberg, *Through the Kitchen Window: The Politics of Home and Family,* Garamond Press, Toronto, 1986.

Using concrete examples from the lives of women, the authors examine the role of housework within the corporate economy.

Marchak, Patricia, *In Whose Interests: An Essay on Multinational Corporations in a Canadian Context,* McClelland and Stewart, Toronto, 1979.

An analysis by a sociologist of how multinational corporations operate in and affect the economy of Canada. The book provides case histories and analysis in a way that unites information from political science, history, economics and business.

McQuaig, Linda, *Behind Closed Doors: How the Rich Won Control of Canada's Tax System,* Penguin, 1988.

A study of the Canadian tax system and of the wealthy that control it.

Myers, Gustavus, *A History of Canadian Wealth,* James, Lewis and Samuel, 1972.

First published in 1914, this muckraker's meticulously documented account of early Canadian history is one of the most important books written on the political economy of Canada.

Ng, Roxana, *The Politics of Community Services: Immigrant Women, Class and State,* Garamond Press, Toronto, 1988.

A careful study of the effects of state funding on the work of an immigrant women's center.

Niosi, Jorge, *Canadian Multinationals,* Between the Lines, Toronto, 1985.

A study of the role and nature of over a dozen Canadian-based multinational corporations.

Ontario Federation of Labour Conference on Education and Training, *Its Our Knowledge,* Our Schools/Ourselves, Toronto, 1989.

The proceedings of a conference on working class education for critical thinking and action for change.

Richardson, Boyce (ed.), *Drumbeat: Anger and Renewal in Indian Country,* The Assembly of First Nations, Summerhill Press, Toronto, 1989.

Promenient native leaders tell about the relationship of their bands and the federal and provincial governments, and the decision to use non-violent direct action to forge their role in Canadian society.

Ross, David and Richard Shillington, *The Canadian Fact Book on Poverty 1989,* Canadian Council on Social Development, Ottawa, 1989.

Data on the extent and character of poverty in Canada.

Ryerson, Stanley B., *Unequal Union,* Progress, 1973.

A history of Canada from 1815 to 1873 that examines how the institution of wage labour and the rise of a class of Canadian businessmen affected struggles for independence and self-determination.

DOING SOCIAL ANALYSIS

Barndt, Deborah, *Naming the Moment,* Between the Lines, Toronto, 1989.

How to do "conjunctural analysis," a process of analyzing the social/cultural/ economic/and political forces at work in a given historical moment, so that appropriate strategies might be chosen.

CUSO Education Department, *Basics and Tools: A Collection of Popular Education Resources and Activities,* Ottawa, 1987.

The handbook provides basic models and principles of experiential adult learning, along with a compilation of role plays, simulation games, exercises and an annotated list of recommended resources.

Czerny, Michael and Jamie Swift, *Getting Started on Social Analysis in Canada*, Between the Lines, Kitchener, 1984.
> Provides analysis and study guides for groups of specific issues in Canada.

GATT-FLY, *Ah-Hah: A New Approach to Popular Education*, Between the Lines, Toronto, 1983.
> A method to get participants to piece together their individual experiences to understand the political and economic systems affecting them.

Kneen, Brewster, *From Land to Mouth: Understanding the Food System*, NC Press, 1989.
> Takes the global food system apart, looks at its components and describes who benefits from it and how.

MacLean, Eleanor, *Between the Lines: How to Detect Bias and Propaganda in the News and Everyday Life*, Black Rose Books, Montréal, 1988.
> Information about how mass media works. Focuses on ownership and control, propaganda techniques, who determines the message, relationship between government and media.

Riches, Graham, *Food Banks and the Welfare Crisis*, Canadian Council on Social Development, Ottawa, 1986.
> Documents the proliferation of emergency food services in Canada and analyzes their role in the "social safety net" and a corporate profit-based food system.

Social Action Commission, Diocese of Charlottetown, *From the Grass Roots: a Critical Consciousness Approach to Social Justice in Prince Edward Island*, Charlottetown, 1987.
> A number of case studies using popular education methodology of activist groups in P.E.I.

CREATING A CULTURE OF HOPE

Arnold, Rick, Deborah Barndt and Bev Burke, *The New Weave*, CUSO/OISE, Toronto, 1983.
> Provides a history of popular education and a tool, the learning loom, for planning popular education workshops.

Adams, Frank, *Unearthing Seeds of Fire: The Idea of Highlander*, John. F. Blair Publisher, 1980.
> The history of the Highlander Education Centre in Knoxville, Tennessee told by Myles Horton, its founder. An inspiring and helpful book about education through action.

Bookchin, Murray, *Remaking Society*, Black Rose Books, Montréal, 1989.
> A thoughful anthropological history from an anarchist perspective: must reading for activists.

Clandfield, David (ed.), *Building A Peoples' Curriculum: the Experience of a Québec Teachers' Collective*, Our Schools/ Ourselves, 1989.
> An anthology of writings by la Maitresse d'ecole, a teachers' collective in Montréal. It combines a lucid critique of the education system with concrete illustrations of alternative practice in the classroom.

Friere, Paulo, *Pedagogy of the Oppressed*, Continuum, New York, 1983.
> The seminal work on popular education methodology.

Gordon, Robbie, *We Interrupt this Program,* Citizen Involvement Training Project, University of Massachsetts, Amherst, 1978.

An illustrated and accessible hands-on manual for community groups using the media. Unfortunately, the examples and analysis are American.

Neighbourhood Action Project, *Neighbourhood Action: Recipes for Change,* self-published, Sudbury, 1983. Available from Sticks and Stones, Box 1058, Station B, Sudbury, Ontario P3E 4S6.

A compendium of exercise, role plays, games and tools for popular education with groups interested in social change.

Starhawk, *Truth or Dare,* Harper and Row Publishers, New York, 1987.

A holistic description and analysis of the state of the world, with ideas, exercises and incentives for working to change it. Starhawk is a witch, the foremost spokesperson in North America for the the old earth-centered spirituality of Europe.

Ura, Michael, *Making the Media: A Guide to Using the Media,* West Coast Environmental Law Research Foundation, Vancouver, 1988.

A short and useable guide to working with media for community groups.

WORKING TOGETHER

Biagi, Bob, *Working Together: A Manual for Helping Groups Work More Effectively,* Citizen Involvement Training Project, University of Massachusetts, Amherst, 1978.

An excellent resource for people working with groups. Contains workshop ideas and hands-on learning situations. Illustrated and approachable.

Centre for Conflict Resolution, *Building United Judgement: A Handbook for Consensus Decision-Making,* Madison, 1981.

As the title suggests, an excellent resource on consensus.

Centre for Conflict Resolution, *A Manual for Group Facilitators,* Madison, Wisconsin, 1977.

An excellent how-to manual for people who want to facilitate groups. Information on planning workshops, group dynamics, problems in meetings and so on.

Hill, Karen, *Helping You Helps Me,* Canadian Council on Social Development, Ottawa, 1984.

A guide for self help groups to getting started, holding meetings and taking action.

ALTERNATIVE ECONOMICS

Changing Work, a magazine published at Box 5065, New Haven CT 06525.

Provides analysis and information about economic alternatives.

Gordon, David (ed.), *Green Cities: Ecologically Sound Approaches to Urban Space,* Black Rose Books, Montréal, 1990.

This project of the Pollution Probe Foundation brings together examples and ideas for an ecolocally sound city.

Kuyek, Joan, *Managing the Household,* United Church of Canada, Toronto, 1990.

A handbook for economic justice work in church groups and others. Includes exercises and analysis for understanding and acting on economic justice issues.

MacLeod, Greg, *New Age Business: Community Corporations that Work*, Canadian Council on Social Development, Ottawa, 1986.

A detailed discussion of three community economic development activities: New Dawn in Nova Scotia, J.A.L. in Québec and Mondragon in Spain.

Melnyk, George, *The Search for Community: From Utopia to Co-operative Society*, Black Rose Books, Montréal, 1985.

A study of co-operative forms from the kibbutz in Israel to Basque co-ops in Spain to Hutterite communities in Western Canada, with an assessment of their effectiveness and shortcomings.

Midwest Centre for Labour Research, "Labour Tackles the Local Economy: Reindustrialization from Below," *Labour Research Review*, Vol.V, No.2, Fall 1986, Chicago.

Good case studies on plant closure strategies in the United States.

Midwest Centre for Labour Research, "New Tactics for Labour," *Labour Research Review*, Vol. 7, Fall 1985.

Some excellent case studies and history on economic conversion.

Pollution Probe Foundation, *The Canadian Green Consumer Guide*, McClelland and Stewart, Toronto, 1989.

Ideas for how the individual can make a contribution toward a safer, greener world with some useful data on polluters and waste.

Southerners for Economic Justice, "Everybody's Business," in *Southern Exposure*, Vol. XIV, No. 5-6, Institute for Southern Studies, Durham, N.C., 1986.

A number of case studies, analysis and tools for community economic development.

Worker Co-op, a magazine published by the Worker Ownership Development Foundation, 348 Danforth Ave, Toronto, Ontario M4E 1A9.

Zalent, Kim, *Economic Home Cookin': an Action Guide for Congregations on Community Economic Development*, The Community Workshop on Economic Development, Chicago, 1987.

A resource for any community groups who want to get involved in community economic development, full of ideas and exercises.

REPOSSESSING POLITICAL POWER

Gaventa, John, *Power and Powerlessness: Quiescence and Rebellion in an Appalachian Valley*, University of Illinois Press, 1980.

Although academic in style, this book provides one of the most detailed analyses of a struggle for power in local communities available.

Johnson, Walter, *The Trade Unions and the State*, Black Rose Books, Montréal, 1978.

An examination in detail of five important strikes in Canadian labour history that show how direct action is often more effective than collective bargaining.

Kahn, Si, *How People Get Power*, McGraw-Hill, 1970.

A book filled with social analysis and detailed information from peoples' struggles in the United States.

Pugh, Terry (ed.), *Fighting the Farm Crisis*, Fifth House, Saskatoon, 1987.

A number of case studies of farmers and others organizing to fight the farm crisis.

Rinehart, James. W, *The Tyranny of Work*, Longman, Toronto, 1975.

An analysis of the modern workplace with a number of case studies of workplace resistance.

Speeter, Greg, *Power: A Repossession Manual: Organizing Strategies for Citizens*, Citizen Involvement Training Project, University of Massachusetts, Amherst, 1980.

Describes different strategies for social change in a non-intimidating style. It contains a number of "how-to" exercises and information about planning, structures, and taking action.

ORGANIZING STRATEGIES AND CASE HISTORIES

Adamson, Nancy, Linda Briskin, and Margaret McPhail, *Feminist Organizing for Change: The Contemporary Women's Movement in Canada,* Oxford University Press, Toronto, 1988.

The authors develop a conceptial framework for understanding feminist practice and reflect on feminist organzing and organizations.

Clairmont, Donald H. and Dennis Magill, *Africville: The Life and Death of a Canadian Black Community,* Canadian Scholars Press, Toronto, 1987.

A detailed study of the growth and removal of Africville, and the struggle of the people to stop it.

Coover, Virginia, Ellen Deacon, Charles Esser, and Christopher Moore, *Resource Manual for a Living Revolution,* New Society Press, Philadelphia, 1978.

The classic on organizing for social change. It looks at change from all levels: personal growth, group dynamics, strategies for non-violent action, and includes a discussion about matters like first aid and cooking for large numbers. A good source book for ideas.

Cunningham, Frank, Sue Findlay, Marlene Kaldar, Alan Lennon and Ed Silva (ed.), *Social Movements/ Social Change: The Politics and Practice of Organizing,* Between the Lines, Toronto, 1988.

Activists from a number of fields describe and analyze their work, including the Dis-Abled Women's Network, the campaign for abortion clinics in Ontario and the Québec Labour Movement.

Diemer, Ulli (ed.), *The Connexions Annual 1989: A Social Change Sourcebook,* Toronto, 1989.

A special annual edition of Connexions periodical, which provides a complete listing of information and ideas about social and environmental alternatives in Canada.

Four Worlds Development Project, *Developing Healthy Communities: Fundamental Strategies for Health Promotion,* University of Lethbridge, 1985.

Develops a medicine wheel approach to health promotion and community development.

Four Worlds Development Project, *Community Development: Discussion Paper Eight,* Lethbridge, Alberta.

Outlines the four worlds community development strategy.

Hellman, Claire, *The Milton-Park Affair: Canada's Largest Citizen-Developer Confrontation,* Vehicule Press, Montréal, 1987.

A detailed and interesting account of one of the most significant struggles in Canadian organizing history.

Kahn, Si, *Organizing: a Guide for Grassroots Leaders,* McGraw-Hill, 1982.

An excellent resource for community organizers filled with organizational expertise and imaginative tactics.

Lee, Bill, *Pragmatics of Community Organization,* Commonact Press, Mississauga, 1986.

A guide for people in the field of social work to community change and citizen participation, the book provides useful and succinct information.

Marshall, Doris, *Silver Threads: Critical Reflections on Growing Old,* Between the Lines, 1987.

A thorough examination of the condition and possibilities for older people in our society by an adult educator who has lived a long time.

Peringer, Christine, *How We Work for Peace, Canadian Community Activities,* Peace Research Institute, Dundas, Ontario, 1987.

A comprehensive compendium of ideas and activities that peace groups have used in Canada.

Roussopoulos, Dimitrios (ed.), *The City and Radical Social Change,* Black Rose Books, Montréal, 1982.

A collection of studies and examples of work for social change in Canadian cities: provocative and useful. Includes work on public transportation, information on neighbourhood councils, and a study of the rise of the Montréal Citizens' Movement.

Ward, Jim, *Organizing For the Homeless,* Canadian Council for Social Development, Ottawa, 1989.

Full of examples from first-hand experience, this book is a good mix of practical organizing ideas and theoretical analysis.

THE SEARCH FOR COMMUNITY

From Utopia to a Co-operative Society

by George Melnyk

2nd printing

Co-ops in capitalist and communist nations are assesed for strengths and drawbacks as Melnyk selects the components that can be adapted to our society and used to link groups already functioning. The result is the "social co-operative," a new citizen-run structure that will respond to our social and economic requirements.

Melnyk offers a fascinating social history of co-operatives, from monastery to commune.
Choice

170 pages
Paperback ISBN: 0-920057-52-7 $16.95
Hardcover ISBN: 0-920057-53-5 $36.95

ECOLOGY AS POLITICS

by André Gorz

translated by Patsy Vigderman and Jonathon Cloud

...the greatest of modern French social thinkers, dares to venture where no one really has before. Fighters for democratic socialism and an ecological society have begun to recognize the other's value, beyond being little more than a tactical means towards achieving their own ends. Gorz, in this exciting and penetrating gem of a book, addresses precisely this question, and offers a connection between the political and the ecological.
Herb Ginis, co-author of *Schooling in Capitalist America*

Gorz's Ecology as Politics *is rich in ways and means to reinvent the future. A very good book.*
City Magazine

215 pages
Paperback ISBN: 0-921618-71-5 $18.95
Hardcover ISBN: 0-921618-72-3 $37.95

COMMUNITY ACTION

Organising for Social Change
by Henri Lamoureux, Robert Mayer, and Jean Panet-Raymond
translated by Phyllis Aronoff and Howard Scott

*...thoroughly readable and immensely useful work...displays the remarkable depth of experience the authors gained through their work...*Community Action *traces the recent developments within Québec's nascent social-activist community. The authors chronicle the successes and failures of various popular movements...an immensely pragmatic work and one that will no doubt become required reading for community activists throughout North America and Europe.*
Quill and Quire

...a capable historical overview of community action...
Ottawa Citizen

190 pages
Paperback ISBN: 0-921689-20-9 $16.95
Hardcover ISBN: 0-921689-21-7 $35.95

VOICES FROM TIANANMEN SQUARE

Beijing Spring and the Democracy Movement
edited by Mok Chiu Yu and J. Frank Harrison
Introduction by George Woodcock

...[the] editors have brought together original documents, translated for the first time into English, including speeches, handbills, posters, manifestos, interviews, and eye-witness reports of the massacre and its aftermath... Voices *is an invaluable primary source for those who want to know more about the spring upheaval.*
Connexions

250 pages
Paperback ISBN: 0-921689-58-6 $19.95
Hardcover ISBN: 0-921689-59-4 $38.95

BLACK ROSE BOOKS

has published the following books of interest

Rita Arditti, Pat Brennan, and Steve Cavrak, Science and Liberation
Christian Bay and Charles C. Walker, Civil Disobedience
Micheline Beaudry, Battered Women
Etienne de la Boétie, The Politics of Obedience
Murray Bookchin, The Limits of the City, *2nd edition*
Steve Butterfield, Amway:The Cult of Free Enterprise
Noam Chomsky, Radical Priorities
Claire Culhane, Still Barred From Prison
Chris DeBresson, Understanding Technological Change
Deborah Harrison, The Limits of Liberalism:The Making of Canadian Sociology
Gary Kinsman, The Regulation of Desire
Frédéric Lesemann, Services and Circuses:Community and the Welfare State
William R. McKercher, Freedom and Authority
Cindy Patton, Sex and Germs
Fran Peavy with Myra Levy and Charles Varon, Heart Politics
Marc Raboy and Peter A. Bruck, eds., Communication: For and Against Democracy
Diana Ralph, Work and Madness:The Rise of Community Psychiatry
Dimitrios Roussopoulos, ed., The City and Radical Social Change
Dimitrios Roussopoulos, Green Politics
Eric Shragge and Linda Davies, Bureaucracy and Community

send for a complete catalogue of books
mailed out free
BLACK ROSE BOOKS
3981 boul. St-Laurent, #444
Montréal, Québec H2W 1Y5 Canada

Printed by the workers of
Ateliers Graphiques Marc Veilleux Inc.
for
Black Rose Books Ltd.